CONVAIR B-36 PEACEMAKER

PEACEMAKER

1941–59

First published in July 2020

A catalogue record for this book is available
from the British Library.

ISBN 978 1 78521 193 5

Library of Congress control no. 2018938902

Published by J H Haynes & Co Ltd,
Sparkford, Yeovil, Somerset BA22 7JJ, UK.
Tel: 01963 440635
Int. tel: +44 1963 440635
Website: www.haynes.com

Haynes North America Inc.,
859 Lawrence Drive, Newbury Park,
California 91320, USA.

Printed in Malaysia.

Senior Commissioning Editor: Jonathan Falconer
Copy editor: Ann Page
Proof reader: Dean Rockett
Indexer: Peter Nicholson
Page design: James Robertson

Forethoughts and acknowledgements

I have been enthralled with the B-36 for almost 70 years, since I
heard the Peacemaker as it droned overhead not far from my home
in Lincolnshire, England, when I was a boy. It was on its way to RAF
Lakenheath in Suffolk and it impressed people there as it did me.

The next time I encountered the B-36 was in the early 1980s when
I had occasion to visit SAC Headquarters at Offutt Air Force Base,
Nebraska, and a Peacemaker was displayed with pride alongside the
case for a very large Mk 17 thermonuclear bomb. This combination had
kept the peace in that vital decade after World War Two and restrained
excessive displays of force by potential aggressors and ideological
opponents of the Free World.

Over these decades since, I have been fortunate to acquire detailed
information, training manuals, familiarisation documents and engineering
drawings of the Peacemaker. And I have had the great good fortune to
have received many recollections of crewmembers and ground crew
directly familiar with the B-36 at an operational level. Men who served
their cause with pride.

So it was with great enthusiasm that I was asked to do a book on this
remarkable aircraft by Haynes, and particularly by my commissioning
editor Jonathan Falconer and by Steve Rendle, who guided me through
the final product. Enormous gratitude to both, who made the project
happen and saw that it survived the odd trauma along the way! I would
also like to thank James Robertson for crafting the design and layout.
I have worked with all three before and would like to pay tribute to their
professionalism and support.

By no means least, I would like to acknowledge the enabling
contribution of Dennis Jenkins. No book is owned by its author but
is rather a compilation of separate elements brought together by
enthusiasts and supporters working to a common cause. Dennis has
made an outstanding contribution to this book and as a fellow aerospace
historian is to be thanked for most of the images published here.

Lastly, thanks to Ann, who continues to put up with the vagaries of
being the wife of an aerospace historian but for whom the tales told
here are as wondrous as they are to me. Thank you Ann for your love,
support and forbearance.

In the end, however, the author must stand solely responsible for the
material he brought together and any errors in this book are mine alone.

David Baker
East Sussex, 2020

CONVAIR B-36 PEACEMAKER

1941–59

Owners' Workshop Manual

America's Cold War 'big stick' ten-engine nuclear bomber that could rain destruction on aggressors anywhere on Earth

David Baker

Contents

OPPOSITE A dramatic underbody view of the B-36 with its unique engine allocation of 'six turning and four burning'.
(Dennis Jenkins)

Introduction

───●───

The B-36 is something of an anachronism: last in a long line of piston-engine bombers, adapted into a hybrid powered both by reciprocating and reaction engines, it was the first of the post-war nuclear deterrent strike systems. But more than that, it was the world's first bomber with a truly intercontinental strike range and it was also a political football kicked around by politicians and opponents of the US Air Force's independent nuclear deterrent.

OPPOSITE A formation of B-36 bombers flies over the Capitol building in Washington, DC, during hearings on the aircraft's effectiveness in 1949. *(USAF/National Archives)*

On the positive side, it was the only true transition bomber bridging the slow and lumbering piston-engine era with the sleek, high-flying jet age. In turn, that would bring speed, efficiency and provide the new independent Air Force with a formidable threat to Soviet hegemony at a time of increased international tension. On the negative side, it was cumbersome, slow, difficult to maintain, prone to engine problems and required major support when deployed to foreign bases.

Yet between those two extremes, the Convair B-36 provided exactly the right capability at precisely the right time, helping forge the world's first intercontinental nuclear strike force, providing the instrument through which miscalculation by a belligerent foreign power carried the gravest consequences for peace. It had the carrying capacity to devastate the Soviet Union in an age when air-dropped bombs were the only means of delivering atomic and thermonuclear weapons, retiring from service just as the Intercontinental Ballistic Missile (ICBM) was about to enter operational readiness.

Replacing the ageing piston-engine B-29 and B-50, an operational contemporary of the all-jet B-45, and preceding the all-jet B-47 and B-52, the B-36 never received an official name but lived up to its informal title: Peacemaker. Through the induction of the B-36 and conversion from the existing inventory of Second World War bombers, Strategic Air Command came of age with this type and under General Curtis LeMay provided a highly credible instrument of strategic warfare, a capability which for ten

years gave the United States total domination in the first decade of the Nuclear Age.

Because of all this, despite the fact that it was never used in anger, the aircraft has a very important position in the history of strategic warfare. It generated layers of experience, building an infrastructure for the global deployment of new airborne delivery systems, and was crucial in testing novel concepts which today look ridiculous but which, at the time, made perfect sense. Concepts such as the fighter-conveyor (FICON) project which proposed carrying small defensive fighters, and fast jet reconnaissance aircraft, deep into hostile territory, and a nuclear-powered bomber capable of remaining aloft indefinitely.

Probably its greatest operational contribution was not as the active end of the nuclear deterrent but as a photographic reconnaissance platform, carrying very powerful cameras with telescopic lenses returning valuable images of strategic targets and regions of tactical interest to the Air Force, the Navy and the Army. This was vital work. In the late 1940s, maps of Russia were generally inaccurate and US defence analysts used captured German cartography to place and locate areas of military interest; the Germans had photographed vast expanses of the USSR by air in the run-up to the attack in 1941 and after. These proved invaluable, but not particularly useful when identifying new industrial complexes and military installations.

In extensively photographing very large areas around the borders of the Soviet Union and its Warsaw Pact allies, the RB-36

played a role beyond its obvious mission, providing maps highly valuable to defining the strategic resources of the USSR and its client states. It directly supported the emerging, and burgeoning, requirements of the Central Intelligence Agency (CIA). Formed in September 1947, less than a year before the B-36 entered service, the CIA had a mandate to provide vital intelligence information about the military, industrial and economic state of the world's countries and soon would acquire responsibility for assessing the political profile as well.

In that regard, the B-36 was, arguably, the last aircraft to carry out such a diverse set of roles: strategic conventional and nuclear bombing, photographic reconnaissance,

surveillance, intelligence gathering and spying, obtaining a catalogue of industrial, civilian and military assets outside the United States. Beyond the era of the Peacemaker, roles would separate off, and dedicated aircraft types would emerge focusing on specific tasks and responsibilities.

In this way too, the B-36 is a unique one-of-a-kind system in the annals of aviation history – the last of the multi-role aircraft embracing such a wide range of tasks and assignments. But it is in its role of strategic nuclear bomber that it is best known and in which it came to best represent the dominance of American air power throughout the 1950s, a legacy which endures today.

ABOVE B-36A 44-92014 during an air show at El Paso, Texas, on 5 December 1948. *(Frank Kleinwechter)*

BELOW A Red Tail B-36B (44-92033) captured in an evocative in-flight view. *(Consolidated)*

Chapter One

The origin of the B-36

The Convair B-36 was conceived, designed and built for strategic warfare – the world's first bomber capable of delivering every piece of air-dropped munition in the US arsenal over intercontinental distances. As a strategic bomber it served the evolving concept of all-out war against resources supporting the manufacturing base for land armies, enemy infrastructure and the full range of its domestic and industrial resources.

OPPOSITE **Trials prompted by William 'Billy' Mitchell in the 1920s demonstrated the value of the bomber, even when attacking shipping.** *(USAF)*

The B-36 was born from an evolved understanding of what was required in 'modern' warfare at a time when totalitarian forces were mobilised in one of the greatest wars in history. It was the product of an application that began several decades before, at a time when there were no aeroplanes and only futuristic ideas tormented the minds of professional soldiers and sailors.

Anticipating the age of aerial bombardment, the first concerns about a potentially significant leap in the science of warfare came in 1899, the year Count von Zeppelin began building his first airship. Fear of attack from the air spurred debate at The Hague on the principles of modern warfare and the moral and ethical acceptance of aerial bombardment by dirigible. Later, in the era of heavier-than-air flying machines, the possibilities opened up by free-flying aircraft silenced those previously working to prohibit the use of aerial devices for dropping projectiles and bombs. No country wanted to be left behind.

The First World War of 1914–18 saw aviation initially support land armies and scouts for naval forces before leaning toward tactical and then strategic bombing as the conflict progressed. Technical limitations and the need to balance experimentation with operational capabilities in the field prevented all-out development of aircraft for striking the enemy's ability to sustain conflict.

By 1918, however, the UK's Independent Force, which grew out of the amalgamation of the Royal Flying Corps and the Royal Naval Air Service into the Royal Air Force, demonstrated the strategic effect of bombing. Henceforth industrial, political and utilities supplying homes with light and heat were considered legitimate military targets. Quickly upon its heels came the use of aerial bombardment to turn citizenry against its leadership, strategic bombing being the use of air power against the full spectrum of a nation's industrial might, including its workforce.

It could be argued that the first use of strategic bombing occurred when Germany used airships and aircraft to strike at the heart of Britain's industrial capability, its maritime trade and at the workplaces of its political leadership – the City of London. To some extent this policy had encouraged wider consideration of reciprocity although it was not on that basis that the Independent Force (IF) was formed.

RIGHT A redundant warship, the USS *Alabama*, receives a direct hit from a phosphor bomb dropped by a DH-4 during Army trials in 1923. *(USAF)*

Nevertheless, led by Hugh Trenchard, initially a reluctant commander of the squadrons assigned, the IF left its mark which would influence debate during the next two decades about the relative merits of strategic bombers or fighters to defend against them.

While terror bombing was demonstrated by Japan in China during the late 1930s, and by the Legion Condor of the Luftwaffe in Spain, this was not strategic bombing but in fact the use of medium and tactical combat aircraft to generate panic and confusion. The lack of a truly strategic force in the Luftwaffe compromised its operational flexibility during the Battle of Britain in 1940 and Germany never did stand up a truly strategic imperative; lacking the equipment and the forces, it retained aerial attack as essentially a support arm of the *blitzkrieg* concept. As a result it failed to erode the industrial capacity of its enemies, principally Britain and Russia, which out-produced the manufacturing and production of munitions of its enemy.

When war broke out in September 1939 between Germany and Poland the United States was averse to engaging its armed forces in yet another European conflict,

ABOVE Huff-Daland produced a series of bombers before it was renamed Keystone, producing the B-4A here seen over the Philippines, emphasising the hemispheric interests of the United States. *(USAF)*

BELOW Facing insubordination over his unforgiving approach to military orders, Mitchell receives a hearing at his court martial. *(USAF)*

especially when it began to shape up as a re-run of the war of 1914–18, with similar potential for major escalation. Publicly boasting of its rapidly expanding Wehrmacht, from 1935 Germany had built in central Europe the largest military force since Napoleon's *Grande Armee*, stimulating arms expenditure in the UK at a greater rate than at any other peacetime period in its history. Presided over by the Baldwin and Chamberlain governments, Britain began preparing for a major war with Germany, developing the Spitfire and the Hurricane to defend the country against aerial attack and investing in radar (rather than the atomic bomb) to consolidate a defensive strategy.

Only a year before Hitler came to power in 1933, Prime Minister Stanley Baldwin proclaimed that 'the bomber will always get through', a phrase which could be taken as a cynical contempt for the fighter advocates or a supportive endorsement of the bomber fraternity! Either way, Britain addressed the under-performing state of extant bombers through a development programme which would attempt to redress the balance, and formed RAF Bomber Command on 14 July 1936 along with Fighter Command, Coastal Command and Transport Command in the same year. Gearing up for war, Britain was doomed to enter the conflict in September 1939 with light bombers such as the Bristol Blenheim and the Fairey Battle, the Handley Page Hampden medium bomber and the medium-range night bomber, the Vickers Wellington.

While anticipating the introduction of the four-engine 'heavies' – the Short Stirling and the Handley Page Halifax – the longer-term requirements of Bomber Command would be met in large part by the Avro Lancaster, itself an outgrowth of the inadequately powered two-engine Manchester. Not before 1942–43 would the RAF be capable of putting up a strong and significantly effective strategic bomber force, joined by the Americans in the Combined Bomber Offensive.

BELOW The Japanese city of Osaka, devastated by a firestorm raid in 1945, the destructive capability of the bomber vindicating the prophetic assertions of Billy Mitchell. *(USAF)*

A new generation

In several respects it can be said that the second phase of strategic bombing began with the Combined Bomber Offensive in the second half of 1942, when the United States joined Britain in the war against Hitler. That would greatly encourage planners to equip the US Army Air Forces with aircraft capable of intercontinental offensives. The US mobilised its own technical resources, quickly supplemented by an escalating capacity in the RAF to drop large quantities of bombs on targets deep in the Ruhr and across the towns and cities of Nazi-occupied Europe. Contested by the Americans, who preferred pin-point bombing of selected industrial targets, the British demonstrated the capacity of massed bomber formations to burn out cities, creating firestorms and widespread panic in the workforce striving to replenish German forces on the battlefield. Either way, both major allies signed up to the concept of strategic warfare. It was within that environment that the B-36 emerged, on a scale far beyond anything that had been anticipated before.

LEFT Gen Curtis LeMay. From planning bombing runs on Germany to the strategist managing firestorm raids on Japan, this outspoken extrovert would push forward plans for intercontinental bombers, paving the way for the B-36. *(SAF)*

The development of US strategic bombing really began when it declared war on Germany in April 1917, and studied the evolution of aerial warfare in Europe over the preceding two years to fix plans for its own use of air power. In plans drawn up for the Expeditionary

BELOW Mass production was key to the resource requirement of long-range strategic bombing campaigns, epitomised here by the Boeing factory producing B-17s. *(Boeing)*

bombers, typified by the Boeing Model 299 – the famous B-17. This aircraft was designed to a concept of self-defence in the belief that single-engine fighters could never be expected to escort long-range bombers all the way to the target and back. Bristling with machine guns, the B-17 was appropriately named Flying Fortress and the Army Air Corps flew it on very long-range flights across Central and South America to demonstrate its performance and boast its capability.

Carrying a crew of eight, the initial XB-17 had four defensive machine gun positions with a bomb-carrying capacity of up to 4,800lb (2,177kg) and, with four Pratt & Whitney S1EG Hornet engines a top speed of 236mph (380kph) and a range of 3,100mls (4,988km). It was the B-17E which would enter the fray from US Eighth Air Force bases in the UK during the second half of 1942. With four Wright R-1820-65 engines it had a maximum speed of 317mph (510kph), a cruising speed of 224mph (360kph) and a range of 2,000mls (3,218km) with a 4,000lb (1,814kg) bomb load.

The B-17E carried nine machine guns and the addition of a ball turret in the under-fuselage position but the B-17G was the definitive development, 8,670 being manufactured by Boeing, Vega and Douglas. Incorporating a new nose turret tested on the B-17F, the G had up to 13 machine guns and a maximum bomb load of 9,600lb (4,354kg). Of course the maximum bomb load compromised range and the assumption that the B-17 would be capable of defending itself proved flawed, driving a pause on the strategic bomber offensive for a redefinition of tactics more akin to that followed by the RAF.

The need for escort fighters pushed development of long-range versions of the P-47 and the P-51 but Luftwaffe pilots found the hail of fire from the bomber formations a formidable obstacle, pushing for high-risk attack in nose-on-nose engagements. With closing speeds of up to 540mph (869kph) or 792ft (241m) per second, a sharp pull-up to fly the length of the bomber's fuselage from nose to tail and away was a tactic performed only by the brave, especially when, in peeling off, the fighter would come under fire from other B-17s in the formation.

Force, advocates of strategic bombing such as William 'Billy' Mitchell and Benjamin D. Foulois opposed the tactical use of air power as favoured by Gen William Pershing. Under post-war restructuring, development of military aviation for varied tasks such as bombing, attack, defence and reconnaissance proceeded on a more or less equal footing.

By the early 1930s, several different all-metal monoplane bombers were competing with each other and the subsidy of trans-continental mail-carrying aircraft, together with the development of trans-Pacific flying boats sponsored the technology for fast, long-range

Opposition to the CBO came from a distinct difference of opinion on the way to employ the bombers: the British wanted large scale bombing of cities to destroy the factories and the homes of industrial workers while the Americans sought to pursue pin-point bombing of critical targets, factories and unique facilities. The debate harked back to a study of strategic bombardment at the Air Corps Tactical School in 1930 from which textbooks called for development of specialised bomb-aiming equipment. That resulted in the Norden and Sperry bombsights and the development of those items preceded the arrival of the B-17 so that when operations began from England in 1942 the US Army Air Corps had distinctly superior bomb-aiming equipment.

The enshrined view that it was morally indefensible to target civilians in war would be a source of robust debate between the Army Air Forces and the Royal Air Force throughout

LEFT The Sperry S-1 operated off a 110 vdc current and divided the controls between opposing hand positions, thereby making it easier to operate than the Norden sight. *(David Baker Collection)*

LEFT The Sperry gyroscope for the S-1 bombsight ran at 24,000rpm, rather than the 8,000rpm for the Norden sight and was therefore less prone to drift. *(David Baker Collection)*

the European war but that dissipated when the US deliberately targeted urban residential areas close to industrial facilities in the war against Japan. The shift in thinking had begun shortly after Pearl Harbor, 7 December 1941, when the Japanese Imperial Navy attacked the US base in a pre-emptive strike before a declaration of war.

Long before this day, in May 1940 after Germany took Norway, attacking France and the Low Countries, recognising that at some point the US would have to become involved, President Roosevelt made unrealistic demands of the aviation industry. He asked Congress to approve a force of 50,000 aircraft. At that date the entire industry had produced only 40,000 aircraft since the Wright Brothers first flew in 1903. In 1940 the US aviation industry could produce only 2,000 aircraft.

The emergency forced politically by the escalating war in Europe and the threat of England falling under the Nazi hammer blows spurred procurement of the Consolidated B-24 Liberator, the Martin B-26 Marauder and of an entirely new type of bomber, the Boeing

B-29. Eventually known as the Superfortress, the B-29 and its contemporaries ran to a new mantra – the replacement of transitional acquisition practices being torn up and replaced by a new flow rate for aircraft design, development, manufacture and introduction to service deployment.

Historically, the Army had bought its aircraft through a process of research, design development and engineering followed by production. An orderly, systematic and predictable cycle to which the US aviation industry had worked for several decades. Because of the limitations of the US aviation industry in fast-track development and manufacture, the Army compressed this conventional acquisition cycle into what became known as concurrency.

The B-24, B-26 and B-29 were the first project types to adopt this flow path, which entered production much earlier in the development stage. This led to detailed design locking in certain vulnerabilities which could have catastrophic results. For instance, the B-26 entered production with a wing too small

Boeing, the winner getting just over $300,000 and the loser being compensated with the balance. The Model 35 was impressive, larger than the B-29, the first prototype of which was then being assembled, but it was unimpressive and unable to meet the stipulated requirement; a problem experienced by the other contenders.

Submitted on 3 May, Boeing's Model 384, and its later 385, failed to impress as they each appeared to be a lacklustre attempt at meeting a compromise position on range. The Model 384 had four engines with tractor propeller arrangements and looked to some extent like a stretched B-29; the Model 385 had six tractor engines with each design featuring defensive armament in two dorsal, two ventral and single tail turrets. Characteristically, the 385 had a high-aspect ratio wing very similar to the B-29.

Within several weeks of the initial request for concept designs, Northrop and Douglas got involved, with Consolidated, Boeing and Douglas submitting design data for their individual concepts. Northrop had been keen to push its flying wing concept and on 27 May the Air Materiel Command requested further details but while it could satisfy the 10,000lb (4,536kg) bomb load the range was a poor 6,000mls (9,654km), far short of that required. Northrop's flying wing was a radical concept to minimise drag and improve aerodynamic efficiency by eliminating the need for tailplanes, a conventional fuselage incorporating crew and bomb-carrying equipment within a blended wing centre-section. Counter-intuitively, it would come to pose the biggest challenge to the B-36.

Other manufacturers got involved, including North American Aviation which proposed a twin-boom layout, a single boom extending back from each inner pair of its four engines and a truncated fuselage emerging from the wing centre-section. Bomb bays were fitted to each tail boom assembly. Designated NA-116, this proposal had very little traction and disappeared from the list of contenders. Nor was the initial proposal from Douglas acceptable, their Model 423 design featuring the same range limitation as the Northrop flying wing. In fact, all four major studies got bogged down in the complexity of producing a workable design to meet the demanding specification.

ABOVE The B-29 was the first production aircraft to have pressurised crew areas, the aft compartment being shown here and accessed from the nose compartment through a tunnel over the bomb bay. *(Boeing)*

BELOW The Boeing KB-50J, a converted B-29 bomber which provided air-refuelling capability, a concept which would have no place in aircraft such as the B-36 with its exceptionally long range. *(USAF)*

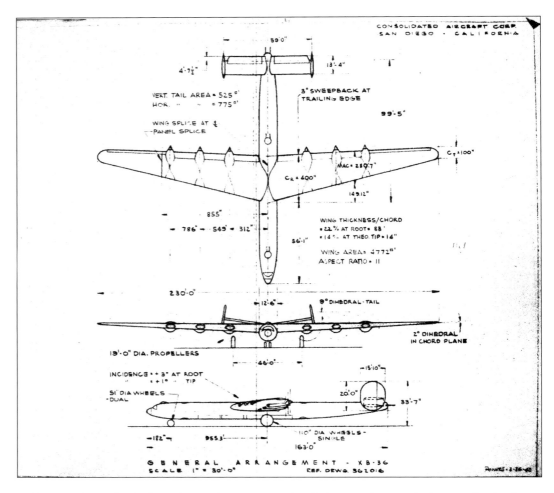

Responding, officials from the newly re-named Army Air Force (AAF) and Air Staff leaders met on 19 August for a conference to discuss the study results and issued an amended requirement, retaining the full range and bomb load but downgrading the speed requirement while setting a service ceiling of 40,000ft (12,192m). Defensive armament was to comprise six 37-mm cannon and eight 50-calibre machine guns to match the need to defend against attack from three fighters simultaneously. Paradoxically, this added to the weight of the aircraft and threatened a solution to the range problem.

As noted above regarding the B-29 story, the German attack on the USSR accelerated plans for aircraft procurement, gathering war clouds making it clear that America would soon have to start fighting the Nazi war machine. Urging an accelerated approach, the AAF leadership anticipated that a prototype could not be ready before early 1944 and consideration of

the design requirement further emphasised a mission radius of 4,000mls (6,436km). A flaw in this cycle lay in the lack of synergy between the availability of design data and the final decision on requirements. The 19 August meeting took place before Boeing received formal approval for its studies while Consolidated had still to complete its final investigation. Nevertheless, the four contractors were pressed to submit their proposals immediately and all were in the hands of the AAF by mid-September, at which point Douglas and Boeing dropped out, the former believing the specification asked the physically impossible.

Perhaps through preoccupation with existing and pending contracts as the aviation and munitions industry went into war-fever, none of the four contenders had provided proper studies to the satisfaction of the customer, the AAF report declaring that 'in no case was sufficient aerodynamic data submitted to permit a complete check' of the performance, 'only one of the design studies contained data giving the amount of fuel carried, and only one study was accompanied by a general arrangement drawing'.

It was arguably difficult to remove the politics of the situation: with a new level of authority within the Army structure, should war come the AAF was proudly expecting to offer great expectations; the White House wanted to push fast with war-winning weapons (aware of how the US had been unable to produce a single home-grown aircraft of any meaningful contribution for the First World War); and industry saw lucrative, lower-hanging fruit with which to expand its contract base. Suddenly, in six months after Air Materiel Division had requested studies into the 'aeronautical art' of the future there was a pressing urgency for a new intercontinental bomber, without wind tunnel tests or any detailed proposal.

But the final determination was that the Northrop and Consolidated concepts were 'within current boundaries' of the possible and within two months had determined, without any further data, that the Northrop flying wing had tremendous potential and that Consolidated's more conventional proposal was worthy of further analysis.

The detailed proposal from Consolidated was sent to the AAF on 6 October 1941 along with a costing analysis and a request for $800,000 to assemble two prototypes. The company was aware of difficulties defined earlier under the fast-track, concurrency management concept and specifically asked that it be kept free of interference and continuous changes and revisions to the requirement. In fact, the B-36 would prove to be one of the most troubled, dysfunctional programmes of the period and continuously in a state of flux, demonstrably exhibited by its evolution long after production orders had been received. But it was not the proposal from Consolidated that had first excited the AAF.

On 22 November 1941, Northrop was awarded a contract for two XB-35 prototype and 13 YB-35 flying wing aircraft with the requirement for the type to enter production via a contract awarded in December 1942 for 200 production models. But the flying wing concept was novel, unproven and lacking in

ABOVE Jack Northrop had a passion for flying wings and put up his own contender, selected for prototyping into the XB-35 with four pusher engines. *(Northrop)*

BELOW The XB-35 in flight, paying the price for a configuration with considerably less drag by presenting an unstable bomb platform which would eventually doom the type to failure. *(Northrop)*

ABOVE The XB-35 42-13603, the first with four pairs of contra-rotating propellers. (USAF)

a wide range of wind tunnel tests and data requirements. Nothing presented by this date could have satisfactorily assured the AAF of its success. Yet the B-35 programme is of great relevance to the story of the B-36 and will become increasingly so.

Formed as recently as August 1939 by John K. (Jack) Northrop at the end of a ten-year period developing flying wing concepts, the company lacked the resources and the capability for serial production. To alleviate these problems the AAF integrated the Glenn L.

Martin Company, cancelling its proposed B-33 in November 1942 so that it could support the contract to Northrop, which was responsible for design and would receive considerable help and support from Martin with engineering assistance and production planning for tooling, jigs and assembly techniques. For its part, Northrop wanted to learn more about the flying wing concept and it built prototype flying wing test aircraft and, in support of the B-35 programme, built four 30% scale N-9M types to evaluate the flying qualities and handling characteristics of the full-size XB-35.

The first N-9M crashed in May 1943 and most of the 45 flights it made were terminated due to mechanical failures. The second N-9M made its first flight in June 1943 and the first drag data on the flying wing was obtained that September. But this was bad news when aerodynamic tests showed a 9–12% increase in drag compared to wind tunnel tests. Also, serious stability and directional control problems were encountered, with spin control, stall characteristics and control at low speeds all indicating major issues. These fundamental

LEFT The wheels on the XB-35 retracted into the nose and outer sections of the mid-wing area, the crew compartment being blended into the low-drag profile. (Northrop)

design issues could not be 'flown out' of the system through subtle changes and were an obstacle to progress with the flying wing.

With production having begun a year before critical aerodynamic and test data with the N-9M revealed serious flaws, the XB-35 became the ultimate example of the folly of concurrency, leaving the engineering staff with little option but to serve dire warnings on the AAF which forced the hand of Materiel Command in giving negative reports. Much of the problem had been the pressure imposed on Northrop by Martin, which urgently sought detailed drawings for production when general design of the prototypes was still in work.

Originally scheduled for late 1943, the first flight was delayed by more than three years and in May 1945 the AAF cancelled the contract and allowed work to proceed only on the two XB-35 prototypes and the 13 YB-35s ordered in November 1941. Along with dubious performance and poor aero-performance, escalating costs added to the aircraft's nemesis. In 1941 the prototyping phase was estimated to cost $4.45million; three years later the total programme had grown to an estimated $25million. Beset by problems pointedly down to concurrency and compressed and overlapping cycles of design, assembly and modification, the first XB-35 would not fly before 25 June 1946.

ABOVE An aesthetic shot of the XB-35 in flight, compromised as a bomber by limited range due to higher than the expected, albeit low, drag and by a delayed development cycle. *(Northrop)*

LEFT The XB-35 was cancelled in May 1945 with work allowed to proceed on only two XB-35 and thirteen YB-35 prototypes. *(USAF)*

Chapter Two

Developing the B-36

On 15 November 1941, Consolidated received a contract to build two XB-36 aircraft at its factory in San Diego, California. Exactly one week later the company engineers concurred with a decision that the Consolidated Model 36 was the one to go with. There had been many interpolations and extrapolations but the world's first intercontinental bomber began to take shape in a war about to go global.

OPPOSITE The general configuration and dimensions of the primary production version of the B-36 would incorporate the several changes made after flight tests with the XB-36, seen here. These would not change throughout the life of the programme. *(Dennis Jenkins)*

Nobody could have predicted that the Empire of Japan under one of its most militant governments ever, would attempt to break a US blockade on its commercial and military interests by attacking Pearl Harbor on 7 December 1941, an act of war which was, according to President Franklin D. Roosevelt, 'a day of infamy'. Japan's entry into one of the biggest clash of arms in history would underpin development of the world's biggest aircraft, by this date already in detailed design, an aircraft that would impose radical solutions on seemingly intractable problems.

Clearly, the B-36 would be required to strike targets across distances unprecedented in aviation history. In efforts to achieve a clean wing in search of maximum range, the Model 36 had six pusher engines installed in the aft wing section which had a span of 230ft (70.1m). Set high on a fuselage with a length of 163ft (49.7m) it supported a twin-fin tail arrangement with a height above the ground of 35.8ft (10.9m). The proposed Model 36 was powered by six Pratt & Whitney X-Wasp, air-cooled radial engines each driving three-bladed propellers sweeping a diameter of 19ft (5.8m).

The thick wing had a root depth of 7.5ft (2.3m) which would allow maintenance access in flight to the six pusher engines. The maximum bomb capacity of 72,000lb (32,660kg) was accommodated in four individual bays with fore and aft pressurised crew compartments connected by a pressurised tunnel, 80ft (24.4m) long and 25in (63.5cm) in diameter positioned along the port side of the bomb bays. This allowed crewmembers to move between fore and aft pressurised compartments. Crewmembers would lie on their backs on a wheeled trolley and move themselves along the tunnel by crossing a rope hand-over-hand and pulling themselves along. Because the aircraft could spend up to two days in the air, bunks, a galley and toilet were located in the aft compartments.

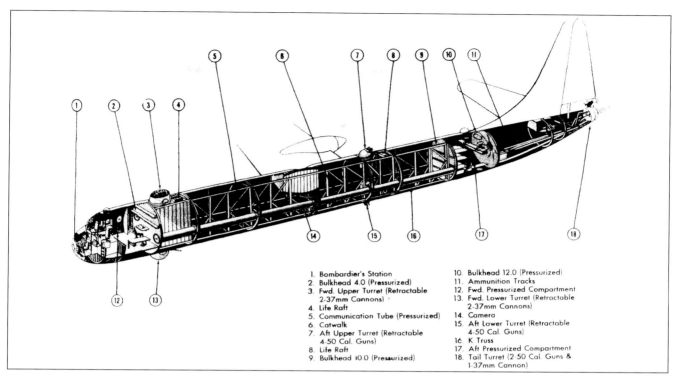

1. Bombardier's Station
2. Bulkhead 4.0 (Pressurized)
3. Fwd. Upper Turret (Retractable 2-37mm Cannons)
4. Life Raft
5. Communication Tube (Pressurized)
6. Catwalk
7. Aft Upper Turret (Retractable 4-50 Cal. Guns)
8. Life Raft
9. Bulkhead 10.0 (Pressurized)
10. Bulkhead 12.0 (Pressurized)
11. Ammunition Tracks
12. Fwd. Pressurized Compartment
13. Fwd. Lower Turret (Retractable 2-37mm Cannons)
14. Camera
15. Aft Lower Turret (Retractable 4-50 Cal. Guns)
16. K Truss
17. Aft Pressurized Compartment
18. Tail Turret (2-50 Cal. Guns & 1-37mm Cannon)

ABOVE The proposed layout for the XB-36 with the original nose section and turret arrangement for the defensive armament, elements of the design which would change significantly due to the 'concurrency' approach to integrated design, development and production. Note the location of the long access tunnel between forward and aft pressurised compartments. (USAF)

RIGHT The forward pressurised cabin containing seating arrangement for up to ten crewmembers and three more in the aft compartment. (Convair)

Defensive armament included five 37-mm cannon and ten 50-calibre machine guns in four retractable turrets in dorsal and ventral positions and a radar-controlled tail turret. Many changes would be made to this configuration as the type went through various stages of modification, responses to changing technical requirements and the inevitable compromises as detailed design and assembly ran in parallel. Initially, the Model 36 had a fuel capacity of 21,116 USgal (79,924 litres) in tanks integral to the wings. The cockpit was conventional side-by-side seating for pilot and co-pilot with engineer and navigator stations behind.

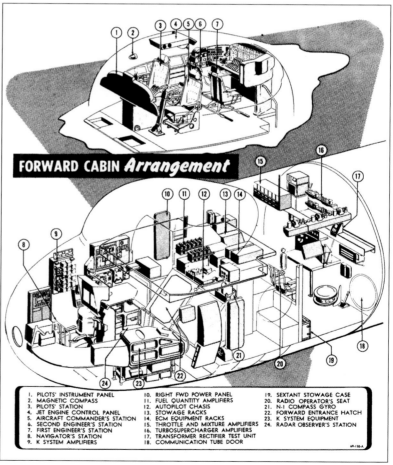

FORWARD CABIN Arrangement

1. PILOTS' INSTRUMENT PANEL
2. MAGNETIC COMPASS
3. PILOTS' STATION
4. JET ENGINE CONTROL PANEL
5. AIRCRAFT COMMANDER'S STATION
6. SECOND ENGINEER'S STATION
7. FIRST ENGINEER'S STATION
8. NAVIGATOR'S STATION
9. K SYSTEM AMPLIFIERS
10. RIGHT FWD POWER PANEL
11. FUEL QUANTITY AMPLIFIERS
12. AUTOPILOT CHASIS
13. STOWAGE RACKS
14. ECM EQUIPMENT RACKS
15. THROTTLE AND MIXTURE AMPLIFIERS
16. TURBOSUPERCHARGER AMPLIFIERS
17. TRANSFORMER RECTIFIER TEST UNIT
18. COMMUNICATION TUBE DOOR
19. SEXTANT STOWAGE CASE
20. RADIO OPERATOR'S SEAT
21. N-1 COMPASS GYRO
22. FORWARD ENTRANCE HATCH
23. K SYSTEM EQUIPMENT
24. RADAR OBSERVER'S STATION

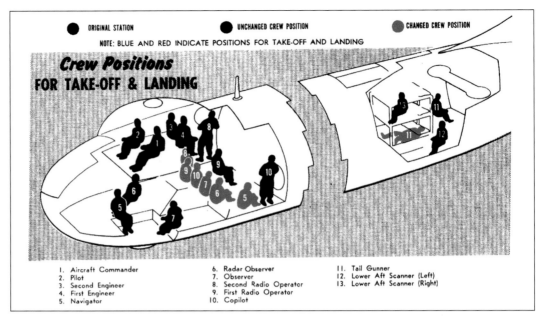

As stated, detailed design would mature over time and there would be many changes to the B-36 that entered service but manufacturing techniques came in for special scrutiny, if only because weight was a serious problem with this large aircraft and savings in manufacturing would bring dividends in range and payload capacity. In an attempt to reduce drag from several thousand pop-rivets, the company conducted research on alternative methods of securing separate elements together, including the use of a special metal

adhesive. Available in both liquid and tape, it was applied progressively throughout the construction of the aircraft to a greater number of structural elements until, by the early 1950s, almost one-third of the exterior surface was bonded using these forms.

Concerned about the fatigue life of this new adhesive, special tests were conducted, revealing a much better performance than mechanical fasteners, a spot-welded technique completing 12 million cycles compared with 18 million for riveted joins and 240

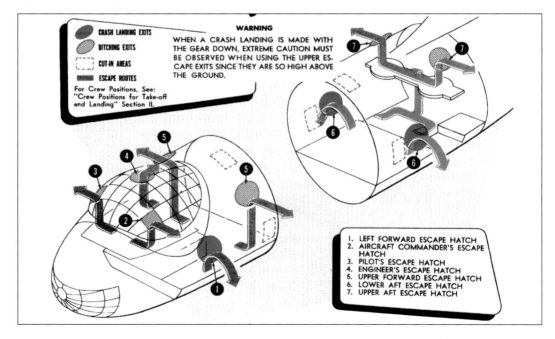

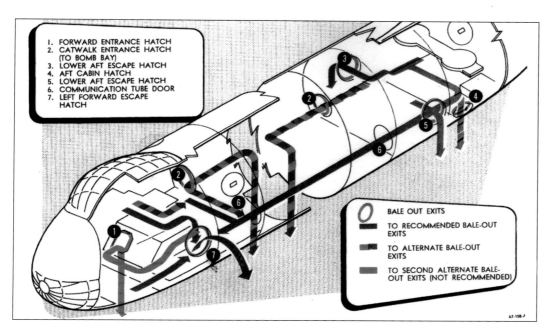

1. FORWARD ENTRANCE HATCH
2. CATWALK ENTRANCE HATCH (TO BOMB BAY)
3. LOWER AFT ESCAPE HATCH
4. AFT CABIN HATCH
5. LOWER AFT ESCAPE HATCH
6. COMMUNICATION TUBE DOOR
7. LEFT FORWARD ESCAPE HATCH

BALE OUT EXITS
⎯ TO RECOMMENDED BALE-OUT EXITS
⎯ TO ALTERNATE BALE-OUT EXITS
⎯ TO SECOND ALTERNATE BALE-OUT EXITS (NOT RECOMMENDED)

67-158-/

LEFT Bale out positions and crew exit routes in the event of an in-flight evacuation. *(Convair)*

million cycles for the new metal-bonding adhesive. This was but one example of the way the programme provided opportunity for pioneering techniques and materials never used before, including new system concepts and engineering design.

A significant research and development effort invested new means of satisfying the hydraulic and electrical requirement, driven in part by the large dimensions of the flying control surfaces. Believing that the standard AAF requirement for a 1,500-psi hydraulic system was inadequate for moving the oversize undercarriage and the large flaps, Consolidated developed a 3,000-psi system with the assistance of engineers from the AAF at Air Service Command, set up at Wright Field, Ohio, in March 1941. Everything associated with this new hydraulic system was functionally redesigned and this would become the standard for all US military aircraft for several decades.

The electrical system for the XB-36 came from Wright Field itself, where a new 400-cycle, 208-volt, three-phase alternating current (ac) system had been developed. This was adopted to replace the direct current (dc) system used on other, and previous aircraft. The logic in this was found in weight saving alone, an ac system weighing less than one-quarter the weight of an equivalent dc system. The ac system was more reliable and less

BELOW The general layout of the aft pressurised crew area with changes in two separate configurations, indicative of the extensive series of modifications and changes driven by operational experience and technical developments. *(Convair)*

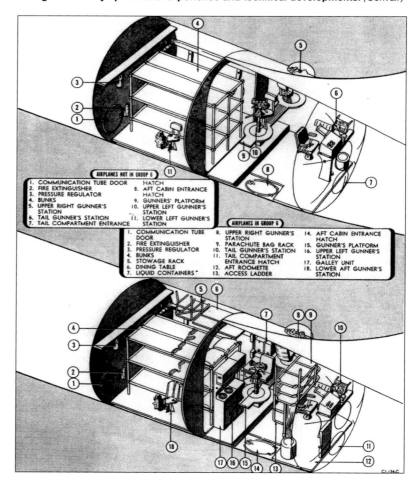

AIRPLANES NOT IN GROUP 6
1. COMMUNICATION TUBE DOOR
2. FIRE EXTINGUISHER
3. PRESSURE REGULATOR
4. BUNKS
5. UPPER RIGHT GUNNER'S STATION
6. TAIL GUNNER'S STATION
7. TAIL COMPARTMENT ENTRANCE HATCH
8. AFT CABIN ENTRANCE HATCH
9. GUNNERS' PLATFORM
10. UPPER LEFT GUNNER'S STATION
11. LOWER LEFT GUNNER'S STATION

AIRPLANES IN GROUP 6
1. COMMUNICATION TUBE DOOR
2. FIRE EXTINGUISHER
3. PRESSURE REGULATOR
4. BUNKS
5. STOWAGE RACK
6. DINING TABLE
7. LIQUID CONTAINERS *
8. UPPER RIGHT GUNNER'S STATION
9. PARACHUTE BAG RACK
10. TAIL GUNNER'S STATION
11. TAIL COMPARTMENT ENTRANCE HATCH
12. AFT ROOMETTE
13. ACCESS LADDER
14. AFT CABIN ENTRANCE HATCH
15. GUNNER'S PLATFORM
16. UPPER LEFT GUNNER'S STATION
17. GALLEY UNIT
18. LOWER AFT GUNNER'S STATION

CI-134C

prone to breaking down and at high altitude was less prone to arcing, another technology development which would become a standard.

Fire extinguishing too benefited from a switch to a methyl-bromide system replacing the standard carbon-dioxide suppressant usually installed within the engine casings. Moreover, it had a lower boiling point and that allowed safe containment at lower pressures in lighter cylinders. As a further example of the evolving nature of systems installation, this new fire extinguishing equipment was not ready for the first XB-36 prototype but would be incorporated in subsequent aircraft as well as the XC-99 (which see later).

These developments were typical of the contributions made by the programme with its tightly compressed layers of detailed design, tests, engineering refinement, systems development and assembly, a seminal example of compressed concurrency with all the flaws and failures that this incurred. But in projecting from the near-term to mid-term requirements, concurrency did stimulate new, sometimes radical, engineering solutions and as such it served as a technology pathfinder.

BELOW The aft rest and bunk area. Equipment here would change significantly according to mark or variant and the operational role, as either a bomber or photo-reconnaissance aircraft. *(Convair)*

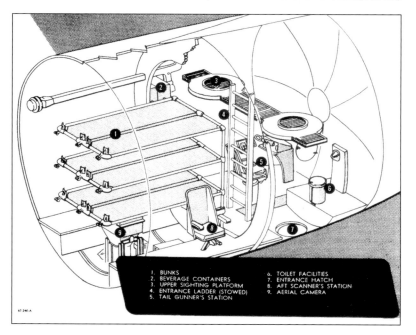

1. BUNKS
2. BEVERAGE CONTAINERS
3. UPPER SIGHTING PLATFORM
4. ENTRANCE LADDER (STOWED)
5. TAIL GUNNER'S STATION
6. TOILET FACILITIES
7. ENTRANCE HATCH
8. AFT SCANNER'S STATION
9. AERIAL CAMERA

Refinements

Wind tunnel tests were a vital element in developing detailed design and began with a 1/26th scale model of the aircraft. It was evaluated in the tunnel facilities of the Massachusetts Institute of Technology (MIT) and at the Guggenheim Aeronautical Laboratory of the California Institute of Technology (GALCIT). As with most new aeronautical designs, the contractor selected a wing profile from the National Advisory Committee for Aeronautics (predecessor to NASA) and selected the NACA 65 profile, a laminar flow wing for high lift and low drag with minimal wind resistance from the way the appendages, including engines, were arranged. But this shape proved unsuitable when tests began in July 1942 and the model was changed to incorporate a NACA 63 profile but with a recommendation to provide a trailing edge forward sweep of 3° from root to tip for improved centre of gravity and balance.

Of singular value to Consolidated was the wooden mock-up set up in a building near to the design and engineering offices and manufacturing plant at its San Diego facility. The company had a history of building large aircraft, notably the PBY Catalina, the B-24 Liberator and the Navy's four-engine P2BY Coronado flying boat which entered service in December 1940. Although production runs for all but the B-24 were limited, the company had experience with both ends of the order spectrum. In fact, its design and engineering experience preceded these types through a distinguished line of training aircraft from the early 1920s, when Consolidated was formed in Buffalo, New York, culminating in the P-30 as the only two-seat, closed-cockpit, retractable landing gear monoplane fighter operated by the Air Corps from 1935.

More B-24s were built for US and allied air forces than any other type of American aircraft, its design and evolution closely managed by I. M. Laddon, the chief engineer on the Catalina. As executive vice-president of engineering, he would be associated with the development of the B-36 in these critical stages of its genesis and production but actual design development was in the capable hands of Harry A. Sutton,

RIGHT **Crew bunks in the aft pressure section, some changes over the life of the B-36 bringing additional levels of crew comfort, especially for the very long reconnaissance flights.** *(Dennis Jenkins)*

who managed the engineering department, and Ted P. Hall, who ran the design group for the early stages of its evolution.

The wooden mock-up proved a stern test rig for the design of the exterior and of the defensive armament, the configuration being crucial to the streamlining of the wetted area, with the undercarriage also coming in for attention due to the extreme weight of the aircraft and the potential forces imposed on landing. When it was inspected on 20 July 1942 it was clear that the design would fall well short of its 10,000ml (16,090km) range requirement. Debate ensued over the desirability of reducing defensive armament to achieve better airflow and reduce drag but that would have significantly diminished the ability of the aircraft to defend itself and negated much of its potential for surviving deep into contested air space.

During August the decision was made to move the programme to Fort Worth, Texas, into the new Government Aircraft Plant No. 4 more than 1,200mls (1,931km) east. But this was a much safer location, given the scare of possible attacks by Japan on industrial facilities along the western seaboard. This freed up the San Diego facilities for B-24 subassembly production for its expanding order book. Added production requirements encroached upon the Fort Worth facility, however, as B-24 production expanded there too and the B-32 Dominator began to roll off the line as well from 1943.

The general expansion of aircraft production driven by the rearmament programme had a significant impact on the short-term needs of the Army and early difficulties in the Pacific against Japan's Imperial Navy intensified the demand for aircraft already in the early production stage. As well as for the B-29 which

RIGHT **Rest time was frequently punctuated with active crew duties in close proximity to crew stations and continuous activity.** *(Dennis Jenkins)*

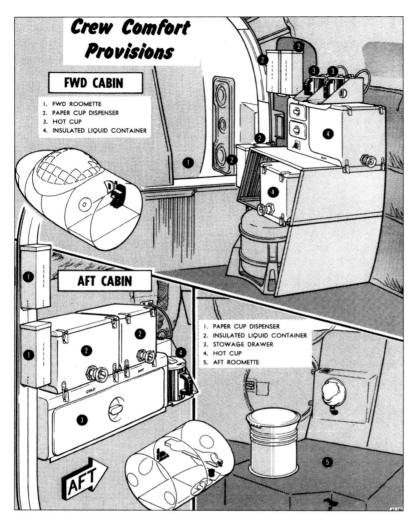

Crew Comfort Provisions

FWD CABIN

1. FWD ROOMETTE
2. PAPER CUP DISPENSER
3. HOT CUP
4. INSULATED LIQUID CONTAINER

AFT CABIN

1. PAPER CUP DISPENSER
2. INSULATED LIQUID CONTAINER
3. STOWAGE DRAWER
4. HOT CUP
5. AFT ROOMETTE

AFT

ABOVE Extended flight operations could see the B-36 in the air for more than 24 hours, drawing in a unique requirement for crew comfort with galley, dispensers and a range of cooking provisions in the forward pressurised section. *(Convair)*

was significantly along in its development. All this argued against an acceleration of long-term projects such as the B-36 which was essentially put on hold so that available, flight-proven types could be granted priority on the production line.

But it was not all bad news. In mid-1942 the AAF agreed to a cargo version which would emerge as the XC-99 (which see later) on the proviso that this would only appear at least three months after the first flight of the XB-36. Consolidated had wanted to fast-track the cargo version so that, unencumbered with the design and integration of defensive armament and combat kit, it could be used to prove out the general configuration and aerodynamic performance of the aircraft including its engines and landing gear. Nevertheless, this was a false expectation because the basic design of the aircraft was still in a state of flux.

In attempts to satisfy unanswered questions regarding the overall design, which had been approved in September 1942 after the detailed analysis of the mock-up, there were worries regarding the twin vertical tails which were thought vulnerable to stress and overload during a hard landing. The company was to apply to the B-36 what it eventually selected for the B-24 and the B-32 (and what Boeing had done to the B-29) – a single, large vertical fin and rudder. This was agreed during late 1942 but only approved by a change order dated 10 October 1943, saving 3,850lb in weight, reducing the base drag and significantly improving stability. The price was a 120-day delay in the delivery of the XB-36 prototype.

This is an appropriate juncture to apply the name Convair, signalled when the Vultee Aircraft Corporation took a controlling interest in Consolidated in November 1942 and changed the name of the organisation to the Consolidated-Vultee Aircraft Corporation (CVAC) from 17 March 1943. It took some time for the name Convair to be adopted officially but it arose naturally from the acronym and is relevant to the story of the B-36 because it was under that moniker that it appeared in service.

Although still some way from a first flight, Convair received a production contract worth about $175 million for 100 aircraft through W33-038-ac-7 in an authorising letter dated 23 July 1943, replacing an earlier letter of intent. But the programme would be compromised both by the success of other bomber types and by the requirement to boost production of those aircraft which could be delivered much earlier for the war effort. Although the B-29 proved temperamental in its early test and development, causing some to question its suitability for rapid production, it was already much further ahead than the B-36 programme. And so, as it neared production readiness, the B-29 was assigned to the war with Japan, leaving the B-24 and the B-17 to fulfil requirements in the European Theatre of Operations.

There had been some concern about the engine selected for the XB-36, with proposals to advance a competing in-line engine, the Lycoming BX which was gaining support for its lower fuel consumption – a key to long range.

But that was rejected although there were significant challenges with the P&W X-Wasp engine, soon to receive the designation R-4360-25 Wasp Major, which was languishing due to a lack of priority. Consolidated was ill at ease with this and sought to have an alternative but the BX had been downgraded due to a shift in resources and manpower to existing programmes, again for the war effort. The War Office was concerned that by having two engines compete for the B-36 programme it would slow completion of the basic design.

Development

With the situation in the Pacific war showing little sign of improvement, in June 1943 the AAF ordered 100 B-36s into production. With Congress closely monitoring the national purse strings (the war budget had grown from 2.4% of GDP to 32% since America's entry into the conflict and would peak at 45% the following year, collapsing to less than 6% two years after Japan surrendered) every weapons programme had to justify itself. With the Navy tasked with seizing the Marianas so that B-29s could hit mainland Japan, the AAF wanted to show a need for very long range bombers before seizure of the islands eliminated the requirement for a successor. The need to effect an irreversible commitment to the B-36 before the war ended was an urgent spur to the production decision. This was verified by the assistant chief of the air staff, Major General Echols, when he said that 'the ordinary procedure would result in a delay of one year in production...and it was very possible that the war would be over before production could commence'.

But there was more to it than that. In 1943

ABOVE Fabrication of the glazed crew enclosure showing the frames and contour where it fits into the upper fuselage mould line. *(Dennis Jenkins)*

BELOW Production brought unique problems due to scale and to the wide range of changes driven by the 'concurrency' approach during development and as a result of flight operations. Here the centre fuselage section of a B-36B (44-92059) is in fabrication. *(Dennis Jenkins)*

the AAF knew, as did military leaders, that communist Russia was a potential post-war threat and there was already a resurgent move to provide the tools for a post-WW2 stand-off with the USSR. Such thoughts had already been sown by Winston Churchill, who would himself ask the War Ministry in Britain to prepare for a strategic war with Russia. The need to fight Hitler from the continental United States had been removed following the establishment of US forces in Britain but the possibility of fighting Soviet Russia from the US was very real.

In more direct terms, the cancellation of the B-35 programme as a potential intercontinental bomber left a vacuum in long-range planning for that class of aircraft and so triggered, albeit with the other considerations, pressure on the government to accelerate the B-36. The possibility of having to use it for raids on Japan was not as unrealistic as it sounds. There was no guarantee that the Navy would seize the Marianas and without those the AAF would have to attack Japan from bases in China,

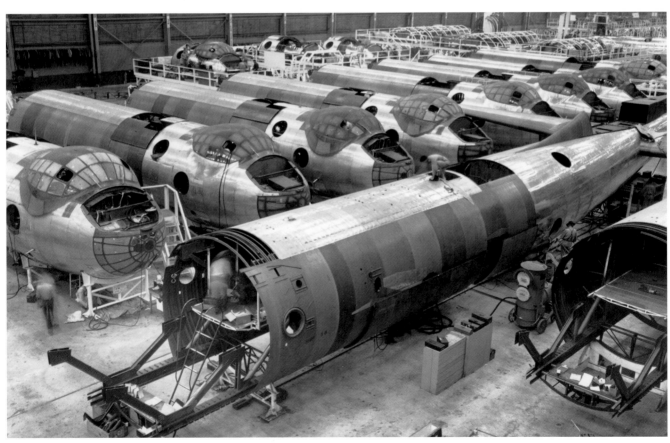

something it was already planning to do until the mainland came within range of Pacific island air bases.

Unfortunately, the programme began to show problems immediately after the production commitment was made. The manufacturer's schedule for a first flight began to slip from the original date of May 1944 and when that year dawned the best estimate had stretched out to June 1945. Some of the delay was caused by technical difficulties which had been glossed over or ignored during 1943. The entire aerofoil design had to be changed and that was not the sort of issue that would normally occur during a production phase. Concurrency again! Then there was a wing flutter problem which would await the flight of the prototype for ground tests before flight trials.

In studies conducted in August 1944, the fundamental flaws with the B-35 programme which brought about its demise prompted the AAF to seek a bomber to succeed the next generation, which turned out to be the B-36. It had to have a top speed of 450mph (724kph) and a service ceiling of 40,000ft (12,320m) while carrying a 10,000lb (4,536kg) bomb load to a target 5,000mls (8,045km) away, or a maximum 80,000lb (36,288kg) over much shorter range. The emergence of the jet fighter in both Britain and Germany was a mild shock to the AAF and played a significant part in the genesis of what would emerge as the B-52. But the infatuation with jet power, as well as the installed desire on the part of the AAF to perfect the flying wing, would bring back the B-35 flying wing concept but this time with jet engines as the B-49 to challenge the B-36. Of which more later.

The definitive contract for 100 B-36 aircraft reworking the deal signed a year previously was signed on 19 August 1944, worth $160million including the full engineering work and spares, a unit cost per aircraft more than three times that of a B-29. But the economics worked in its favour, with a B-36 working out at half the operating cost per ton/mile than a B-29. As the war neared its end, on 25 May 1945 the entire range of munitions and war

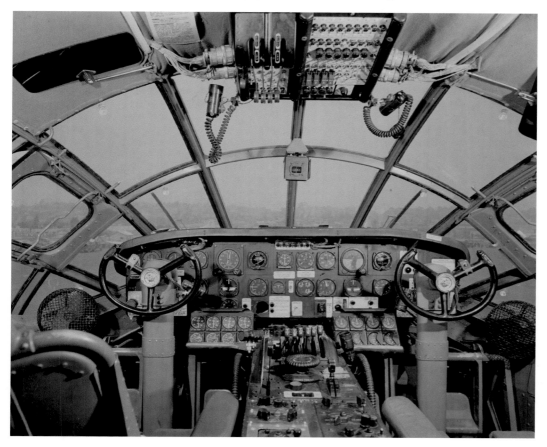

LEFT The full flight deck of the B-36 underwent a major change in arrangement following initial test flights with the XB-36, as seen here with the definitive configuration and change to the top glazing.
(Dennis Jenkins)

ABOVE The nose configuration was dictated by the requirements of the offensive and defensive capabilities, providing a bombardier and nose gunner positions below and in front of the upper flight deck. *(Dennis Jenkins)*

crew compartment, applicable from the second prototype as seen in accompanying images. Technical developments too introduced new equipment which added weight, 3,500lb (1,588kg) and more from the radio and radar equipment which was now imperative.

To avoid a penalty in base drag, design engineers worked to incorporate the requisite Western Electric AN/APQ-7 Eagle radar antenna within the leading edge of the wing. Some B-24 and B-29 aircraft carried the Eagle radar but with an antenna carried transversely under the fuselage giving the appearance of an additional wing. This effort was unnecessary as the APQ-7 was replaced by the APQ-23 X-band, high-altitude bombing radar in the B-36. But the problematic engines too gaining weight added an extra 2,304lb (1,045kg) overall.

Potentially more serious was the main landing gear for the tricycle undercarriage. As originally designed, the aircraft would have one tyre each side with a diameter of 110in (279cm), at 1,475lb (669kg) the largest tyres manufactured by the contractor, Goodyear Tire & Rubber. Each had a 225lb (102kg) inner tube pressurised to 100psi (5,175mmHg). The wheels were 46in (116.8cm) in diameter, weighing 850lb (385kg) to which were attached triple-disc brake units each weighing 735lb (333.3kg), for a total wheel assembly

contracts was cut back by 30% but as peace fell upon the world the B-36 went unscathed, largely as a result of the achievements of the strategic bombing campaign and the effect of the atomic bomb, which the AAF was determined to integrate as a deterrent against future aggression.

Several changes had been made to the design of the B-36 over the preceding two years and some new requirements inserted, including a different nose gun arrangement and work toward a different configuration of

RIGHT Under instruction. A Pratt & Whitney R-4360-5 cutaway training model provides a reference point for familiarisation and engineering instruction on the massive and powerful engine. *(Dennis Jenkins)*

adding a total 8,550lb (3,878kg) to the overall weight of the aircraft – much more than the empty weight of a P-51D Mustang.

Optimised in design to fit the undercarriage into the wing space, the single wheel each side imposed too great a weight on the runway, only three in the world being capable of supporting the enormous weight of the aircraft which necessitated a concrete depth of at least 22in (55.9cm). All three runways (Fort Worth, Texas, Eglin Field, Florida, and Fairfield-Suisun Field, California) were in the continental United States and there were already plans to deploy the B-36 overseas for which there were no suitable runways. A bigger risk was the consequences of a blown tyre on landing, potentially catastrophic for the aircraft.

A solution was sought by Maj Gen Edward M. Powers, the Assistant Chief of Air Staff for Materiel, Maintenance and Distribution who worked with Consolidated to design a multi-wheel bogie of a unique type, which would serve as the genesis for a new and evolving design of landing gear, and would become a standard concept for many aircraft types several decades later. The B-36 design adopted a four-wheel unit each side with 56in (142.4cm) tyres in a compact unit which, being bulkier in side elevation, necessitated a bulge in the upper wing and in the wheel well doors to accommodate it. Yet these drag-inducing bulges were offset to some extent by the 2,600lb (1,179kg) saving in weight over the original design.

LEFT The controversial landing gear incorporated a large 110-in diameter tyre and wheel seen here in an early test rig. Wheels of this size were impractical and could not have been used on most runways due to the foot pressure in the contact area being greater than the bearing strength of concrete on most airfields.
(Dennis Jenkins)

Roll-out and flight tests

Due to priority being given to existing production aircraft and development of new and promising types such as the B-29, the first XB-36 (42-13570) was not rolled out until 8 September 1945, six days after the signing of the Japanese surrender. As it emerged for the second time from its Fort Worth Experimental Building (the first time had been a quick in-and-out when it was 82% complete to turn the aircraft around 180 degrees) from those who had not seen it during assembly, it brought gasps of disbelief – the largest aircraft ever produced for the AAF.

Performance predictions had been modified from the original estimates, and further still from

the design requirement set originally by the Air Corps several years earlier. Gross weight had gone from an estimated 265,000lb (120,204kg) to 278,000lb (126,100kg) and its projected top speed had fallen from 369mph (593.7kph) to 323mph (519.7kph), with the service ceiling now estimated at 38,200ft (11,643m) instead of 40,000ft (12,192m). Now more closely matched on speed with the B-29, it could carry a 72,000lb (32,659kg) bomb load with a range of 5,800mls (9,332km) against the B-29's bomb load of 20,000lb (9,072kg) over a range of just over 2,900mls (4,666km). Realistically

BELOW The 110-in diameter tyre on B-36 42-13570, giving the aircraft an ungainly appearance and an impractical solution to the challenge of getting the heaviest aircraft then entering production with the lowest possible impact pressure.
(Dennis Jenkins)

the B-36 was much less than twice the weight of the B-29 while carrying more than 10 times its bomb load to 5,500mls (8,849kg).

But the delays caused by general war production were also due to faulty workmanship in materials provided by contractors, and by labour union problems at the Aluminum Corporation of America which provided Convair with most of its metal. This played back into the

general condition of the first XB-36, which was judged unsuitable for anything other than as an aerodynamic test vehicle for early flights. Which was inevitable given that concurrency had worked to bequeath to the production models an aircraft significantly different to that of either of the two prototypes.

With this in mind, on 27 April 1945 a decision was made to prepare the second prototype (42-13571) closer to the production standard than that originally intended. It would have a raised flight deck in a new two-deck structure, a new bulbous canopy and redesigned forward compartment, the two aft bomb bays would be positioned together instead of being separated by aft dorsal turret bays and there was provision for the newly mandated nose turret. This aircraft, in that redefined guise, was re-designated YB-36 and became the first of the series to roll out of Building 4 at Government Plant No 4 at Fort Worth.

The issue over defensive armament for the B-36 became quite controversial toward the end of the war and departed greatly from the original mock-up in July 1942. There, the upper and lower forward turrets were each equipped with two 37-mm cannon controlled by a gunner in each turret. The aft upper turret would have had two 0.50-calibre guns, the lower aft turret four 0.50-calibre guns, these controlled via two upper and two lower sighting blisters. Because of this, the fire control system would be compromised since it would have to cope with alternate control and double parallax computations. Finally, two 37-mm tail guns would be controlled by a gunner located remotely in the aft crew compartment.

Largely at the behest of contractor General Electric, by early 1944 the defensive arrangement favoured eight retractable turrets, four on top and four below, with a single tail turret, all of which would carry two 20-mm cannon controlled through a single sighting station, eliminating complexity and removing gunners from exposed and vulnerable positions in the proximity of the turrets. Much of this concept had come from the B-29 and from the Northrop P-61 Black Widow night fighter. The greatest change came in adapting the equipment from the dc to the ac electrical system in the B-36. GE got to work fast and by

spring 1945 it had two fully working systems.

A further addition was made in January 1945 when the nose turret was added and on 15 July the AN/APG-3 tail radar, applied to the B-29, was added to the B-36, but by adopting that the two lower forward turrets were removed to accommodate the radar, replacing the APG-7 Eagle originally specified. That brought control of the radar-directed tail turret under the authority of the radar operator situated in the forward cabin. But it was not easy upscaling the equipment from the B-29 configuration to the B-36 and not until early 1946 did the fire control electronics finally get free of interference with just about every other system on the airframe!

As further evidence of the overlap between development and production, the solution was not finally resolved until long into delivery of the production aircraft but compromise solutions in efforts to save money and time continued to confound reliability well into service use. In fact, the unified fire control system (2CFR87A-1) was installed in the YB-36 during late 1947, with the modified B-1 upgrade intended for the B-36A and the much improved C-1 for the B-36B.

After two preliminary taxi runs, the XB-36 took to the air for the first time shortly after

10.00am on 8 August 1946 at the hands of Beryl A. Erickson and G. S. 'Gus' Green, with flight engineers J. D. McEachern and William 'Bill' P. Easley, flight test engineer Robert E. Hewes, flight test analysts W. H. Vobbe and A. W. Gedeman, and observers W. I. Daniel and Joe M. Hefley. In a relatively uneventful flight lasting 37 minutes in which the undercarriage remained down and the No. 2 flap failed to

ABOVE Displaying the initially less rounded nose section and the 110-in diameter tyres on single main landing gear wheels, the XB-36 demonstrates its handling qualities for the company public relations camera.
(Convair)

LEFT Convair test pilot Beryl A. Erickson took the B-36 on most of its test flights and demonstrated the aircraft's handling characteristics.
(Convair)

retract, the heaviest aircraft ever to take to the air performed as expected. About 7,000 Convair employees watched the flight, conducted at 3,500ft (1,067m) and a speed of 155mph (249kph) over the downtown area of Fort Worth with a throbbing reverberation that many people around the world would come to know was the unmistakable sound of six Wasp engines.

The second flight with the XB-36 took place six days later with the same crew in a flight lasting 2hr 43min, using the same personnel but also with Maj Stephen P. Dillon, the flight acceptance officer. In the spirit of encouraging support from the senior AAF leadership, the sixth flight demonstrated the aircraft to Gen Spaatz but it was a superficial display of the dramatic proportions of the aircraft. It was not all good news. Later flights early in the test phase indicated that the maximum speed would be no more than 320mph (515kph) and that several problems would have to be solved prior to service introduction. Arguably the more important, inadequate engine cooling prevented the aircraft climbing above 30,000ft (9,144m) and propeller vibrations threatened the structural integrity of the airframe.

A development programme for a two-speed cooling fan helped solve that problem but the vibrations were a persistent issue, offset by strengthening of structural parts including the flaps. Eventually, a new propeller would be introduced and the early test work involving

the XB-36 proved invaluable in catching up with modifications and the redesign of critical elements. But the XB-36 never did manage to get above 37,000ft (11,277m). Other problems began to give the aircraft a bad name in the technical press, especially when a propeller shattered, taking with it part of the wing flap which plummeted into a field. Concurrent with the flight tests, wind tunnel measurements showed a disturbingly poor stall characteristic which prompted the adoption of slots in the outer wing sections; this proved unnecessary when flight trials showed the stall conditions acceptable.

The XB-36 was a test-bed, lacking any military equipment and unrepresentative of the initial production aircraft. Kit was a vital tool for bringing up the production aircraft to an acceptable standard but the policy of concurrency, while significantly compressing the schedule from first flight to service introduction generated much more work and additional cost. It impacted the flight trials too. But adverse publicity was attracted when the XB-36 was publicly ridiculed after a trailing airspeed indicator suspended 75ft (22.8m) below the aircraft broke loose. It smashed through the roof of a school, demolishing the toilet – as a mischievous press pointed out, the giant behemoth's first bombing target!

Numerous instances of failing equipment, near-crashes and under-performing tests dogged the flight trials with the XB-36, the last of which, lasting 5hr 10min, took place on 13 January 1948. But it did serve a useful purpose, in that it could be used to evaluate equipment destined for the production model, the B-36A. The XB-36 was finally turned over to the Air Force in June 1948 and on its 32nd flight, that month too saw it fitted with the new four-wheel bogie landing gear with which all production aircraft were fitted. Also, new and improved R-3640-41 engines of 3,500hp (2,610kW) rating were fitted to this

POST-WAR CONVULSIONS

When the war ended the US Army Air Forces had more than 63,000 aircraft on hand, of which more than 2,800 were in the category of Very Heavy Bombers (B-29s) and 11,000 were Heavy Bombers (B-17s and B-24s). The price of a bomber had risen from $187,700 for a B-17, to $215,500 for a B-24 and $509,000 for a B-29. The category for B-29s was new and the type introduced the classification which would soon embrace the B-36.

Technology too played into the balance between cost and capability, with the clear advantage in jet aircraft for high altitude flight and higher speed. Within a few weeks of the war's end, scientists and engineers were scrambling to apply results from advanced German research into high-speed aerodynamics and new methods of propulsion including not only the jet but rocket propulsion too.

The end of the war also brought about massive de-armament on a colossal scale, the number of aircraft in the inventory crashing to little more than 25,000 in two years, when the US Air Force obtained its independence from the Army. All these factors fed in to controversy about the future direction of air power and the choice over the type of aircraft required for national defence, even regarding which service should have control over the strategic deterrent. The Navy wanted the super-carrier; the Air Force wanted the B-36.

aircraft before handover and all the flight test equipment was removed.

It arrived at Strategic Air Command for training purposes on 19 June 1948 just one week before the first B-36A production aircraft was delivered. Within weeks the XB-36 was back at Fort Worth's Experimental Building where it spent the rest of that year and 1949 as the YB-36, while the B-36A took up the role of flight test evaluation and familiarisation. In April 1949 the British test pilot John Pegg, the experimental pilot for the Bristol Brabazon, familiarised himself with the aircraft during a visit to Fort Worth; the two aircraft were similar in size and unique for their era.

On 26 March 1950 the XB-36 took to the air for the one and only time equipped with a track-type landing gear on each main leg. An experimental test for a design of undercarriage which some thought might allow heavy aircraft to operate from unprepared strips proved as bizarre as it was noisy. The tread applied a force of only 57psi (383kPa) to the runway compared with 156psi (1,075kPa) with the four-wheel bogie. Consisting of a series of roller wheels and drive sprockets, a wide track-treaded belt provided a continuous loop rolling mat which on landing left a trail of component parts shed from the device as the aircraft clattered to a stop. The device was never intended for B-36 production but

the availability of the XB-36 allowed trials with a concept considered for heavy transport aircraft. It was never used operationally.

The final flight with the XB-36 conducted by Convair came four years to the day after the first flight, when the aircraft was delivered to Wright-Patterson Air Force Base (formerly Wright Field). With the decision that it would cost too much to upgrade it to production standard, the XB-36 was placed in storage back at Fort Worth in October 1951. It was officially retired on 30 January 1952 and was towed to the north end of the plant where engines and other equipment were removed and it was left to the vagaries of the weather. In May 1957 it was towed across to Carswell Air Force Base, its undercarriage was removed and it was used for fire training where it was ultimately consumed during exercises. In all, the XB-36 had made 30 test flights over an accumulated duration of 88hr 50min.

As described earlier, the second XB-36 was completed with several of the important changes and equipment upgrades developed during the assembly of the first airframe. Re-designated YB-36 on 7 April 1945 and as a precursor to the production B-36A, 42-13571 made its first flight on 4 December 1947 lasting 1hr 50min, retaining the original single wheel per main landing leg but without armament or equipment which would be built

BELOW The YRB-49 was powered by eight Allison J-35-A-15 turbojets at a rated thrust of 5,000lb and the flying wing boasted a top speed of 493mph (793kph). But the type was unsuited to the role for which it was designed. *(USAF)*

in to production aircraft. In June 1944 the AAF had ordered Convair to build a nose mock-up which incorporated a turret carrying two 30-mm cannon and the revised two-level flight deck and bulbous canopy. Inspected in early November, it was cleared as the production standard and in April 1945 the YB-36 was directed to have this new arrangement together with the third and fourth bomb bays moved closer together.

During the third test flight, on 19 December 1947, the YB-36 achieved an altitude of 40,000ft (12,192m), somewhat better than the best that could be achieved with the XB-36. After 89 hours of flight tests, on 27 May 1948 the landing gear was replaced with the production-standard, four-wheel bogie per leg. With the new R-4360-41 engines replacing the 3,000hp R-4360-25 engines, the first flight in this configuration came in June, a configuration which Convair flew for 36 additional test flights accumulating a further 97.5 hours. All the while, General Electric was making incremental changes and some modifications to the defensive armament.

Turned over to the Air Force on 31 May 1949, it was integrated as a B-36A and was delivered back to Fort Worth in October 1950 where it was converted to an RB-36E configuration, standing in for the first B-36A which had been subject to destructive testing. The YB-36 would continue flying for the Air

Force, adding a further 1,952.5 flying hours before it was retired in 1957. It was given to the Air Force Museum at Wright-Patterson AFB but did not survive the building of the new museum and it was scrapped. Some parts of the aircraft were acquired by Walter Soplata who placed them on his farm in Newbury, Ohio.

ABOVE The YRB-49A with a modified engine arrangement placing four jets in the wings and two on external underwing mountings. *(Northrop)*

BELOW Another publicity view of the YRB-49A with the vertical control surfaces applied in an unsuccessful effort to mitigate the aircraft's poor stability and flight control, making it a very unstable bomb platform. *(USAF)*

Chapter Three

Type evolution and production

When the B-36 entered service it was at the start of a type development programme that would see it mature into a truly intercontinental bomber with enormous capacity for both conventional and nuclear bombs. As the 'big stick' threatening retribution on an unacceptable level, it was the ultimate nuclear deterrent.

OPPOSITE Core fuselage assemblies in Building 4 of the Fort Worth facility prior to reaching the major mating area where they will be integrated with wings, tails and other subassemblies. In the foreground, aircraft B-36B 44-92059, accepted in August 1949. *(Dennis Jenkins)*

The B-36 was a big aircraft and the full length of the main fabrication facility at Fort Worth was committed to the production of the aircraft with three major divisions of responsibility: Major Components; Major Mating; Final Assembly.

The Major Components section was the reception area for parts and components arriving from other fabrication facilities and from subcontractors, and it occupied one-third of the south end of the facility. Major Mating introduced the wing sections to each other and where they were mated to the centre-section of the fuselage and the bomb bays.

Final Assembly divided work into 11

substations in progressive assembly of the completed aircraft up the line with landing gear, leading edge and trailing edge systems and equipment, internal systems and subsystems, and the six engine nacelles were installed. Along with these, the engine build-up assemblies provided the mountings, with turbo-superchargers added, intercoolers were installed, the electrical system and shrouding were put in place, the fuel and fire extinguishers were added and associated engine mounting equipment laid up. Then the engines were hung on their mountings and the cowl structure was installed.

The Wasp engines were received from Pratt & Whitney in crates, unpacked and suspended on a six-point overhead rack assembly for building up the ancillary equipment, positioned at a suitable height for access by technicians and assembly workers. Both engine and airframe had evolved in synergy and Pratt & Whitney was concerned enough to work closely with Convair on correcting any anomalous faults discovered on installation. The engine was crucial to the desired high-altitude performance of the aircraft, one of its key selling points, and P&W worked very hard with Air Force engineers to achieve better performance.

At the eighth assembly station the outer wing panels were attached and due to the dimensions of the facility the aircraft had to be set at a diagonal angle to get clearance within the 200ft (61m) wide bay for the 230ft (70m) wingspan. From there, the aircraft was crabbed down the rest of the line on dollies and at the terminal end of the line the canopy, instrumentation and control surfaces were assembled and emplaced, followed by the turrets and government-furnished equipment (GFE) for communications, navigation and propellers. It was at this point that the insignia and production identification and assignment markings were added and appropriate areas spray painted using stencils for the B-36A and B-36B, with decals used on the later marks.

The final station saw roll-out from the factory, removal of the dollies and transfer of the completed aircraft to the Field Operations area in the north yard for the final inspection. Flight tests by Convair and by Air Force pilots

BELOW One of the greatest burdens imposed upon the newly formed US Air Force with the introduction to service of the B-36 was its high maintenance requirement, increasing the number of personnel required to carry out essential activities for servicing and inspection. *(Dennis Jenkins)*

followed prior to the aircraft being signed off for delivery to the Air Force.

However, major manufacturing problems ensued, due almost exclusively to the unprecedented size of the aircraft, with the sheer mass of equipment and installed subsystems together with the problems of so many integral fuel tanks and the large number of seals and joints. Fuel leakages would blight the programme continuously and the problem was never fully solved until, three years into production, the manufacturer worked with Proseal and jointly developed a solution with Coast Paint & Chemical Company of Los Angeles. This was produced specifically for the B-36 and the entire interior surface of all six integral fuel tanks were coated with Proseal.

CENTRE The spacious main gear wheel well provided open areas for work but some of the conduits in this area were difficult to access and, due to concurrency of development and operational activities, frequent changes made it difficult for mechanics to keep current. *(Dennis Jenkins)*

RIGHT Routine maintenance activity on a B-36 at Carswell AFB showing the access to the engine catwalk, activity photographed in April 1949. *(USAF)*

A potentially major manufacturing challenge was in the use of magnesium panels which were engineered in primarily secondary structures. Here too there were problems in establishing quality bonding. Some areas used Metlbond, another product specially developed by Convair for this aircraft. It was found to be particularly useful in those areas where vibration affected light structures and in areas where conventional airframes would focus stress at rivet joints. But the greatest challenge of all was to integrate all the corrective solutions into a unified production upgrade. Not least of all the production and manufacturing problems was the daunting task of oversize components; the only place where the massive main landing gear struts could be manufactured was at the US Naval Gun Factory!

B-36A

The first production version of type and the first to enter service with the US Air Force, the B-36A lacked many of the systems required by the specification and for effective operation as a strategic bomber. Initially, the first 13 aircraft under contract were designated YB-36 when that number of pre-production airframes were envisaged. Fortunately for the Air Force, only 22 were built (44-92004 to 44-92025). Similar to the YB-36, the B-36A had six R-4350-25 Wasp engines but initially

without any defensive armament, only the tail turret being added later to this variant.

The type could carry a full 72,000lb (32,659kg) bomb load over a combat radius of 2,100mls (3,379km) or a 10,000lb (4,536kg) load to a combat radius of 3,880mls (6,243km). With no war load and with full tanks it could be ferried over a distance of 9,136mls (14,700km). These were unprecedented performance figures and the general enthusiasm displayed by the Air Force to news media, especially the aviation press, had one eye on its deterrent factor as much as its applicability to real war situations. The B-36A was far from an effective tool for conflict and was a poor shadow of what later variants would become.

Optimistic too were the claimed performance figures, attributing a top speed of 345mph (555kph) at 31,000ft (9,449m) carrying a 10,000lb (4,536kg) bomb load.

Officially manifested crew numbered 15 personnel but eight of these were gunners who had no armament, the remaining crewmembers being the two pilots, the radar-bombardier, navigator, flight engineer and two radiomen. For most of the time the crew had their hands full as the performance and lack of reliability haunted the B-36 programme in these early days of operational trials and testing in an active environment.

The first B-36A took to the air for the first time on 28 August 1947, ahead of the first YB-36, and carried the new four-wheel bogie arrangement but with limitations on the undercarriage, maximum take-off weight was 310,380lb (140,788kg). Ironically, the first B-36A beat the YB-36 into the air by several months but from the outset this was used for publicity and took pride of place at several public events both at Fort Worth and at nearby Carswell AFB where it was displayed to full public view.

Its future lay in its use as a destructive test frame for structural loads analysis and for that purpose it made two flights, one of which lasted 7hr 36min around the pattern at Fort Worth before carrying only enough equipment for a ferry flight to Wright Field at the hands of pilots Col Thomas P. Gerrity and Beryl Erickson. Delivered to Air Materiel

RIGHT J. E. Massey inspects the port main landing gear of the first B-36A (44-92004) in August 1947. *(Dennis Jenkins)*

BELOW Subject of substantial attention from the public relations photographer, B-36A 44-92014 on show at St Louis Air Show on 17 October 1948, displaying the fully glazed nose and spacious positions for the nose gunner and radar-bombardier. *(Dennis Jenkins)*

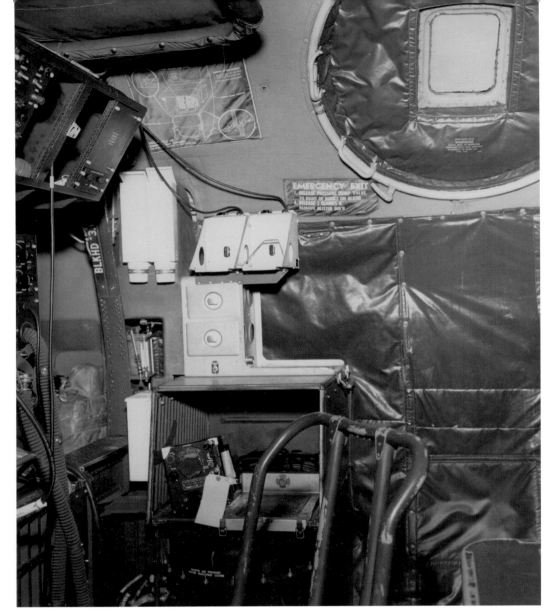

RIGHT The essential coffee pot, viewed aboard B-36A 44-92014. *(Dennis Jenkins)*

BELOW The B-36H and J series had a slightly remodelled facility for hot drinks as seen here. *(USAF)*

BELOW RIGHT The crew trolley on which personnel could move through the tunnel between forward and aft pressurised compartments. *(USAF)*

Command in May 1948 on its second and last flight, the Air Proving Ground Command at Eglin AFB received the aircraft for climate tests on 18 June 1948.

By this date, on 22 March 1948 it had been announced that the 7th Bombardment Wing (BW) at Carswell would be the first unit to deploy the B-36A operationally and that the first of those (44-92004) would be delivered shortly, that date eventually stretching out to 26 June. In the interim, significant progress was made getting the aircraft into a fit state for delivery. On 8–9 April, 44-92013 completed a demonstration flight lasting 33hr 10min covering 6,922mls (11,137km) in a continuous loop between Fort Worth and San Diego. In a 'real-world' simulation of an operational

flight, the aircraft was loaded with ballast to compensate for the lack of armament and the absence of a 10,000lb (4,536kg) bomb load, dummy 500lb (226.8kg) bombs being dropped from 21,000ft (6,400m) over the Air Force bombing range at Wilcox, Arizona. Halfway through the flight two engines gave trouble, cutting the average speed to a lowly 214mph (344kph).

The same aircraft made another simulated long-range flight on 13–14 May 1948 when, at a gross weight of 299,619lb (135,907kg), it remained airborne for 36hr 8min covering 8,062mls (12,972km) carrying 10,000lb (4,536kg) of dummy bombs and a ballast of 5,796lb (2,629kg) simulating defensive armament. This was a mission simulation

ABOVE The engineer's panel on the B-36A displaying the six throttle levers for the reciprocating engines. *(Dennis Jenkins)*

OPPOSITE The B-36 pilot's display panel with the (larger) trim wheel and the (rotating) rudder trim on the central console. *(Dennis Jenkins)*

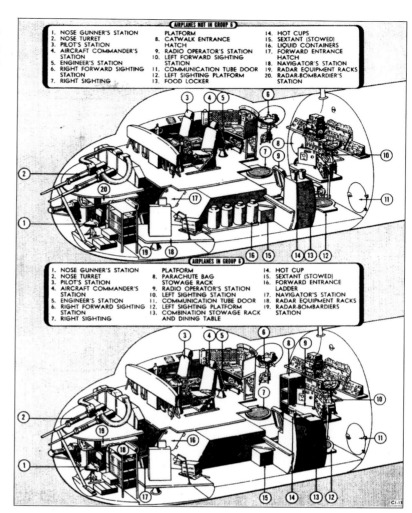

AIRPLANES NOT IN GROUP 6

1.	NOSE GUNNER'S STATION		PLATFORM	14.	HOT CUPS	
2.	NOSE TURRET	8.	CATWALK ENTRANCE	15.	LIQUID CONTAINERS	
3.	PILOT'S STATION		HATCH	16.	LIQUID CONTAINERS	
4.	AIRCRAFT COMMANDER'S	9.	RADIO OPERATOR'S STATION	17.	FORWARD ENTRANCE	
	STATION	10.	LEFT FORWARD SIGHTING		HATCH	
5.	ENGINEER'S STATION		STATION	18.	NAVIGATOR'S STATION	
6.	RIGHT FORWARD SIGHTING	11.	COMMUNICATION TUBE DOOR	19.	RADAR EQUIPMENT RACKS	
	STATION	12.	LEFT SIGHTING PLATFORM	20.	RADAR-BOMBARDIER'S	
7.	RIGHT SIGHTING	13.	FOOD LOCKER		STATION	

AIRPLANES IN GROUP 6

1.	NOSE GUNNER'S STATION		PLATFORM	14.	HOT CUP	
2.	NOSE TURRET	8.	PARACHUTE BAG	15.	SEXTANT (STOWED)	
3.	PILOT'S STATION		STOWAGE RACK	16.	FORWARD ENTRANCE	
4.	AIRCRAFT COMMANDER'S	9.	RADIO OPERATOR'S STATION		LADDER	
	STATION	10.	LEFT SIGHTING STATION	17.	NAVIGATOR'S STATION	
5.	ENGINEER'S STATION	11.	COMMUNICATION TUBE DOOR	18.	RADAR EQUIPMENT RACKS	
6.	RIGHT FORWARD SIGHTING	12.	LEFT SIGHTING PLATFORM	19.	RADAR-BOMBARDIERS	
	STATION	13.	COMBINATION STOWAGE RACK		STATION	
7.	RIGHT SIGHTING		AND DINING TABLE			

RIGHT Extracts from the manuals for the B-36 show the forward pressure compartment and crew dispositions in two separate group production specifications. Throughout the programme many changes were made to various configurations within the two pressure compartments and in other arrangements of equipment and systems or subsystems. *(Convair)*

BELOW B-36A 44-92009 in flight on 15 April 1948 showing the clean lines of the 'cigar with a high-span wing!' *(Dennis Jenkins)*

RIGHT President Harry S. Truman takes a photo-call from the side hatch of B-36A 44-92010.
(Dennis Jenkins)

THE COLD WAR

Many of the decisions regarding the service deployment of the B-36 were influenced by the Cold War, effectively settling upon the world shortly after the Second World War as deep ideological differences dissolved the wartime alliance that had seen Britain and the United States supply equipment and materiel to the beleaguered Soviet forces in a combined bid to rid the world of fascism and Nazism.

The political intention of the USSR to maintain occupation of several countries as buffer states in Eastern Europe stemmed from their concern that the West would seek to destroy communism and potentially pose a threat to Russia itself; it was not uncommon for Soviet leaders to regard the United States and Western European countries as enemies-in-waiting and likely to conduct a pre-emptive strike. The US' possession of the atom bomb, and its demonstrated willingness to use it reinforced that assumption. It spurred the USSR to prioritise on developing its own atomic weapons and to seek a means of attacking the USA by ballistic missile without having to use manned bombers to fly over hostile airspace.

During the operational tenure of the B-36, the Russians tried to starve out the people of West Berlin at a time when Moscow had control over half of Germany, executed leaders of democratic movements in Poland and Czechoslovakia, set up client states in countries throughout Asia and invaded Hungary to crush a revolution from ordinary people attempting to gain their freedom and overthrow their Soviet occupiers. Throughout, the Kremlin sought to demonise the United States, accusing it of global hegemony and specifying that fact through the example of new and powerful weapons in the hands of its former allies.

The B-36 itself was put up as an indicator of America's political objective, and the rhetoric from senior US Force leaders such as SAC's Gen Curtis LeMay, doing little to mask advocacy for the use of this aircraft to destroy Soviet industry and to eliminate it as a military threat before it grew strong and militarily equal. In this regard, when viewed objectively the B-36 served as a very real threat to the USSR at a time before it had adequate defensive capabilities from early warning stations, radar and fighters capable of addressing the new threat. As such, it is no surprise that the unofficial name of the mighty B-36 was 'Peacemaker'.

flying a profile close to that envisaged for the B-36. The first 369mls (593.7km) were at 5,000ft (1,524m) followed by a power climb to 10,000ft (3,048m) for a further 30 minutes when the aircraft climbed to 25,000ft (7,620m) for a maximum speed bombing run which also incorporated 17 minutes of evasive manoeuvres and a return to base at the same altitude.

In further flight proving trials, on 18 May another B-36A dropped twenty-five 2,000lb (907kg) bombs from an altitude of 31,000ft (9,449m) across the Naval Range at Corpus Christi, Texas, part way on a 7,000ml (11,263km) flight. A maximum capacity bomb load of 72,000lb (32,659kg) was dropped during a flight on 30 June 1948, by far the greatest weight of bombs dropped by a single

aircraft and a record that would stand for a long time until just eclipsed by the Boeing B-52 during the Vietnam War.

With these trials satisfactorily logged, the first B-36A (44-92015) delivered to Carswell AFB arrived on 26 June 1948, having taxied over the perimeter at Fort Worth. Bearing the name *City of FORT WORTH*, the aircraft was assigned to the 492nd Bomb Squadron (BS). Only eight months later the last B-36A was delivered, 20 of the total production lot serving with the 7th BW at Carswell for training and familiarisation as well as additional flight testing. But their reliability was poor, the readiness level fell far below 50% and the operational life was short, the last airframe being rebuilt into an RB-36E and delivered as such in July 1951.

BELOW Carswell AFB and maintenance time on 44-9212, one of 22 A-series B-36 bombers built for the Air Force and accepted between August 1947 and February 1949.
(Dennis Jenkins)

THIS PAGE With its enormous carrying capacity, the B-36 made light work of carrying spare engines between locations on deployment. Panniers either side of the forward fuselage section carried two reciprocating engines each, as demonstrated on B-36B 44-92026. *(Dennis Jenkins)*

B-36B

The first variant of this type made its initial flight on 8 July 1948 when Beryl Erickson took 44-92026 into the air at Fort Worth. Initial tests showed a considerable improvement over the A-series, with a top speed of 381mph (613kph) and a service ceiling of 42,500ft (12,954m). Trials demonstrated that an average speed of 300mph (482.8kph) could be maintained at 40,000ft (12,192m). The first B-36B was accepted by the Air Force on 25 November 1948 and assigned to the 7th BW at Carswell AFB, joining the B-36As in their training role. The 11th BW also stood up with the B-36B, the first of its aircraft (44-92050) delivered on 18 March 1949.

Equipped with a full suite of operational equipment, the B-36B had the essential advantage of the 3,500hp (2,608kW) R-4360-

ABOVE Directly comparable to a previous shot of a B-36A, this B-series aircraft (44-92033) viewed from the starboard three-quarter rear displays the evocative arrangement of the pusher engines. *(Convair)*

BELOW Given scale by the relative size of the workforce crawling over it, B-36B 44-92057 is coming together in the general mating section of the Fort Worth facility. *(Dennis Jenkins)*

41 engine which had water injection and replaced the earlier engines used on X, Y and A series aircraft. But this came at the price of substantial modifications to the structure of the wing and this served as a template for retrofit to some of the A-series aircraft. In addition, the sixteen 20-mm cannon were installed in all eight turrets, including the six retractable turrets in the fuselage, and the nose and tail turrets. Two blisters in the forward fuselage

and four in the rear fuselage were used for the computing gunsights. As noted, the tail turret was directed using the AN/APG-3 gun-laying radar and a periscope gunsight was mounted in the bombardier's station. The B-36B also incorporated armoured panels to protect the outer wing fuel tanks. Because the inner tanks were empty by the time the aircraft reached hostile air space, to save weight the inboard tanks were left unarmoured.

Originally, Convair planned to equip this variant with the Farrand Y-1 retractable periscope bombsight but the Norden M-9 sight was used when delays brought about by development problems rendered them unavailable for production. But the Y-1 was eventually retrofitted to some B types, as evidenced by a flat, glazed nose section. The crew complement of 15 included the two pilots, the radar-bombardier, navigator, flight engineer, two radiomen, three forward gunners and five rear gunners. Invariably, problems with the defensive armament left little time to address potential targets, as much of the time was devoted to sorting out mechanical and electrical problems with the guns and the radar.

Of not a little embarrassment which brought some furrowed brows in the Pacific, on 7–8 December 1948, the seventh

ABOVE A clear view of distinctive features on the aft section of the fuselage as 44-93043 moves out of the assembly line. *(Dennis Jenkins)*

LEFT Carswell AFB on 26 May 1950 where two B-36Bs from the 7th BW (44-92073 in foreground and 44-92084) undergo routine maintenance. Note the various applications of steel and magnesium plating on fuselage and wings. *(Dennis Jenkins)*

ABOVE A B-36B at the Albuquerque, New Mexico, Air Show in August 1949 reveals the sliding aft upper turret doors and the round-tip propellers of the early series. *(Frank Kleinwechter with scanning by Don Pyeatt via Dennis Jenkins)*

BELOW Bearing the insignia of the 7th BW and the motto 'Death from Above', this B-36B (44-92041) was spotted at El Paso, Texas, on 5 May 1949 and clearly shows the port side of the forward fuselage with upper canopy and nose gun arrangement. *(Frank Kleinwechter via Dennis Jenkins)*

of Strategic Air Command was 'Peace is our Profession'. Notwithstanding complaints from several sectors of the general public, including the clergy who challenged the use of that name in that it invoked the real peacemaker, who was 'not built by Consolidated', the name was never officially adopted and became the moniker applied by enthusiasts, advertisers and the pro-defence orientated media.

But a contest over much more than just the name of the aircraft was being fought with consequences which could have doomed the B-36 to cancellation after the initial 100 had been delivered. Defence matters and national security were becoming an increasing concern to government and politicians alike, as the Russians hardened their stance over West Germany, isolating the people of West Berlin

with a blockade which only left air routes open to access from the West. In contravention of the agreement signed at the end of the Second World War, Moscow tried tough tactics to blackmail the West into preventing an independent West Germany from ever rising again. Moreover, on 29 August 1949 the USSR detonated its first atom bomb and the US no longer had a monopoly on nuclear weapons. But Russia lacked the means to deliver such a device and most professional analysts were not unduly concerned, seeing in this test more of a laboratory demonstration than a new instrument for strategic conflict.

Nevertheless, the judicious use of the public purse on expensive military programmes was never far away from the political debate and since the US Air Force stood up as an

ABOVE A more detailed view of the nose section of B-36B 44-92035. (Dennis Jenkins)

B-49 CHALLENGE

The Navy carrier programme was not the only challenge to the B-36 in the late 1940s, for the XB-35 reared its competitive head again in the guise of the newly emerged jet-powered derivative, the YB-49. Cancelled for its poor handling qualities and lack of performance, the YB-35 piston-engine, flying wing bomber prototype was redeveloped into the jet-powered YB-49. The second and third YB-35 (42-102367 and -102368) were converted under a contract signed on 1 June 1945. Bearing the initial designation YB-35B, this was quickly changed to YB-49. The original four Wasp reciprocating engines were replaced by eight Allison J35-A-5 turbojets each rated at 4,000lb (18kN) and buried in the wing, four either side of the centre-section to the forward end of which was buried the cockpit. Low drag intakes were designed into the wing leading edge.

The control and handling difficulties were alleviated with the provision of four vertical stub-tails extending just above and below the wing inboard and outboard of the engine groups. Wing fences were added for additional stability, extending forward from the vertical fins to the leading edge to apply the stabilising effect previously provided by the propellers and shaft housings. A crew of seven was contained within the centre-section of the wing with the pilot located centrally beneath a bubble canopy; a six-man relief crew could be carried in the tail cone for long-duration flights.

The first of the two converted aircraft made its initial flight on 21 October 1947, more than a year after the planned date due to engineering problems with the design of the vertical fins, joined for its test programme at Muroc AFB by the second aircraft on 13 January 1948. Over a period of more than 20 months, the two aircraft completed 169 test flights with Northrop and Air Force pilots, demonstrating a maximum speed of 520mph (837kph) with a service ceiling of 42,000ft (12,800m). The aircraft had a range of 4,000mls (6,400km) carrying a 10,000lb (4,536kg) bomb load, half the range of the XB-35. But the stability problems were still there and never completely corrected, the aircraft being useless as a stable bombing platform due to violent pitching and yawing.

In March 1948 Northrop proposed a reconnaissance version, the YRB-49A, and the Air Force accepted this the following month with a production for 30 aircraft of this type on 12 August. Ironically, on 5 June the second YB-49 had crashed north of Muroc Dry Lake killing the pilot Captain Edwards and four other crewmembers. By the end of 1949 Muroc had been renamed Edwards Air Force Base in his honour. The YRB-49A would have six Allison J35-A19 jet engines in the wings, two on each side, and two more suspended in pods beneath the wing leading edge. Photographic equipment was to have been installed in the tail cone below the centre section.

Lacking confidence in Northrop to handle such a major production contract, the Air Force stipulated that Convair would build all but one of the 30 aircraft on order. When it became apparent that the six-engine YRB-49A would be slower than the swept-wing Boeing B-47 Stratojet the Air Force Board cancelled the entire programme, formally signed off in December 1948. Those funds saved from the YRB-49A were allocated to the B-36.

The only YRB-49A built (converted from the tenth YB-35, 42-102376) flew for the first time on 4 May 1950 and continued to fly on test until early 1952 when it was flown to Northrop's Ontario International Airport for installation of a stability augmentation system. By this time funds had run out and it remained there until scrapped in November 1953. Long before that date, the B-36 had seen off all its competition as well as the challenge from the US Navy.

independent service in September 1947, the Navy had contested its self-serving assumption that it alone held the strategic leverage in air power and the long arm of retribution. Accordingly, the B-36 ran headlong into a Navy bid to get the money to build a super-carrier with which it asserted the United States would have a more robust and survivable weapon than the manned penetrating bomber.

This contest had been hardened by the decision from President Harry S. Truman to freeze the 1949 defence budget to $11billion, for the financial year starting 1 July 1948. The USAF had planned to increase the number of combat groups from 59 to 70 but the frozen budget required a reduction to 48 groups and the cancellation of $573million in contracts, the penalty payments alone amounting to $56million. Moreover, along with production cutbacks came the cancellation of the proposed Boeing B-54 (an improved version of the B-50, itself a development of the B-29), in return for prioritisation on the B-36.

BELOW Among this line-up of B-36Bs at Carswell AFB, in the foreground is 44-92036 sporting a canopy weather cover with successive airframes in the series 44-92xxx displayed by the BM number on the forward fuselage. *(Dennis Jenkins)*

at 40,000ft (12,192m), the test was declared inconclusive. It was only the outstanding demonstration of long range strike capacity from the B-36B that saved the day for the big bomber, many claiming that the B-36 had the best and most articulate advocates while the Navy 'brass' appeared truculent and offensive.

B-36C

The performance of the B-36B had provided a baseline configuration ripe for development, improvement and expanded capability. Confidence in the type from Convair and now the Air Force provided encouragement to seek ways of eliminating its weaknesses. These included a list of performance increments under consideration for improvement, headed by the poor speed of the aircraft. Along with improved reliability and systems operability, the aircraft would benefit from different engines and with the production order clearly heading for an increase beyond the 100 initially contracted for, attention switched to that issue. The B-36 would serve the Air Force until the B-52 entered service which would itself be accompanied in service by an operational infrastructure including aerial tankers and base facilities, which was not expected to be achieved until at least 1955.

Ironically, just as the B-52 was transitioning in concept from turboprop to jet, the B-36 was looking in the reverse direction, with several concepts examined for turboprop conversion. Most favoured of those was the 5,500hp (4,101kW) Wright T-35 or the 10,000hp (7,457kW) Northrop T-37 Turbodyne, with either tractor or pusher engines buried in the wing. Several studies were conducted but none were taken up. Yet the search for improved speed forced development of the B-36C with the Variable Discharge Turbine (VDT).

As early as March 1947 Convair had proposed that 34 of the 100 aircraft on order

TOP **On its way to the Chicago Air Fair on 3 July 1949, this B-36B (44-92041) survived to fly for a further six years, being written off on 10 January 1956.** *(Frank Kleinwechter via Dennis Jenkins)*

ABOVE **B-36B 44-92027 with a bomb at right of picture.** *(Dennis Jenkins)*

Under existing defence plans, the Navy had begun work on a 65,000 ton (58,968 tonne) super-carrier the USS *United States* (CVA-58) but under the new cost cuts this was cancelled by Louis A. Johnson, the Secretary of Defense. Johnson had been a director at Convair and accusations of manipulated interests followed, especially when money from the carrier programme was used to bolster B-36 production. By this date the range and capability of the B-36 had been demonstrated but when Russia produced its new jet-powered MiG-15 interceptor on 1 May 1949 doubts over the survivability of the giant bomber surfaced.

The Navy used this in what was quickly known as the 'Revolt of the Admirals' and challenged the Air Force to an exercise in which the B-36 could be tested for survivability in mock-attack from jet fighters. When North American test pilot 'Chuck' Yeager (the pilot who first took the Bell X-1 through the sound barrier) reported that it was difficult to hold his F-86 Sabre stable

Figure 1-5. Flight Engineer's Station

RESTRICTED

ABOVE The general arrangement of the flight engineer's station in relation to the upper flight deck in the forward pressurised section. The three flat panels are designated A, B and C from left, with the auxiliary fuel control panel at top of C. *(Dennis Jenkins)*

RIGHT The pilot's seat on a typical B-36B layout varied little from the A-series types. *(Walt Jeffries Collection via Mike Machat)*

be fitted with VDT engines, which had also been approved by the Air Force for use on the B-54, before that aircraft was cancelled. But the Pratt & Whitney R-4360 VDT had to drive tractor, rather than pusher, propellers which meant the wing having to support a 10ft (3m) shaft extending through the entire wing chord. That required redesign of the trailing edge flaps and the internal cooling system as well as changes to the forward fuselage to resist vibrations.

Calculations were optimistic that the VDT engines would boost top speed to 410mph (660kph), provide the aircraft with a 45,000ft (13,716m) service ceiling and retain the 10 x 10 range and bomb load originally required by the Air Force. Pushing the innovation to the customer, Convair funded airframe modifications for one aircraft by deleting three B-36s from the original contract and this was approved by the Air Force in July 1947.

After a year-long analysis and significant engineering study, Convair discovered that the cruising speed over a range of 7,250mls (11,665km) was 262mph (421kph), some 23mph (37kph) slower than the existing aircraft. This disappointing result pressed hard upon the Air Force. The projected speed was troublingly low and this brought fresh calls for cancellation, the Air Force beginning to look at the aircraft as more suited to maritime patrol and reconnaissance duties than as a manned penetrating bomber.

But the Berlin blockade on 18 June 1948 saved the day when the political leadership pressed upon the Air Force to do nothing to undermine the apparent strength of the United States and to preserve the sole very long range bomber capable of seriously threatening the Soviet Union. There was also a concern that by shutting down the B-36 production line the considerable government investment in Plant 4 at Fort Worth would be underutilised, a production capacity which may very well be needed as the Cold War intensified.

The VDT aircraft had been given the designation B-36C and five airframes (44-92099 to 44-92103) had been cut out of the 100-aircraft production order to compensate for cost inflation and to pay for the new project. The Air Force had no alternative but to cancel its order for the five C-series aircraft and to finish them to B-36D specification, with jet engines supplementing the reciprocating engines. A solution had been found to the slow speed of the aircraft but not in the way originally intended.

B-36D

The giant bomber only truly came of age with a supplementary propulsion system in the form of four jet engines, significantly improving the aircraft's performance and its operating potential. Reassuringly, it came when the Soviets under Joseph Stalin were escalating tension in East Berlin and the certain knowledge they had about plans to appreciably improve the performance of the B-36 was in itself a counter to that.

The search for an effective performance increase was motivation for extensive development of optional programmes for supplementary propulsion. When the VDT proved ineffective and totally unsuited to the B-36, the idea of using jet engines to augment the reciprocating engines was a natural progression. Between 1945 and 1948 considerable improvement in jet engine efficiency made their use desirable. Not yet as an exclusive replacement for the propeller-driven arrangement but as a supplement during which the jets could be turned on and off as required, thus considerably reducing the disadvantage they had of high fuel consumption. As said earlier, the all-jet force of B-47 and B-52 forced a parallel investment in air-to-air refuelling tankers so that they could reach their targets.

Intensive studies at Convair into structural loads analysis and optional locations for supplementary jets followed the traditional practice of the time in seeking ways to give heavy aircraft the opportunity to use shorter runways. RATO – or Rocket Assisted Take-Off – was well developed and would be used with the B-47 as well as a wide range of other aircraft. Some RATO-boosted fighters such as the F-100 and the F-104 would use this technique for zero-launched take-off, the lightweight fighters literally hurled into the air from an inclined mobile launch ramp, with a

ABOVE The radio operator's station as viewed during the Electronic Countermeasures programme in 1955. *(Don Pyeatt via Dennis Jenkins)*

BELOW The Loran hyperbolic navigation set installed in a B-36B. Developed during the Second World War it was similar to the British Gee system but operated at lower frequencies for longer range. *(Dennis Jenkins)*

view to operating them from hidden locations far from conventional airfields.

But Convair used the loads analysis for identifying the best location for the engines employed in a more conventional fashion. Its engineers proposed a pair of General Electric J-47 turbojet engines and the number of modifications required for this adaptation were far less than those required for the cancelled VDT of the defunct B-36C. Convair promised the Air Force that it could have a flying conversion ready within four months of go-ahead but haste was not commensurate with the squeezed budget and authorisation to proceed was not received before 4 January 1949. Nevertheless, having continued to work on the detailed design of the augmentation, the first flight occurred as early as 26 March 1949, but of a converted B-36B (44-92057) and not a contracted B-36D as frequently misidentified.

Because of the unavailability of the J-47, the converted B-36B had four Allison J35-A-19 engines standing in for the J-47s. As usual, Beryl Erickson was at the controls for the first flight, this time with co-pilot Doc Witchell, when the aircraft took to the air for a 3hr 15min flight, the first with jet pods.

The second B-36B modified to carry jet pods (44-92046) was fitted with the J-47-GE-11 engine for high altitude testing. The first two B-36B aircraft thus converted did not have the extensive sequence of modifications identified for the production B-36D in the

following text. In an attempt to reduce vibration, endemic in the B-36, 44-92057 was used to test the 16ft (4.87m), four-bladed propeller but little difference was noted. It did, however, begin a development programme which would result in the square-top shape adopted for the B-36H (which see).

In the ultimate expression of concurrency, the new arrangement of 'six turning, four burning' involved the last eleven B-36Bs being completed to B-36D standard on the assembly line in the form of seven reconnaissance versions (RB-36D, for which see later) and four bomber configurations. It was then decided to retrofit all B-36Bs into the D-series standard. After the first four B-36Bs were converted (44-92026, 034, 053 and 054) the modification work transferred to the San Diego plant, leaving the Fort Worth factory to produce all new production-line B-36Ds.

The D-series type adopted the same 3,500hp (2,608kW) T-4360-41 reciprocating engine which had been fitted to the B-36B and although there would be a modest update to the -41 series engine, this would remain the engine for subsequent variants of the bomber. The D-series also set the maximum gross weight which had increased to 357,000lb (161,935kg) and this would be retained across subsequent variants. It also set the trend toward maximising the quantity of magnesium applied to the external surfaces and replacement of the fabric-covered flying control surfaces. To this date, earlier variants had a retractable tail bumper but this was eliminated from the D-series on, although it was still to be seen on the modified B-36Bs into the D-series configuration.

A new contract to cover the B-36D was signed off on 19 January 1949 to cover 39 additional aircraft over and above the 95 already under the original contract (five having been deleted to compensate for added work on the jet pods conversion). Further contract extensions increased the added production lot to 75 aircraft by October that year, the first of several production extensions. The first new-build production B-36D, originally ordered as a B-36B, flew on 11 July 1949 and the Air Force received its first D-series (49-2653) on 22 August 1950. It went straight to the 11th BW at Carswell but spent its life as a test aircraft at Eglin AFB while the 26 new-build D-series aircraft were all delivered by August 1951. The last carried the serial 49-2655 and was delivered later than its immediate predecessors as, by arrangement with Convair, it had been used to evaluate various improvements to crew comfort.

Conversion work at San Diego on B-36Bs began with a complete overhaul with new

control surfaces, and snap-action bomb bays doors which would become standard on this and all subsequent aircraft. These doors could open and close in two seconds and this reduced drag. Two sets of doors were provided, one for the forward bays and the other for the rear pair and all B-36Ds came with the ability to carry the Mk. 3 Fat Man atomic weapon in the forward bay. This location was chosen because it was the

ABOVE A pleasing air-to-air shot of a B-36D (44-92057) handed over to the Air Force in January 1951 and used for flight test evaluation with J35 and J-47 engines. *(Dennis Jenkins)*

LEFT Night maintenance on a pair of Peacemakers, the second aircraft being 49-2657, built on the line as a B-36D and delivered in November 1950. *(Dennis Jenkins)*

easiest to get to and would allow best access for arming the bomb in flight. Also replaced was the much improved AN/APG-32 tail radar over the APG-3 installed in the B-36B, although here too the converted B-36Bs initially had the older equipment.

Work also involved removing all the outer wing panels for strengthening, engines and associated accessories being sent to Kelly AFB for re-sealing of the integral fuel tanks and the fitting of new auxiliary tanks in the inner wing sections. In addition, 13gal (49.2 litre) of oil for the jets was stored in 20gal (75.7 litre) tanks in the outer wing sections. Two 4,800gal (18,168 litre) supplementary fuel tanks were incorporated into the inboard wing sections. These consisted of four bladder-like fuel cells manufactured from rubber with nylon fabric impregnated. These were not self-sealing or armoured but the exact capacity differed by up to 100gal (378 litres). It was still possible to house the single 3,000gal (11,355 litre) auxiliary tank in bomb bay No. 3. Variability appears to have been common as some flight manuals indicate such tanks in one, two or all four bays, probably a product of field modifications due to various tests and exercises.

The factory modifications also provided an opportunity to update the electronics and to fit new variants of existing equipment. It was expected that the D-series would have the much improved K-3 bombing and navigation system but this proved problematical and initially the K-1 was installed offering very little advantage over the APQ-24, which had been standard in the B-36B. Special outdoor work docks were set up but the reassembly work was carried out on four aircraft simultaneously

BELOW The photographer provides a useful shot of the excellent vision afforded the crew, together with control displays on B-36D 44-9264, converted to Featherweight III configuration.
(Dennis Jenkins)

in Building 3, only the tail missing due to the height of the roof.

The first converted B-36B (44-92043) had been at San Diego since 6 April 1950 and was returned to the air as a B-36D on 5 December following which, after two further flights, it was sent back to the Air Force on 17 December. The last reworked aircraft ordered as a B-36B (92081) was re-delivered back to the Air Force on 14 February 1952. Significant re-qualification of the aircraft was required and extensive checks were carried out on navigation equipment and especially on the defensive armament, with tests at Fort Worth consuming 200,000 rounds of 20-mm cannon shells by the end of 1950!

The B-36D was a completely new aircraft in several respects and much more than a mere type change or upgrade. The new engines produced an impressive step up in performance, although some early boasts claimed a top speed of 439mph (706kph) at 32,120ft (9,790m) and a service ceiling of 45,020ft (13,722m). After much publicity surrounding these optimistic projections, and the end of the budget cycle for that year, the figures were revised downward to 406mph (653kph) at 36,200ft (11,034m) and a ceiling of 43,800ft (13,250m). In service use, indisputably the aircraft was more flexible and increased operational capabilities: with jets on and all six reciprocating engines, the take-off run was reduced by 2,000ft (610m) and the rate of climb doubled to 900ft/min (274m/min).

Operationally, the B-36D could operate well above the normal operating ceiling of the jet fighters of the day, which were in any event unstable at that height due to the reduced atmospheric pressure on their low aspect-ratio wings. It fitted very well within the operational expectations of a long range bomber force and was a suitable precursor to the B-52, which it had already influenced in both design and operating capacity. To a limited extent, it had the best of both worlds. At cruising altitude the B-36D could shut down the jets and two, even three reciprocating engines, continuing to operate well on just three of its ten engines. This conserved fuel and operational practice (see later) routinely operated the jets only for take-off, for climb out and for a dash across the target.

In projecting the new and significantly expanding capability of Strategic Air Command, the propaganda effect of the aircraft was enormous, drawing crowds whenever there was an open day at Fort Worth, at air shows where it appeared, and certainly during visits to overseas bases. On 16 January 1951 six B-36Ds arrived at RAF Lakenheath in the UK, having flown from Carswell and staging through Limestone, Maine. Under the operational name UNITED KINGDOM, it was the first overseas goodwill visit but it also sent a strong message to the Soviet Union, that here was a bomber uniquely capable of striking the USSR from the USA and that it was sufficiently operationally flexible to operate from NATO air bases in the UK and, if necessary, Western Europe. The visit was led by Col Thomas P. Gerrity, the commander of the 11th BW at Carswell AFB and the six aircraft returned on 20 January.

The appearance made a great impression on the British public and on the RAF too; to compare the enormous size of the B-36, a Gloster Meteor was posed under one wing of the aircraft for Pathe News to film the two together. It was also the first time anyone outside the United States had heard the extraordinary, and quite unique sound of the B-36, as can be testified to when this writer experienced the aircraft on that very visit

ABOVE Landing gear maintenance on B-36D 49-2050, built as a B-series but converted. *(Dennis Jenkins)*

DRIVING THE B-52

The years 1948 and 1949 proved decisive for the future pattern of bomber types destined to enter service over the next decade. With the B-36 secure, the very existence of this aircraft played an enabling role in deciding both the capabilities and the mission function of the B-47 and the B-52. As such, it is relevant to show how the Peacemaker influenced those choices.

Overall, defence budgets were held at around $13billion for much of the immediate post-war period, and although very high compared to pre-war levels, they would not allow the Air Force to have the 70 groups it sought. But the Air Force fought its corner and Congress did vote a supplement toward achieving that, only for the money to be vetoed out by President Truman who was fixated on not allowing the defence budget to undermine the economy. In a series of meetings held from December 1948 it was decided that of the 48 groups, four would be heavy bomber groups equipped with the B-36 while one would be for reconnaissance versions of the Peacemaker. But these additional aircraft would be of the B-36D with supplemental jet engines and carry increased performance. It was also decided to increase the complement of each group from 18 to 30 aircraft.

This was the long awaited turning point for the B-36 and far from allowing it to limp along as it had been for many years, it was now clearly the aircraft of choice for the strategic bomber role of the future, and along with that the nuclear deterrent for Strategic Air Command. The imminence of the ten-engine B-36D played a highly significant role in shaping the design of the B-52. Originally defined as a straight-wing, turboprop bomber, the B-52 had been conceived right at the end of the war, taking advantage of the latest research into aerodynamic shapes, much of which had been acquired from German research facilities.

Powered by four turboprop engines, the Boeing Model 464-35 had a projected top speed of 445mph (716kph) but in 1948 the Air Force was beginning to look again at turbojet engines which, until this date, had used too much fuel to be considered appropriate for long-range aircraft. Now that problem was being solved and in May 1948 the Air Force asked Boeing to come up with an all-jet version which resulted in the 464-40 substituting turbojet engines for the turboprops. The top speed increased but the range was less than desired, Boeing submitting its -40 design but continuing to work on the turboprop version. The Air Force rejected both concepts.

Less than three weeks after Convair made its B-36D proposal, on 21 October 1948 Boeing dispatched a team of engineers and senior staff to Wright Field to discuss how they could deliver a suitable bomber to eventually succeed the B-36. Over the following weekend Boeing design draughtsmen worked in their hotel to redesign what would become the B-52, abandoned the straight wing and conventional fuselage, adopting a swept-wing, streamlined design powered by eight jet engines placed in four nacelles under the wings. With a 30-page report in hand and a hand-carved model, they reported to the evaluation committee on 25 October. The new Model 464-49 would have a range of 8,000mls (12,872km), a cruising speed of 520mph (836kph), a top speed of 572mph (920kph) and a 60,000lb (27,216kg) maximum bomb load.

Boeing's chief aerodynamicist, George Schairer, said that the Air Force had directly compared their turboprop design with the promised B-36D and found it wanting. He claimed that had it not been for the competitive pressure of the B-36, they would never have come up with their radically different design evolution. In that regard, the definitive evolution of the Peacemaker played a direct hand in development of the B-52.

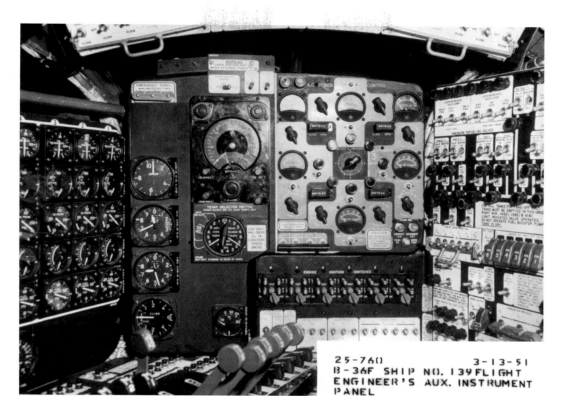

25-760   3-13-51
B-36F SHIP NO. 139 FLIGHT
ENGINEER'S AUX. INSTRUMENT
PANEL

18 August. It turned out that the new engines quickly settled in to a reliable service life with maintenance tasks reduced due largely to the adoption of fuel injection.

Paradoxically, a disproportionate number of accidents were suffered by the B-36F, the first on 6 March 1952 when 50-107 burned out after a main landing leg failed in the parked position on the ramp at Carswell AFB. From 20 March special inspections and repairs were conducted on existing B-36Fs before a team from Carswell decided to inspect all B-36s across the inventory. Some modifications were carried out as a result, aircraft being recycled through facilities at San Diego, Fort Worth and San Antonio. Shortly thereafter, on 5 August 1952 fuel exited through the No. 3 tank vent on 49-2679 and was ignited by exhaust from a power unit nearby, completely destroying the aircraft, which had been on the inventory of the 7th BW/436th BS.

Induction of the B-36F came in parallel with the development of the REAC (Reeves Electronic Analogue Computer), a massive device containing 625 vacuum tubes, heralding the dawn of the computer age which would replace manual solutions to complex mathematical problems previously using slide rules or written expressions conducted by women trained in high mathematics who had been themselves defined as 'computers'! With a price tag of $77,000 ($760,000 in 2019 money), REAC was officially described as an 'all electronic differential analyser for speed dynamic solution of simultaneous differential equations'. It was said that the device could solve in one calculation lasting 108 man-days the work of an equivalent 2,950 man-days if conducted manually.

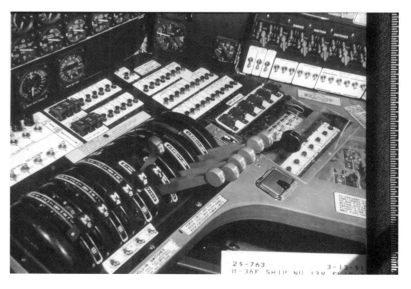

25-763   3-13-51
B-36F SHIP NO. 139

Significant changes to the flight engineer's station on the B-36H reflected the compulsive need for two seats, for which on earlier models there was only one despite the presence of two engineers. Paradoxically, throttles and instruments for the jet engineers were still retained at the pilot's station. *(Dennis Jenkins)*

Weighing 5,800lb (2,630kg), it had been developed by the Reeves Instrument Company of New York and was similar to a new generation of analogue computers which had been delivered to General Dynamics for their work on the 1947 Atlas concept for an ICBM. It was this development that made possible the new missile designs ten years later which would be introduced to SAC and compete with the manned penetrating bomber as the lead concept for strategic nuclear deterrence.

B-36G

This was the designation applied to a radical new development proposed in 1950 as a swept-wing, four-jet bomber based on the B-36 and aimed directly at the requirement for which the Boeing B-52 had been submitted. It involved two B-36F aircraft and the designation was changed to YB-60, information about which can be found in a later chapter.

B-36H

Essentially the B-36F but with the K-series electronic countermeasures equipment moved into the forward pressurised compartment to ease maintenance, this variant did have a reconfigured flight deck with an additional station for a flight engineer and featured an improved instrument panel for the two pilots. There were also changes to the lighting at all crew stations. A revised flight deck arrangement had been pursued for some time, the original layout being considered inadequate. The mock-up for the new arrangement had been inspected in August 1950, about the same time the B-36D was being delivered.

Despite general approval, it was recommended that subtle changes should be included, such as altering the pilot's gyro horizon, considered too small and generally regarded as unreliable. Additional space on the flight deck was recommended by moving the flight engineer's panel aft by 12in (30.5cm). It was also felt that the pilot's pedestal should be shortened by 6in (15.2cm) to enhance the emergency escape of the co-pilot and the assistant flight engineer.

Improvements to the defensive armament system included the same C-2 which had been fitted to the later B-36Fs but the C-3 was incorporated on Block 5 aircraft with dynamic gun mountings to help alleviate the fire dispersion problem, a persistent failing with the B-36. The solution proposed was to mount the gun on a spring cushion attachment which allowed it to move back and forwards on tracks along the line of fire. This transmitted some of the shock through the springs instead of it being transferred to the turret.

A new AN/APG-41 gun-laying tail radar which encompassed twin tail radomes was incorporated in the B-36H from 51-5742 and, as mentioned earlier, this was essentially two APG-32 units coupled so that one could track immediate threats and the other scan for other

LEFT A totally redesigned flight deck and display panel for the B-36H which was also retained for the J-series model, with control boxes for the nuclear weapons in bays 1 and 4 at the top of the anti-glare shield. *(Dennis Jenkins)*

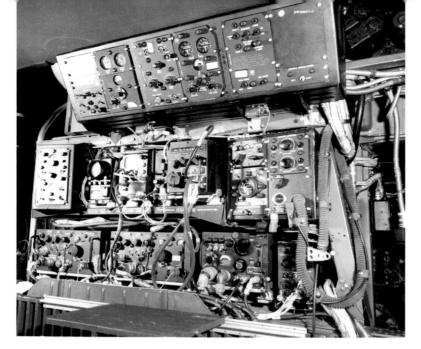

ABOVE Taken during tests in 1955, this is a part of the left-hand side panel, looking forward, for the defence electronic countermeasures panel. *(Don Pyeatt via Dennis Jenkins).*

undetected incomers. The left-hand radar could scan aft from 60° right to 80° left while the right-hand unit, also facing aft, could scan 80° to the right and 60° to the left.

The B-36H had the square-tipped propeller blades fitted as standard and that improved vibration levels and provided greater efficiency at higher altitude. Overall, flying performance of the B-36 had been compromised by the original propeller design consisting of three 19ft (5.79m) blades. The four-bladed, 16ft (4.8m) propeller was eventually fitted to the XC-99 (described in a later chapter). The H also carried an improved ECM package and two A-6 or A-7 dispensers with 1,400lb (635kg) of chaff, a system installed on late B-36Fs.

The B-36H was announced initially on 5 November 1950 and a total of 83 were built to this specification. It made its first flight on 5 April 1952, eight months ahead of deliveries to SAC, a delay effected when a B-36F pressure bulkhead failed incurring a halt to new deliveries until the problem was solved. In that incident, an RB-36F had experienced a failed pressure bulkhead at 33,000ft (10,058m) after which all flying was restricted to below 25,000ft (7,620m).

One tragic accident occurred during a visit by 18 B-36Hs from the 7th BW/492nd BS at Carswell to RAF Fairford in the UK during February 1953, a simulated mission with the code name Styleshow. One of the aircraft developed technical trouble en route and returned home, the other 17 heading on across the Atlantic after staging through Goose Bay, Newfoundland. Sixteen aircraft landed safely but one (51-5719) had to hold due to bad weather and missed two GCA approaches, largely due to inexperienced staff at the base. The aircraft had to be abandoned in flight but the crew were saved with no injuries. The exercise proceeded with training missions out of Fairford. Fourteen aircraft returned home on

CENTRE AND LEFT Indicative of the early nature of the radio operator's station, provisions were made for sending Morse Code via a telegraph key whereas the B-36H had a more sophisticated system. *(Dennis Jenkins)*

13 February but two remained in the UK for specialised training. Of those returning to the US, a further misdirection from the Goose Bay GCA caused 51-5729 to fly into a hill, killing two of the 17 crew on board. The 13 remaining aircraft arrived back at Carswell on the 21st, followed by the two remaining aircraft from the UK two days later.

One sub-variant, the tanker-bomber conversion listed as the 'XIV', referred to the Mark XIV refuelling reel which was installed in B-36H 51-5706. The Air Force had never seriously considered a tanker version of the B-36 bomber, despite SAC operating a range of such derivatives, including the KC-97 and the KB-29 and facilitating in-flight refuelling for the B-47 intermediate, medium-range bomber. The general design of the B-36 made that an unlikely possibility and the aircraft itself emerged from an era in which mid-air refuelling was a novelty and not an operational choice.

Nevertheless, in 1951 SAC considered a B-36 tanker-bomber (Tanbo) for refuelling its incoming generation of all-jet bombers at high altitude and speeds and 51-5706 was converted with a probe-and-drogue system following an authorisation of 15 January 1952. When that conversion was complete in May, the aircraft reappeared with a large hose reel in bomb bay No. 4 together with bladder tanks for jet fuel installed in the other three bomb bays. As a possible operational option, the aircraft carried the hose, fuel transfer pumps and hydraulically operated extendible boom on a special frame that could be readily removed. In times of national emergency the aircraft could be returned to use as a bomber in less than 12 hours to carry a thermonuclear device in that aft bay. Only the bladder tanks were a permanent installation.

The modifications provided close to 16,000gal (60,560 litres) capable of being transferred at a rate of 600gal/min (2,271 litres), equal to the full internal capacity of a B-47 but would probably have topped up three aircraft in turn. Tests started in March 1953 with a Republic F-84 but the reel mechanism, made in the UK, was not wholly compatible with the conversion and testing ended on 27 May that year. But the aircraft was not wasted and was handed over to the development

ABOVE The search radar scope (at the centre) at the radar-bombardier's position with the bombsight (to the lower left) which incorporated a Farrand Y-3 periscope carried vertically down through the fuselage to the underside of the aircraft. *(Dennis Jenkins)*

programme for a stand-off missile capability with the Bell B-63 Rascal.

One concern regarding the concept of the manned penetrating bomber was its vulnerability and a development by the German Air Force in the Second World War was picked up and exploited for application to manned bombers after the war. The Air Force had been impressed by the use of the Fieseler Fi-103, the V-1 flying bomb, when applied as an air-launched weapon using the Heinkel He-111 from December 1944. Under a programme run

BELOW The Bell XGAM-63 Rascal air-to-surface stand-off missile was mooted as a solution to the vulnerability of the relatively slow-flying B-36 and tests showed positive results but the weapon was eventually aligned with the B-47. *(USAF)*

by former V-2 director Walter Dornberger, in May 1947 Bell Aircraft Company received an Army Air Force contract to develop a stand-off, air-to-ground missile which could be launched from the B-29, the B-50 and the B-36.

The programme requirement began in March 1946 as Project Mastiff which anticipated a stand-off weapon capable of delivering a nuclear device across a range of 300mls (483km) providing clearance between the carrier aircraft and the target, reducing vulnerability to air defences and expanding its distance from the nuclear blast. Named Rascal, the GAM-63 (later the B-63) was propelled by a triple-chamber Bell XLR67-BA-1 rocket motor delivering a total thrust of 10,440lb (46.4kN), two chambers being shut down after a boost phase, leaving the single chamber as a sustainer for propelling the missile to its target. It had a maximum speed of Mach 2.95 with a range of 100mls (161km) and an accuracy, or cep (circular error probability, in which 50% of warheads would fall), of 30,000ft (914m).

On 7 July 1952 the Air Materiel Command authorised Convair to develop a conversion programme using B-36H 5-5710 with the designation YDB-36H and adapt 12 H-series into the director-bomber configuration, a production option for those being signed on 26 May 1953. The initial design recognised that Rascal could be carried submerged within the existing bomb bays, Nos. 3 and 4 being assigned to modification providing for a semi-submerged configuration with the missile. Wind tunnel tests were carried out on the semi-exposed configuration and found acceptable and a mock-up was built for final configuration decisions as well as a new forward pressurised compartment with the associated controls.

Rascal (B-63) had a total length of 32ft (9.75m) and a set of trapezoidal aero-surfaces, a single pair fore and aft with the larger pair being aft with a span of 16.7ft (5.1m). The two vertical aft fins spanned a height of 12.5ft (3.8m) and the missile had a total loaded weight of 18,200lb (8,255kg) fuelled with

BELOW Change came frequently to the B-36. This flight deck layout for the B-36D was a significant step beyond the earlier A- and B-series aircraft. *(Convair)*

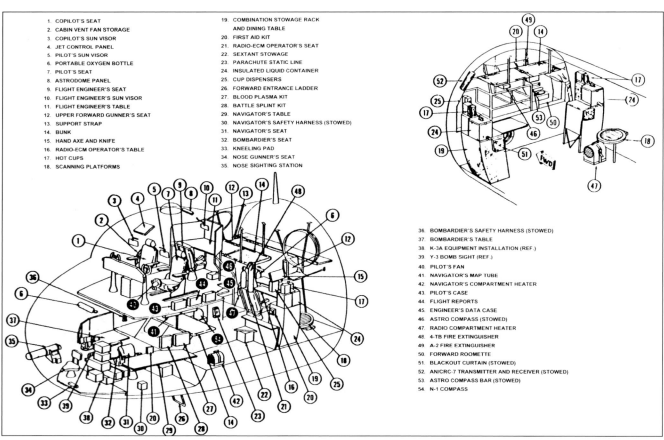

1. COPILOT'S SEAT
2. CABIN VENT FAN STORAGE
3. COPILOT'S SUN VISOR
4. JET CONTROL PANEL
5. PILOT'S SUN VISOR
6. PORTABLE OXYGEN BOTTLE
7. PILOT'S SEAT
8. ASTRODOME PANEL
9. FLIGHT ENGINEER'S SEAT
10. FLIGHT ENGINEER'S SUN VISOR
11. FLIGHT ENGINEER'S TABLE
12. UPPER FORWARD GUNNER'S SEAT
13. SUPPORT STRAP
14. BUNK
15. HAND AXE AND KNIFE
16. RADIO-ECM OPERATOR'S TABLE
17. HOT CUPS
18. SCANNING PLATFORMS
19. COMBINATION STOWAGE RACK AND DINING TABLE
20. FIRST AID KIT
21. RADIO-ECM OPERATOR'S SEAT
22. SEXTANT STOWAGE
23. PARACHUTE STATIC LINE
24. INSULATED LIQUID CONTAINER
25. CUP DISPENSERS
26. FORWARD ENTRANCE LADDER
27. BLOOD PLASMA KIT
28. BATTLE SPLINT KIT
29. NAVIGATOR'S TABLE
30. NAVIGATOR'S SAFETY HARNESS (STOWED)
31. NAVIGATOR'S SEAT
32. BOMBARDIER'S SEAT
33. KNEELING PAD
34. NOSE GUNNER'S SEAT
35. NOSE SIGHTING STATION

36. BOMBARDIER'S SAFETY HARNESS (STOWED)
37. BOMBARDIER'S TABLE
38. K-3A EQUIPMENT INSTALLATION (REF.)
39. Y-3 BOMB SIGHT (REF.)
40. PILOT'S FAN
41. NAVIGATOR'S MAP TUBE
42. NAVIGATOR'S COMPARTMENT HEATER
43. PILOT'S CASE
44. FLIGHT REPORTS
45. ENGINEER'S DATA CASE
46. ASTRO COMPASS (STOWED)
47. RADIO COMPARTMENT HEATER
48. 4-TB FIRE EXTINGUISHER
49. A-2 FIRE EXTINGUISHER
50. FORWARD ROOMETTE
51. BLACKOUT CURTAIN (STOWED)
52. AN/CRC-7 TRANSMITTER AND RECEIVER (STOWED)
53. ASTRO COMPASS BAR (STOWED)
54. N-1 COMPASS

JP-4 jet fuel and a WFNA (White Fuming Nitric Acid) oxidiser. With Rascal in bomb bays Nos. 3 and 4, the guidance electronics package was installed in bay No. 1, leaving bay No. 2 effectively free to carry bombs or decoys.

The operation of Rascal was semi-automatic in that its guidance package would be pre-set to launch automatically when the carrier-plane reached a determined location where the aim point and the target aligned. The action releasing the missile to fall free from an altitude of 42,500ft (12,954m) pulled a lanyard which ignited the rocket motor but if that failed, a timer would do the job after a pre-set interval. After ignition the missile would climb to 50,000ft (15,240m) and the missile control operator would guide Rascal to its target by means of a video link, conducting minor refinements to the pre-planned trajectory.

Mock-up inspection took place on 18 November 1952 and the first flight of the YDB-36H took place on 3 July 1953. Beginning on 31 July, the next six flights determined drag levels and by installing the B-63 for

passive compatibility tests, accumulated 20hr 5min flying time by the time the sixth and last flight was conducted on 16 August. Counter-intuitively, the pilots reported no difference in drag or in handling, reporting that they would not know the Rascal was installed from the performance of the aircraft alone.

The first air launch occurred on 30 September 1952, but from a specially modified Boeing DB-50D, followed by the first unpowered drop test from the YDB-36H on 25 August 1953 prior to a grounding while Bell engineers installed the guidance system. It was returned to the Air Force on 22 July 1954. Before that, on 6 July 1954 the tanker-bomber B-36H (51-5706) was handed over to SAC and before the end of the month it was recorded as the first production Rascal launcher. On 22 December 1954 it flew to Holloman AFB to join the Rascal test programme.

In engineering terms, the requirement for any converted B-36H to be returned to normal bomber condition within 12 hours was easily beaten by ground crews who

BELOW The flight deck and forward fuselage arrangement for the B-36H and J-series aircraft reflected significant changes in equipment. While the lower deck was retrofitted to earlier types, the flight deck was unique to the H and J aircraft. *(Convair)*

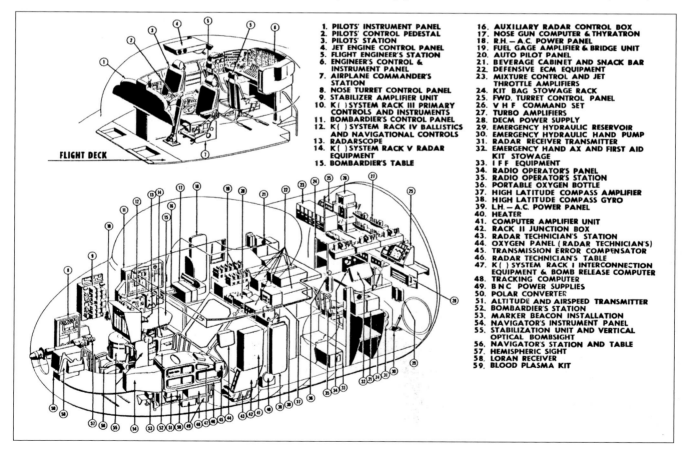

1. PILOTS' INSTRUMENT PANEL
2. PILOTS' CONTROL PEDESTAL
3. PILOTS' STATION
4. JET ENGINE CONTROL PANEL
5. FLIGHT ENGINEER'S STATION
6. ENGINEER'S CONTROL & INSTRUMENT PANEL
7. AIRPLANE COMMANDER'S STATION
8. NOSE TURRET CONTROL PANEL
9. STABILIZER AMPLIFIER UNIT
10. K( ) SYSTEM RACK III PRIMARY CONTROLS AND INSTRUMENTS
11. BOMBARDIER'S CONTROL PANEL
12. K( ) SYSTEM RACK IV BALLISTICS AND NAVIGATIONAL CONTROLS
13. RADARSCOPE
14. K( ) SYSTEM RACK V RADAR EQUIPMENT
15. BOMBARDIER'S TABLE
16. AUXILIARY RADAR CONTROL BOX
17. NOSE GUN COMPUTER & THYRATRON
18. R.H. — A.C. POWER PANEL
19. FUEL GAGE AMPLIFIER & BRIDGE UNIT
20. AUTO PILOT PANEL
21. BEVERAGE CABINET AND SNACK BAR
22. DEFENSIVE ECM EQUIPMENT
23. MIXTURE CONTROL AND JET THROTTLE AMPLIFIERS
24. KIT BAG STOWAGE RACK
25. FWD. TURRET CONTROL PANEL
26. V H F COMMAND SET
27. TURBO AMPLIFIERS
28. DECM POWER SUPPLY
29. EMERGENCY HYDRAULIC RESERVOIR
30. EMERGENCY HYDRAULIC HAND PUMP
31. RADAR RECEIVER TRANSMITTER
32. EMERGENCY HAND AX AND FIRST AID KIT STOWAGE
33. I F F EQUIPMENT
34. RADIO OPERATOR'S PANEL
35. RADIO OPERATOR'S STATION
36. PORTABLE OXYGEN BOTTLE
37. HIGH LATITUDE COMPASS AMPLIFIER
38. HIGH LATITUDE COMPASS GYRO
39. LH. — A.C. POWER PANEL
40. HEATER
41. COMPUTER AMPLIFIER UNIT
42. RACK II JUNCTION BOX
43. RADAR TECHNICIAN'S STATION
44. OXYGEN PANEL (RADAR TECHNICIAN'S)
45. TRANSMISSION ERROR COMPENSATOR
46. RADAR TECHNICIAN'S TABLE
47. K( ) SYSTEM RACK I INTERCONNECTION EQUIPMENT & BOMB RELEASE COMPUTER
48. TRACKING COMPUTER
49. B N C POWER SUPPLIES
50. POLAR CONVERTER
51. ALTITUDE AND AIRSPEED TRANSMITTER
52. BOMBARDIER'S STATION
53. MARKER BEACON INSTALLATION
54. NAVIGATOR'S INSTRUMENT PANEL
55. STABILIZATION UNIT AND VERTICAL OPTICAL BOMBSIGHT
56. NAVIGATOR'S STATION AND TABLE
57. HEMISPHERIC SIGHT
58. LORAN RECEIVER
59. BLOOD PLASMA KIT

FLIGHT DECK

ABOVE AND BELOW
Carried by the B-36J 52-2220, donated to the USAF Museum, these views of the flight deck show the final configuration of display and controls changes to the last series of type. *(Dennis Jenkins)*

accomplished that in 3hr 12min. But some concern was expressed over the ventral fin being moved 90° to the right so as to provide ground clearance for take-off, a hand pump being used to lower it to the flight position after getting airborne. Should the B-36 have to return without dropping the Rascal, the reverse procedure would be necessary but an electrically operated pump was recommended for ease and the safety of the aircraft.

By this time SAC had migrated the Rascal concept to the B-47 and in 1953 it was

decided to modify B-47B 51-2186 and this aircraft appeared as the YDB-47, carrying a single missile under the starboard side of the fuselage just below the wing, since its size precluded it from being set in the bomb bay. Technical difficulties with Rascal delayed its development and in June 1955 the Air Force decided not to deploy the missile on the B-36, but to adopt it for the B-47 instead. Within two years the programme had been cut back and was cancelled on 29 September 1958.

Although of only passing moment in the story of the B-36, the Rascal programme was another indication of how this aircraft was right at the beginning of so many technical and engineering developments which would be pursued over several decades by the Air Force, an evolution of stand-off and cruise missiles carried and launched from strategic bombers. What would follow was a development path that would carry the B-52 into an entirely new operational role, outliving SAC itself. Rascal was followed by Hound Dog, the first tests of which were conducted in April 1959. Carried by the B-52, it entered service at the end of that year and was declared operational from July 1960. After 15 years of service, it too was replaced, by the AGM-69 SRAM (Short Range Attack Missile) and then by the AGM-86 ALCM (Air Launched Cruise Missile) from December 1982. A new generation of long-range cruise weapons is currently in development.

B-36J

This was the last production variant of the B-36, defined by two additional fuel tanks in each outer wing section which increased capacity by 2,770gal (10,484 litres) bringing the total load to 36,396gal (137,759 litres). This series also had the first significant gross weight increase, from 358,000lb (162,388kg) to 410,000lb (185,977kg) and could be recognised on the ramp by the adoption of a single elongated radome which covered the two antennae of the APG-41A gun-laying radar in the tail, although this had been adopted for later production B-36H types as well.

The first B-36J (52-2210) took to the air in July 1953 and was accepted by SAC in the

September and, watched by 11,000 people, the last of 33 (52-2827) was rolled out of the factory on 10 August 1954 and delivered to the Air Force four days later, the last of 385 B-36 types built. Top speed was reduced to 422mph (661kph) due to the added weight from the heavier and beefed-up landing gear. The last 14 B-36Js were produced as Featherweight variants (see next section), the only ones to get the lightweight treatment on the production line, the rest being modified after delivery.

In service, later B-36Js had the newly introduced high-altitude finish consisting of anti-radiation white paint to protect the underside of the fuselage and certain underside areas of the wing for the flash effect of thermonuclear weapons. When the B-36 had been introduced the fission weapons did not create the blast effect or the heat and light intensity that accompanied the fusion, or thermonuclear, bombs. This scheme was eventually applied to all B-36s in service.

Featherweights

With the acceleration in Cold War tension, the B-36 became embroiled in a wide range of planning for accelerated response and rapid strike capability. The preceding generation of piston-engine bombers relied on pre-attack staging and latterly on the emerging concept of air-to-air refuelling, initially with a reel and hose and then by flying boom, which became standard. As noted, the B-36 did not lend itself to aerial refuelling and only cursory attention was given to its potential role as a tanker-bomber.

Other means were sought to prevent the need for pre-strike positioning, a euphemism for tanking up prior to a bombing mission. With both the United States and the USSR building nuclear stockpiles, it was not possible to rely on foreign bases for pre-attack staging; these may have been destroyed long before the B-36s got there. Moreover, foreign bases were costly to maintain, requiring valuable stores and logistical support along with manpower and an amenable political regime. The Pentagon was getting increasingly concerned over the cost and dubious strategic advantage in overseas bases and the dilemma of substantive requirements for airborne operations fed into that concern.

With an already unprecedented range, other means were sought to extend even further the range and the flight duration of bombing missions and this is where the Featherweight programme came in. Calculations on flight paths and range showed that operations from only one base, at Limestone AFB, Maine, could support direct operations from CONUS (Continental United States) to deep inside the USSR where most of the targets were located. A major problem was altitude at remote pre-staging bases and the revised doctrine of how to wage a global war involving nuclear weapons fell parallel to the determination that, with lightweight thermonuclear devices now becoming available, each aircraft would have added value by carrying a much heavier punch and more than one atomic weapon.

It was coincident with the decision to build a force of intercontinental ballistic missiles (ICBMs) that SAC, which would have responsibility for those as the second leg of the deterrent from the end of the decade, sought a solution that only the B-36 could provide. The intermediate B-47 medium bomber had aerial refuelling which the B-36 did not, but the overall capacity of the aircraft to deliver more range was a real possibility due to its size and weight; a large and heavy aircraft can deliver more weight reduction than can a smaller and lighter aircraft.

In early 1954, just as decisions were being made about the overall configuration of SAC after the B-36 was retired and a new generation of weapons would become available by the end of the decade, a strongly contested debate began to develop over the balance between missiles and manned aircraft, introducing the phrase 'push-button warfare' from those already involved in the balance of procurement, seeking efficiencies through unmanned strike systems and fewer maintenance and support personnel than required for aircraft.

The two sides were contested by Gen Bernard Schriever, campaigning strongly for a greater reliance on rockets and missiles, and Gen Curtis LeMay who sought to prioritise the manned air fleets that had been essential for winning the Second World War. Schriever would get his missiles at the cost of manned air fleets of tankers and bombers, which would be reduced because of that, but in 1954 there was all to play for. So it was that a concerted effort began to put the B-36 through a major weight reduction programme, expand the demonstrated capability of the aircraft and further validate its existence.

There were three proposed Featherweight concepts under discussion. Under Configuration 1, immediately prior to their use on real-world bombing missions, all extraneous equipment would be removed, including all the retractable turrets, the auxiliary bomb racks for conventional bombs, and the crew comfort upgrades already introduced on production aircraft. Configuration II would repeat much of the above but also remove unnecessary ECM equipment, external protuberances causing increased drag, with periscopes and high altitude equipment added in addition to flush covers for all sighting blisters. These changes could be carried out at depot level and shaved 4,800lb (2,177kg) from the weight of an operational aircraft. Tests showed that Category II weight-shaving increased range by 25% with guns fitted and to 39% without defensive armament.

Configuration III was the most stringent weight reduction programme proposed, involving complete removal of all the defensive armament, but leaving the tail turret and upper and lower aft sighting blisters in place. These could be replaced with Plexiglass and the lower blisters were a convenient location for engineers to check for leaks. Chaff dispensers would be retained with ECM equipment upgraded with lighter, and improved, derivative equipment. The crew comfort equipment would also be largely removed as would the astrodome on top of the cockpit. By eliminating most of the guns, two crewmembers could be removed but because insulation would be taken out, heated flight suits would be provided, equipped with integral communications sets; weight saving raised the ceiling which would add to crew discomfort without those new suits.

Overall, Configuration III Featherweight

measures reduced weight by 15,000lb (6,804kg) and this increased range by 25–40% over the Configuration II increases, depending on the specific model. Overall, by reducing drag and lightening the airframe, the top speed of the B-36D was increased to 418mph (672kph) and for the B-36H to 423mph (680kph). But the greatest operational advantage carried the rated ceiling to 47,000ft (14,325m) and to more than 50,000ft (15,240m) on some flights, testified to by the crew on several test missions. Several crews swore they achieved 55,000ft (16,764m).

Configuration I changes were not adopted in total but most of those proposed changes were applied at depot level. Configuration II changes were adopted universally and those aircraft carried a (II) suffix to their series identification (e.g. B-36D (II), or B-36D-II) with a similar identification code for the Configuration III types (B-36D-III). Rapidly, the entire fleet of aircraft went through the Featherweight programme but there were other, more subtle changes during this renewed lease of life afforded to the B-36. They each were given improved, and enhanced, support for the thermonuclear role (including the new anti-flash paint scheme) and ECM equipment was relocated to the aft fuselage from positions in bomb bay No. 4 and some aircraft had a modified bombardier's scope.

Formalised on 16 June 1954, the shift back to a bomber priority for the B-36 recognised the increasingly important role the B-47 was playing in reconnaissance and the Featherweight programme acknowledged that, although there was some concern on SAC's part for eliminating one crewmember. On 1 October 1955 all RB-36 reconnaissance wings were re-designated heavy-bombardment wings but in reality reconnaissance duties were still a very ready option.

Featherweight aircraft modification began in February 1954 with the final converted aircraft returned for operations six months later, the last bomber being delivered in November 1954 followed by the last modified RB-36 in May 1955. The anti-flash paint (also known as a 'high altitude' finish) was universally applied from late 1954 and was conducted when the aircraft entered planned modification cycles. But, emblematic of the pace of technological

change, the B-36 was to spend more time in modification and maintenance than any other aircraft operated by the Air Force – which, considering it was conceived before the US entered the Second World War, could be expected. But this was also a product not only of the pace of change but in the concurrency model where metal had been cut before the final configuration had been signed off.

As an example of the intensity of this activity, in mid-1953 SAC and Convair entered into a rolling cycle of modification and modernisation which would see every B-36 going through a commonality update and improvement programme, in parallel to the Featherweight treatment. Known as the Specialised Aircraft Maintenance (SAM) scheme, an RB-36E (42-13571, the original YB-36) was the first aircraft to enter the cycle with the last aircraft (52-2216) redelivered back to SAC on 29 April 1957. This process required 59 days per aircraft and 38 maintenance docks in work simultaneously on 13 aircraft a month.

THIS PAGE Handed over to the US Air Force in August 1954, the last Peacemaker, B-36J 52-2827, in final roll-out. *(Dennis Jenkins)*

Chapter Four

Variants and derivatives

The B-36 spawned more
adaptations, roles and redesigns
than any other US Air Force
type, following its design role
of conventional bomber with
nuclear bomber, reconnaissance
version and cargo-carrier as
well as swept-wing and nuclear-
powered derivatives.

OPPOSITE **Displaying the magnesium panel in non-reflective finish, this RB-36 (49-2688) shows off the modified appearance of the D-series in reconnaissance configuration.** *(Dennis Jenkins)*

RB-36 reconnaissance variants

An important role to come out of the Second World War was the adaptation of aircraft to reconnaissance duties, standard aircraft modified to that job as required for tactical or strategic purposes. All combatant forces grew their reconnaissance capability on the specific operational capabilities of selected aircraft designed specifically for air combat or bombing. LeMay was particularly concerned to have all his bombers adapted for reconnaissance duties and this applied to the RB-29 as well as the RB-36, the RB-45, RB-47, and RB-57. Only the B-52 escaped this adopted role with a designated variant specifically assigned to reconnaissance.

In the immediate aftermath of the Second World War, the Air Force was aware that its potential enemy, Russia, was a largely unmapped country and that it had to rely on captured Luftwaffe photographs and German maps created before and during Operation Barbarossa and the attack on the USSR in June 1945. In fact, many of the Russian maps were deliberately incorrect, accurate maps only being available to Soviet government personnel. With the atomic bomb, the Air Force needed detailed information about ports, industrial facilities, marshalling yards and military bases, frequently misidentified and incorrectly placed on published maps.

Accordingly, with the extreme range of the B-36, LeMay sought, and obtained, a high priority for a reconnaissance version of the B-52 and that began with a remanufactured YB-36 and 21 of the operationally inadequate B-36A converted to RB-36E standard by way of an upgrade to B-36B standard and then fitted for reconnaissance. Over time, 142, around one-third of all B-36 aircraft produced, were reconnaissance versions and it is arguably in that role that the B-36 was of more operational use. Although, the sheer presence of the B-36 as a bomber in the SAC inventory sent a very clear message to the Soviet hierarchy and the freshly minted communist state of the People's Republic of China.

The origin of the B-36 reconnaissance

BELOW An RB-36D rolls off the production line at Convair's Fort Worth facility signalling the emergence of arguably the most operationally useful of all variants. *(Convair)*

programme dates back to early 1948 when Convair and some specialist reconnaissance camera companies were asked to produce mock-ups of equipment, the first being shown on 17 March 1949, reviewed by the Air Force over the next several months. The designations for these aircraft were the RB-36E (the 'E' series being exclusively reworked A-series aircraft) and the RB-36D, which were entirely new-builds. The only real difference between the two derivations were their origin on the production line and all were brought to the D-series standard. In this regard the usual variant suffix letter applied more to the production lot than to the particulars of a specific variant.

A special board comprising 75 Air Force officers and civilians, set up to evaluate all new types prior to entering production, examined the reconnaissance variant on 21 November 1949 and in an inspection lasting five days approved the modifications, of which there were a substantial number. The crew complement changed significantly, with roles and responsibilities changed, the total

complement growing from 15 to 22 personnel, additional crewmembers being assigned to the cameras and photographic equipment as well as electronic reconnaissance systems. By the 1950s considerable attention was being paid to the identification, location and frequency mapping of radio communications and radar sites and this role was added to the traditional one of taking pictures from a great height.

Substantial modifications were made to the bomb bay area, the No. 1 bay being converted to a 4.87m long housing for up to a maximum 23 cameras with 14 in a pressurised compartment. The No. 2 bay would house photo-flash bombs and the through-tunnel was modified into two separate sections, a very short one running from the forward compartment to the new pressurised photo compartment and which did not require a transfer cart, and a second tunnel from the aft end of the photo compartment, through the aft three of the four original bomb bays to the aft pressurised section, that retaining the cart. The Nos. 3 and 4 bomb bays were modified into an electronics equipment

ABOVE Reserved exclusively for the A- and B-series conversions to reconnaissance aircraft, an RB-36E (44-92020), originally a B-36A, seen in an evocative view. *(Dennis Jenkins)*

RIGHT The cramped crew quarters of an RB-36H (50-1110) are evident as 1st Lt James Shively (front left) occupies the navigator seat with photo-navigator Capt William Merrill behind. Nose gunner and weather observer A1C Albert Brown (top centre) is to the left of radar observer Capt Franklin O'Donald.
(Dennis Jenkins)

compartment. These facilities required the forward and aft bulkheads to be converted into pressure domes and changes to the bomb bay doors were made together with switching to aluminium for the exterior skin since magnesium could not stand the pressure cycles. This allowed easy visual identification of the reconnaissance versions, together with the various windows, covered with sliding doors when not in use.

The primary cameras employed were the K-17C, K-22A, K-38 and K-40. There was a facility serving as a darkroom to allow cartridges to be reloaded with new film in flight. The maximum complement of cameras had two fixed and five remotely controlled locations, designated as the trimetrogon, vertical, split vertical, multi and the forward oblique positions. The trimetrogon is an arrangement of three fixed cameras, one pointing downwards, and two either side of the groundtrack at a 30° depression angle, 60° from vertical with overlapping images for stereoscopic views of undulating topography. These were controlled from the photo-navigator's station in the nose or from the photographer's station in the photographic

LEFT SSgt John McCarl occupies the radio operator position in RB-36H 50-1110.
(Dennis Jenkins)

ABOVE The AMQ-7 sensor instrument boom on the Integrated Electronic and Weather Reconnaissance System (IEWRS) on an RB-36, August 1955. *(Don Pyeatt via Dennis Jenkins)*

RIGHT Another functional element of the IEWRS was the APS-23 scope seen here in an RB-36. *(Don Pyeatt via Dennis Jenkins)*

compartment. The two oblique cameras were controlled from their respective positions by the photographer operating switches. The vertical camera could also be used for night photography when it would be operated in conjunction with 88 T-86 or M46 photo-flash bombs each weighing 45kg. These bombs were located in bay No. 2 and a photocell trip would expose the film when the flash went off. The remotely controlled cameras would be used in conjunction with determinations of altitude, speed and settings on the intervalometer, a device which measures brief intervals of time and can trigger exposures at previously set intervals. Two C-1 radarscope cameras were also carried in the photo compartment together with one A-6 movie

RIGHT The ARA-25 IEWRS antenna housing on the inside of the RB-36 fuselage. *(Don Pyeatt via Dennis Jenkins)*

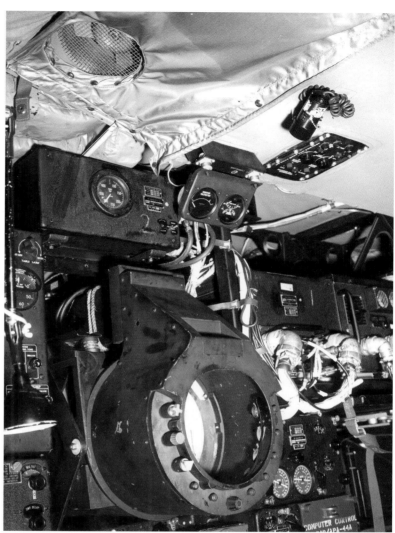

camera and these items could be operated by the photo-navigator who was located in the forward fuselage.

At first, the Nos. 2 and 3 bomb bay positions were covered with a single set of doors, 33.6ft (10.2m) in length, the No. 3 bay containing an auxiliary fuel tank or additional flash bombs. Of course no bombs were carried on the reconnaissance versions, permitting removal of the Norden or periscope bombsights and the No. 4 bay supported a single pallet with electronic eavesdropping equipment. In the external positions where the two aft bomb bays would normally be found, three large radomes were installed and through these, operators could record and analyse communications and radar signals, allowing identification and frequency mapping of Soviet defence and acquisition radars. Some degree of weight-reduction was possible, engineers at Convair taking the opportunity to install different bulkheads on each end of the place where the bomb racks would normally be supported. Also, some of the fuselage frames were lightened and changes were made to the wing spar which also helped reduce weight.

Operationally, flying the RB-36 differed little from the bomber version, but the bombardier was replaced with the photo-navigator in the extreme nose with excellent views of the ground below and to either side. As would be the practice for a bombing run, the pilot would hand over control of the aircraft to the photo-navigator who would position the flight path over the desired groundtrack and steer the aircraft from that point. He would also operate the cameras. The photographer in the photo-compartment was responsible for the film magazines and for changing cassettes as necessary, also controlling the heating and the dehumidifier as well as looking after the technical performance of the cameras.

Standard on all RB versions of the B-36, ferret ECM (Electronic Counter Measures) was installed in bomb bay No. 4 with most of the defensive ECM and its electronics situated in the forward fuselage as it was for the bomber versions but there was a considerable amount of location-shifting required when the B-36 was modified to carry atomic bombs; the aircraft itself had never been designed to carry these weapons and some structural changes were

BELOW A characteristic feature of the reconnaissance variants was the installation of ferret electronic countermeasures in aerodynamically streamlined radomes in the position of the No. 4 bomb bay, the shorter doors of No. 3 bay seen to the right of the picture. *(Don Pyeatt via Dennis Jenkins)*

required when the ECM equipment was moved to bomb bay No. 4. The bulkheads for the reconnaissance versions were redesigned and that formed a major part of the structural changes that were useful for the aircraft carrying gravity atom bombs.

It is worth mentioning at this juncture that similar modifications were adopted for the weather reconnaissance aircraft, conducting missions to get meteorological data through a weather observer station in the extreme nose. Radio altimeters were attached to the underside of the horizontal tail and the associated electronics were added to the aft pressurised compartment. A probe for measuring barometric pressure, temperature and humidity was attached to the starboard side of the extreme nose behind the glazed panelling. An equipment rack for a radiosonde was installed at the operator station for the intermediate frequency ECM operator. The sonde dispenser was mounted to the floor of the centreline in the rear pressurised compartment in the place where the strike camera was installed on the bomber versions. The controls for the sonde were situated in the high-frequency ECM station on the starboard side of the aft compartment

and at the lower gunner's blister on the same side of the fuselage.

International events accelerated the use of bombers as reconnaissance aircraft: the communist coup in Prague in February 1948, the blockade of Berlin four months later and the detonation of the Soviet A-bomb in August. Two months after that the North Korean forces mounted a devastating attack on South Korea, the trigger, as briefly mentioned earlier, for the

ABOVE A close-up of the search radome in the forward fuselage with electronic countermeasures receiving antennas. *(Dennis Jenkins)*

LEFT Introduced on Phase II of the electronic countermeasures programme, the dual APT-16 transmitters operated at separate frequency levels, the electronics packages being situated beneath the table. *(Don Pyeatt via Dennis Jenkins)*

ABOVE The lower aft right-side gunner's position on RB-36H 52-1352 with the escape rope which, when pulled, would allow rapid escape after the blister had been opened and the sight pivoted in and down in the direction of the chair.
(Dennis Jenkins)

light up defensive radars but there were none. The first overflight took place on 10 May 1948 when 1/Lt Poe flew from Misawa Air Base, Japan, flying over the Kuril Islands, followed on 10 March 1950 with the first overflight of the Soviet Union to take pictures of the naval base at Vladivostock. But SAC wanted flight profile simulations of attack routes from CONUS bases to Soviet targets for assignment of nuclear weapons. This was different to the general intelligence information sought by the Air Force through the RB-45 and the RB-47 and smaller aircraft such as the RF-80, RF-86, RF-100 and the Navy's F2H-2P, initially known as SENSINT (Sensitive Intelligence).

RB-36D

Responding quickly, the first reconnaissance version destined for SAC, RB-36D 44-92088 made its first flight on 14 December 1949. Piloted by George Davis and Francis Keen, that flight lasted 7hr 1min. This aircraft was delivered to SAC ahead of the first B-36D bomber configuration as were the next six reconnaissance versions of the D-series, albeit originally ordered as B-36Bs. The first arrived with SAC in June 1950. These aircraft were operated by the 28th SRS (Strategic Reconnaissance Wing) at Rapid City AFB, North Dakota, now Ellsworth AFB, and all 24 had been delivered by May 1951.

Early evaluation included a calibration of the cameras on a photo target comprising a set of white lines against a black background set up at a parking lot at Convair, where employees were asked not to leave their car! Some of these test flights could be long. Fifteen hours into one such run, Beryl Erickson and Francis Keen were given a call to divert to Eglin AFB to participate in a synchronised air show with a 15sec window to appear at full throttle and all engines at maximum revs. As the only B-36D with jet pods, the Air Force wanted to impress. Streaking across the airfield and closely followed by two B-36Bs dropping a full load of 500lb (227kg) in front of the grandstand, the RB-36D pulled up and steep into a climbing bank. No rehearsal and not even a day's work – back to the scheduled test profile, a further 32 hours in the air and a landing 47hr 45min after take-off.

suspicion that the Soviet Union was preparing to attack Western Europe along with an attack on the Continental United States (CONUS). Determined to obtain intelligence information on the disposition of Soviet forces, in December 1950 President Truman authorised the first overflights of the USSR but specified that these should be undertaken by the new B-47 and the fourth of its type was assigned the task, cancelled when it was destroyed in a fire at Eielson AFB, Alaska.

Operations with the reconnaissance versions of the B-36 supported SAC requirements which were focused on attack profiles in the event of a major war with the USSR. Attacks from CONUS would be made over the Arctic and knowledge about Soviet defensive systems across the vast coastline of Siberia was largely unknown.

Since the end of the war, B-17s and B-29s converted for reconnaissance ('weather') duties had been probing the Arctic region, flying up and down the Soviet northern territories trying to

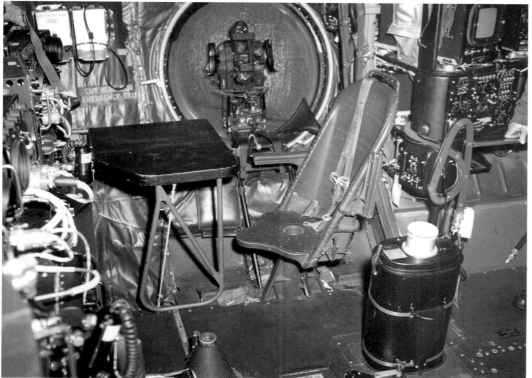

ABOVE The B-36 Norden bombsight at the photo-navigator's station in the lower pressurised section of the forward fuselage. *(Dennis Jenkins)*

LEFT The weather reconnaissance modifications were common on the RB-36, the dispenser for a radiosonde being located on the floor to the side of the right lower gun blister as seen here looking outboard. *(Don Pyeatt via Dennis Jenkins)*

RIGHT A view of the open MA-1 radiosonde dispenser chute. The equipment stack for this was situated in the intermediate frequency operator's station for the electronic control measures station in the aft pressure compartment. *(Don Pyeatt via Dennis Jenkins)*

FAR RIGHT The radar controls in the weather reconnaissance equipment on the RB-36. *(Don Pyeatt via Dennis Jenkins)*

RIGHT The operator station for bomb bay No. 1 in the RB-36. *(Don Pyeatt via Dennis Jenkins)*

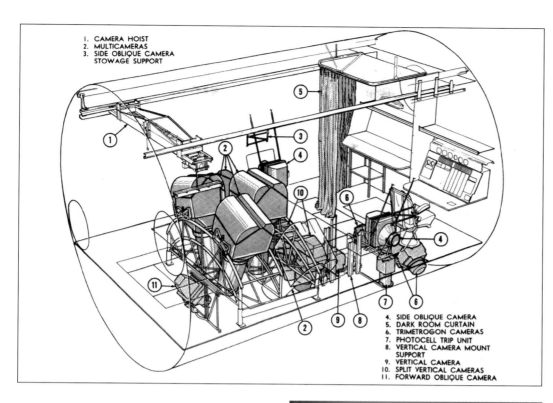

1. CAMERA HOIST
2. MULTICAMERAS
3. SIDE OBLIQUE CAMERA
   STOWAGE SUPPORT

4. SIDE OBLIQUE CAMERA
5. DARK ROOM CURTAIN
6. TRIMETROGON CAMERAS
7. PHOTOCELL TRIP UNIT
8. VERTICAL CAMERA MOUNT
   SUPPORT
9. VERTICAL CAMERA
10. SPLIT VERTICAL CAMERAS
11. FORWARD OBLIQUE CAMERA

LEFT The camera compartment on the RB-36 was sufficiently flexible to support a variety of different camera types for specific mission objectives. Note the provision of a darkroom for processing the film onto positives. *(Convair)*

The new capabilities of the reconnaissance version were demonstrated on 16 January 1951 when an RB-36D (44-92090) landed after a flight lasting exactly 51hr 30min. Flown by a Convair test flight crew, this flight was not that far beyond the duration of many operational flights, routine missions of more than 30 hours being considered normal. RB-36D 44-92088 spent its entire life flying test missions, was given the designation ERB-36D and was the one modified to carry the phenomenally complex Boston Camera.

Developed by Dr James Baker at Harvard University and officially designated K-42, it was built by the Boston University Optical Research Laboratory. It had a focal length of 240in (609.6cm) folded through a series of mirrors and was equipped with a lens with an f/8 stop and 1/400th/second shutter speed. The K-42 weighed 6,500lb (2,948kg) and had a resolution of 28 lines/mm which allowed it to show a golf ball from an altitude of 45,000ft (13,716m). This is still the largest camera ever built and produced photographs on negatives 18 x 36in (45.72 x 91.44cm) from film stored on two 18in wide reels. Spectacular in concept and highly impressive, the camera was tested for about a year from 1954 but serious problems

LEFT One of the cameras available for the RB-36, the Fairchild K-17C system offered vertical and oblique photographs by means of a shutter between the Bausch and Lomb Metrogen lenses, using interchangeable cones. *(NASM)*

LEFT Adopted as a standard day reconnaissance camera on the B-36, the Fairchild K-22A used a 24in (61cm) Eastman Kodak Ektar lens and focal plane shutter. *(NASM)*

with vibration produced a high percentage of smeared photographs, unusable for sensible intelligence purposes. It was removed from the ERB-36D and because of the amount of work required to restore the aircraft to operational use, it was scrapped in 1955.

RB-36E

Product of the original order to adapt existing B-36B aircraft into reconnaissance versions, the next series to fly was the RB-36E, based on YB-36 42-13571 which was remodelled into the new role. The first RB-36E (44-92024) took to the air on 7 July 1950 and was delivered to the 28th SRW at Rapid City AFB on 28 July, the last of the 22 of this series being delivered on 27 April 1951. Of course all these aircraft flew without the jet pods provided to the RB-36D.

RB-36F

ABOVE A close-up of the tail of RB-36 49-2704 with access work gantry. *(National Archives)*

BELOW An RB-36F (49-2707) tail serves as backdrop for a posed gathering of crew, with the rear access ladder just visible. *(Dennis Jenkins)*

The 36 aircraft in this series were contracted under the same order of 13 April 1949 which launched the B-36D series. The first RB-36F took to the air on 30 April 1951, the last being delivered in December 1951. The basic

aircraft were similar to the B-36F which the reconnaissance equipment was that applied to the RB-36D. It was on one of these aircraft that a pressure bulkhead failed causing a temporary altitude restriction.

RB-36H

This variant was by far the most prolific of all reconnaissance variants, 73 aircraft of this series being produced after the contract was announced on 5 September 1951. The

ABOVE An RB-36E (44-92020) used frequently for a set of posed public relations photographs showing radomes and ECM receiving antennas. *(Dennis Jenkins)*

LEFT A line of RB-36H reconnaissance bombers (52-1384 in foreground) on the maintenance line at Fort Worth, Convair being one of the first manufacturing companies to receive contracts for depot maintenance. Note the exposed tail radar. *(Dennis Jenkins)*

26-1404   2-20-52
RB-36E NO. 16 - BOMB BAY
SECTION STA. 6. 2 - LKG. FWD
CVAC FT. WORTH TEX.

```
26-1401              2-20-52
RB-36E NO. 16 - CAMERA
COMPARTMENT 5.0 BLKHD.
LKG. FWD.
CVAC FT. WORTH TEX.
```

```
26-1399              2-20-52
RB-36E NO. 16 - PILOTS
PEDESTAL
CVAC FT. WORTH TEX.
```

THIS SPREAD
Following an accidental ground collision with (former B-36A) RB-36E 44-92019, another RB-36E (44-92022) suffered only minor damage but the fuselage of 019 split at the location of the forward turret bay. Here, the work to restore it to service is carried out at Travis AFB, California, as the only field-remanufacture on record since the airframe could not be flown back to Convair. *(Dennis Jenkins)*

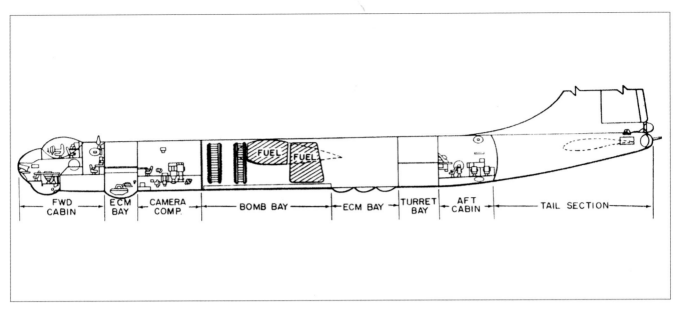

FWD CABIN   ECM BAY   CAMERA COMP.   BOMB BAY   ECM BAY   TURRET BAY   AFT CABIN   TAIL SECTION

ABOVE The general configuration of the RB-36 showing the location of the camera compartment and work station for photographers and film processors, and the additional fuel tank which could be fitted to one of the bomb bays.
(Convair)

agreement had been reached the preceding year which provided serial numbers bearing the fiscal year 1950. As with the RB-36F, in this variant the airframe was identical to the B-36F while the reconnaissance package was unique to all variants modified into this role.

Cold War capers

Many claims have been made about overflights of denied airspace conducted by the B-36 but in reality these were very few and the details of those which were carried out are obscure and many of them still classified. Of all overflights more than 80% were conducted by SAC RB-47s, since they had the advantage of air-to-air refuelling, speed and height. But the intensity of overflights was great. Between July 1946 and December 1956, almost 200 military overflights took place, those before the first reconnaissance mission of 10 May 1948 being with general observation aircraft. These far outnumber the 24 U-2 missions between July 1956 and May 1960.

The separate intelligence-gathering requirements of SAC and the Air Force together with the various US intelligence services added to a considerable database of detailed photographic and electronic information. It was made more acute in 1952 when general intelligence appeared to show that the Russians were building air bases in northern Siberia for their Tu-4 bombers, preparatory

to using the arctic route to hit North America in the event of war. That concern resulted in Project 52 AFR-18 assigned to SAC and briefed personally by LeMay. It was successfully mounted in October 1952.

Because of Soviet agents living as normal American families in the US, these penetration flight plans were highly secret, the air crew only being told by the commander when they had flown a routine training circuit of CONUS and headed off out to foreign parts out of non-residential areas. These clandestine destinations helped maintain secrecy from covert agents and LeMay was totally convinced that they were necessary on all B-36 flights as well. This has led to many urban myths, exaggerated by not a few seeking to dramatise the importance of their flights. They were all important, and not demeaned simply because they did not wander across the Soviet Union carrying atom bombs! But the reconnaissance missions conducted by the B-36s so modified were just as vital as the bomber versions and their highly professional crew.

Nevertheless, in support of the overall war-fighting strategy of SAC, the largest overflight ever conducted was Operation Home Run, involving RB-47s flying 156 penetration flights from Thule AFB, Greenland between March and May 1956. They flew to areas right along the arctic seaboard of the USSR almost as far west as Murmansk and as far east as Provideniya, a coastline 3,666mls (5,900km)

of the B-52. If used in aggression it was reasoned that the nuanced value of escort aircraft would be irrelevant and the value of protection from various aircraft in a fleet of intruding bombers once again fell into favour. But reconnaissance missions were lone flights and were an entirely different proposition: devoid of bombs, the cavernous bays on an RB-36 was ready and available for a protective parasite.

Moreover, and increasingly favoured, a fast reconnaissance fighter could be carried by an RB-36 to the perimeter of hostile airspace, release the camera-carrying fighter to carry out a high-speed dash and return for a pick-up and withdrawal to a safe air base. In this way, with the radius of action for an RB-36 so equipped, and the 2,000ml (3,218km) range of a recce-fighter, the total system would have a range of 12,000mls (19,308km). For this duty, the Air Force chose the swept-wing RF-84F Thunderflash, an aircraft specifically adapted for reconnaissance duty. The YF-84F (49-2430) was chosen for the tests, similar to the F-84E except for the relocation of the horizontal tail, canted downwards to clear the

underside of the RB-36 during departure and approach. Early development tests showed a high level of flutter at the tail of the parasite but modification to the profile of the remaining segments of the remodelled bomb bay doors solved the problem.

By this time the Air Force was getting excited about this extension of its capabilities

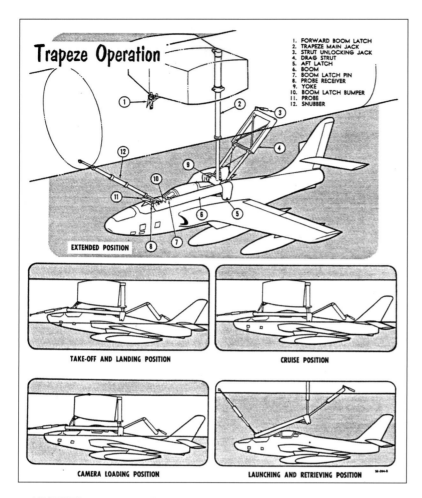

Trapeze Operation

1. FORWARD BOOM LATCH
2. TRAPEZE MAIN JACK
3. STRUT UNLOCKING JACK
4. DRAG STRUT
5. AFT LATCH
6. BOOM
7. BOOM LATCH PIN
8. PROBE RECEIVER
9. YOKE
10. BOOM LATCH BUMPER
11. PROBE
12. SNUBBER

EXTENDED POSITION

TAKE-OFF AND LANDING POSITION

CRUISE POSITION

CAMERA LOADING POSITION

LAUNCHING AND RETRIEVING POSITION

ABOVE The trapeze configuration for carrying an RF-84F seen here in deploy and retrieve positions. Note that the horizontal tail of the fighter was given anhedral to allow it to fit into the underbelly of the mothership. *(Convair)*

BELOW The general arrangement of the GRB-36 with the RF-84F retained within the original area of the bomb bay with additional fuel tanks for the fighter. *(Convair)*

and wanted to show off its new adaptation; there had been criticism of the B-36, that it was too slow and lumbering a platform to have relevance in the jet age and this was an ideal way to show that a relatively low-cost asset (the jet parasite), when carried to the border of a hostile state could do a valuable job made possible only by the availability of a carrier-plane to place it in harm's way and recover it with valuable intelligence information. Accordingly, the Air Force revealed the FICON as it existed at this time, during the National Aircraft Show in Dayton, Ohio, during August 1953. In a flurry of B-36 appearances, two flying directly in to the show from Japan and two more from the UK, the YF-84F and the JRB-36F performed several hook-ups. Later that year, other public demonstrations were conducted at Eglin and Carswell.

As 1954 began, Convair boasted a contract from the Air Force for 10 RB-36Ds and 25 RF-84Fs, the carrier-plane modified according to Featherweight Configuration III with the new ECM equipment. But this was a reduction from the 30 RB-36s and the 75 RF-84s that the Air Force wanted, comprising the efficiency of the conversion and virtually relinquishing the work to individual changes on the production line. The converted aircraft received the designations GRB-36D-III and the RF-84K, the first carrier-plane taking to the air on 28 July 1954, flown by Ray Fitzgerald and Fred B. Perry. Although testing on the carrier-plane was over by 22 September, the first RF-84K was not ready before 17 December. But in the intervening period problems hit the programme

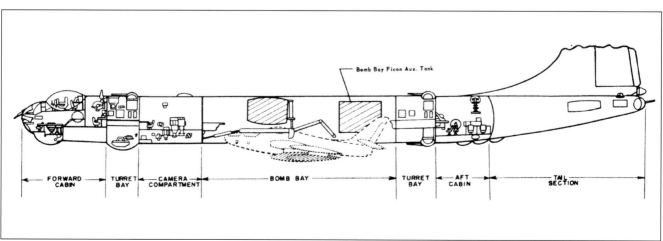

Bomb Bay Ficon Aux. Tank

FORWARD CABIN | TURRET BAY | CAMERA COMPARTMENT | BOMB BAY | TURRET BAY | AFT CABIN | TAIL SECTION

and a trapeze jack failed on the carrier-plane. However, this did not interrupt delivery of the first aircraft to the Air Force in February 1955, followed in August by the first RF-84K.

The general preferred operating procedure had the RF-84F take off independently and join up with the carrier-plane but it was also possible to carry the parasite into the air hung semi-buried in the under-fuselage, displaying minimal ground clearance with its two underwing drop tanks requiring the rotation off the runway to be handled sensitively. Convair had to use ramps to jack up the GRD-36 but two pits were built at Fairchild AFB to accept the parasite, offering it up to the carrier-plane rolled in over the pit.

A standard mission would release the parasite at a distance of 800mls (1,287km) to 1,000mls (1,609km) from the target, at a nominal 2,810mls (4,521km) from take-off. Specially sculpted doors (known as 'plug-and-clearance' doors) enclosed the parasite in the converted bomb bay area and these closed over the opening after releasing the RF-84F. After flying its planned penetration flight the parasite would return to the GRB-36D and return to base. The carrier-plane was fitted with an APX-29A IFF/rendezvous set and the bay had a catwalk area with hand holds and safety wires. With a 1,140gal (4,315 litre) supplementary fuel tank on the port side of the fuselage containing JP-4 jet fuel, the carrier-plane could refuel the parasite should that be necessary.

Training on the new configuration began at Convair in late 1955 during which 13 pilots from Fairchild AFB went through a rigorous familiarisation with the new concept, returning to their home base for more extensive, pre-operational training before assignment to classified missions. These included a wide range of potentially clandestine flights, some of them for night operations, re-rendezvous with the carrier-plane aided by a system of lights installed in the under-fuselage of the GRB-36D. The GRB-36D went into operational service with the 99th SRW at Fairchild operating RF-84Ks from the 91st SRS of the 71st SRW based at Great Falls AFB, Montana, and then at Larson AFB, Washington.

The parasite concept had great value to SAC and their operational use has never been

ABOVE A close-up view of bomb bay No. 2 and the fittings and retention equipment for the FICON concept with the RF-84F.
(Dennis Jenkins)

fully declassified. Moreover, the pilots who flew a lot of those operations were subject to special terms of constraint and secrecy. Undoubtedly, several penetrations into Soviet airspace were carried out, the GRD-36Ds staying in international airspace and releasing their parasitic snoopers to go about their own business. On several flights, the carrier-plane crew knew nothing of the sortie being carried out, or of the targets selected for photo-reconnaissance but it is clear that these RF-84K flights gathered up electronic intelligence as well as photographic, with some 'special' missions conducted in the brief interval between the start and finish of parasite operations.

With the advent of the Lockheed U-2 a new era in spy plane operations began and the FICON concept faded away. Conceived in 1954 under a veil of utmost secrecy, Lockheed started work on the U-2 originally as a concept for the Air Force but it quickly became an adopted asset of the CIA, which began

covert overflight operations in 1956, before switching to the Air Force as a high-altitude reconnaissance system. From there the story is well known: at President Eisenhower's direction a succession of covert overflights took place right across the Soviet Union and on one mission from Peshawar, Pakistan, to Bodo, Norway, Francis Gary Powers was shot down, arrested and put on trial for spying, later to be exchanged after less than two years in jail for a top-level Russian KGB spy under the name Rudolf Abel.

From then on emphasis on reconnaissance departed to niched and highly specialised intelligence gathering missions with the A-12 from 1963 by the CIA and the SR-71 operated by the Air Force from 1966. From which began an inevitable migration to satellites in space, the first operated under the Corona programme which introduced the age of spying from the advantage of Earth orbit during the early 1960s. But it had been the B-36 which had seen the most bizarre form of overflight espionage during a brief period in the mid-1950s on missions so important that there is largely a veil over them 65 years later.

But FICON was not the only parasitic project, one which started after FICON but

ABOVE The RF-84F is fully retracted into the shoe containing the upper part of the fighter's fuselage with the cockpit which would be entered in flight. *(Dennis Jenkins)*

RIGHT Its main landing gear jacked up to allow the RF-84F to be positioned for installation on the restrain and deploy mechanism, GRB-36 49-2696 prepares for a test flight. *(Dennis Jenkins)*

which reverted to the air defence capability and may therefore be addressed as a successor to Goblin but utilising the ubiquitous line of F-84 aircraft. Promoted by ex-German scientist Dr Richard Vogt, and known as TOM-TOM, it began as a way of extending the range of bombers and reconnaissance aircraft by attaching free-floating fuel tanks articulated to the wing-tips of the aircraft to which they were attached and with an aerofoil profile to allow them to provide lift and reduce drag. They could also increase the range and altitude by increasing the aspect ratio of the wing; range would be increased by the extra fuel, altitude achieved by the adaptation of the fixed wing planform, and weight removed by jettisoning them when empty.

From this idea emerged the concept of parasitic escort fighters which could 'ride' on their own wings but passively attached to the carrier-plane and with their engines shut down. This 'free' ride could dramatically extend the operational capability of the parasites, advocates said and the Tom-Tom concept pressed by Vogt was a direct product of trials carried out in Nazi Germany during 1944 and early 1945. Post-war, preliminary trials had been carried out by the Air Force using a

Douglas C-47A and a Culver PQ-14B with an attachment sufficiently flexible to allow three degrees of freedom, but riding on its own lift. The first attempt at coupling up in flight occurred on 19 August 1949 and it was not successful.

Nevertheless, this small-scale evaluation showed promise and, with the B-36 programme under way, the Air Force took the idea a step further, initiating a full-scale air-tow concept using a B-29 to tow two F-84 fighters in Project TIP TOW. Republic modified two F-84D-1RE aircraft and designated them EF-84D with wing tips carrying flexible mountings to attach to suitably adapted wing tips of an EB-29A (44-62093). Despite some modest success the risks were very high and in a catastrophe on 24 April 1953, all three aircraft plunged into Peconic Bay, Long Island, after one of the two parasites flipped over and struck the B-29 wing, killing all on board.

Along with this programme, two RF-84F-5-REs (51-1848 and -1849) were modified to carry wingtip hook equipment and on 8 May 1954 the FICON JRB-36F test aircraft was assigned to what was named the Tom-Tom project. This time the entire coupling system design and manufacture was consigned to

LEFT Special controls on the GRB-36 flight deck for the FICON configuration.
(Dennis Jenkins)

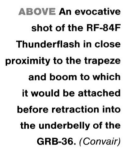

the Thiebolt Engineering Company and a fixed mock-up was attached to the wing of JRB-36F and an RF-84F and on 30 September 1954 some 7hr of proximity flight tests were conducted. A retraction mechanism firmly clasped the parasite and made electrical and hydraulic connections to allow the fighter to shut down its engine. But following the TIP TOW crash tests were wound down.

On 2 November 1955 the first aerial hook-up was accomplished with a fighter on the port wing and on 26 September 1956 the final hook-up resulted in violent oscillations that broke the connecting sleeve and the parasite fell away free to land safely, as did the JRB-36F. The programme was cancelled and thus ended the dream of using parasitic free rides to augment the range of the escort fighter or to carry to enemy territory a fast reconnaissance system, superseded by much more efficient methods of extending range or obtaining vital intelligence information.

XC-99 Cargo Carrier

Seeking to capitalise on a successful long-range bomber design, early in its development phase Consolidated set to work on a cargo version which it tried to sell, to the Air Force and to commercial airlines. First to order a military transport version, the AAF ordered a single prototype (43-52436) on 31 December 1942 with the designation XC-99, on the basis that this would not interfere

with development of the B-36 bomber. Then named Consolidated, the manufacturer was keen to get under way with this as an aide to development of the B-36, because without the added inconvenience of military equipment it would be an exemplar for the bomber on to which was being hung a complexity of government-furnished equipment. A 'clean' configuration would more effectively advance detailed design of the B-36.

Both military and commercial versions of a derivative would have essentially the same wing as the B-36 but the fuselage would be very different. In fact, Pan American Airways asked Consolidated to come up with a flying boat based on the same six-prop tractor design of the B-36 but with a very different fuselage incorporating a hull, twin-fin tail and no landing gear.

The attraction of flying boats focused on the lack of appropriate airfields and landing strips in many places the developing airline industry was now visiting. Pan American had pioneered the routes across the Pacific Ocean on a series of flying boat designs placed with Sikorsky and in the mid-1930s had turned to Boeing for the 314 Clipper to service its routes all the way from the West Coast to the Philippines. Intriguingly, the Clipper too had been a derivative of a long range bomber design, the wing and engines of the Boeing XB-15 bomber were taken as the basis for the commercial Clipper, but with a flying boat hull. Now Pan American wanted Consolidated to do the same, adapting the wings and engines of the B-36 for its bigger flying boat with longer range.

Dubbed 'Super Clippers', the flying boat derivative of the B-36 would be able to carry up to 204 passengers in relative luxury as well as 15,000lb (6,804kg) in baggage and freight. The flying boat would be powered by six 5,500hp (37,922kN) Wright T-35 turboprop engines each driving a triple-propeller with 19ft (5.79m) blades. The Super Clipper would incorporate a mix of day seats and sleeper berths with a large circular staircase at each end of the pressurised cabin. Special gourmet meals would emerge from the comprehensive galley with toilet facilities on a par with five-star hotels.

Anticipating a burgeoning business after the war, seeing peace just around the corner, Pan American had ordered 15 Super Clippers in February 1945 and allowed the company newspaper *The Eagle* on 25 May to announce with a flourish that this was its passenger liner of the future, boasting unprecedented luxury and range. With enormous progress in both engines and airframes due to the requirements of the war years, airlines had a rich choice of capabilities and unique opportunities, to take ostensibly military aircraft and adapt them for new commercial uses after the war.

Without landing gear, saving 6,500lb (2,948kg), the different hull and the wing floats added weight which required 3,000lb (1,360kg) of additional fuel for a range of 4,200mls (6,758km) at a cruising speed of 332mph (534kph) with a service ceiling of 29,200ft (8,900m). The usual take-off run of 4,760ft (1,451m) for the B-36 was stretched to 5,680ft (1,731m) for the flying boat, a Super Clipper requiring 48 seconds to unstick from the water.

It was a fitting prescient for the wide-body airliners of the future and could have easily become a standard trans-Pacific service had the airline not fallen out of love with flying boats. Within a year or so the extensive experience of building large airfields and very long runways advanced commercial flying in leaps and bounds and very quickly the inconvenience of moving people to coastal departure points for transfer to flying boats made this approach far less

BELOW Seen here at Kelly AFB, San Antonio, Texas, the Consolidated XC-99 (43-52436) transport aircraft emerged as a very early adaptation of the initial B-36 concept. *(USAF)*

attractive than the current generation of airliners. Pan American chose to back the Lockheed Constellation and its fleet of DC-7s and the Super Clipper was retired as a paper-aeroplane.

Meanwhile, the Air Force was much less sanguine about its XC-99 heavy-lifter, the wings and parts common to the B-36 being produced at Fort Worth with the new fuselage coming together at San Diego, which would receive the rest of the aircraft. Much about the XC-99 reflected the XB-36 design, including the single wheels each side in a tricycle configuration, until replaced by the four-wheel bogie before it as formally accepted by the Air Force, and initially powered with the R-4360-25 engines pending the newer -41 series engines along with the B-36 fleet.

The fuselage had a length of 182.5ft (55.63m), just over 20ft (6.1m) longer than the B-36, with two decks in the fuselage which had a height of 20ft (6.1m) and a width of 14ft (4.26m) presenting a cargo volume of 16,000ft^3 (452.8m^3). It was capable of carrying 100,000lb (45,360kg), up to 400 fully kitted troops or 300 litter patients. With maximum load, the XC-99 had a range of 1,720mls (2,767km) or up to 8,100mls (13,033km) with a 10,000lb (4,536kg) load. It had a cruising speed of 292mph (470kph) and a maximum speed of 335mph (539kph) at 30,000ft (9,144m). Total crew complement included two pilots, two flight engineers, the navigator, a radio operator and two scanners, the latter situated on the lower deck in the aft fuselage to watch the engines and landing gear. Soundproofing and carpeting was provided along with black fluorescent lighting for night operations.

Two cargo doors were provided underneath the fuselage, one in the aft fuselage and another forward of the wing. In addition, two pairs of clamshell doors were provided aft of the rear sliding door which required it to be open to operate them. The side doors could be opened in flight to drop cargo but the clamshell doors could not be opened in flight due to structural limitations. Two ramps could facilitate the loading of cargo or wheeled vehicles to either the forward or aft aperture. These two cargo compartments were separated by the wing carry-through structure and electric hoists were provided for moving cargo around for dropping through the underside doors, each one capable of moving 4,000lb (1,814kg) or twice that on a coupled, double-hoist.

The upper cargo compartment was provided with two openings, one above the forward sliding door and the other above the aft door with a ladder at the front and at the rear to allow crew access. Five canvas bunks were provided on the flight deck and toilet and drinking water supply but no provision for preparing food, but five additional toilets could be installed when it was configured as a troop carrier, with seating for personnel on canvas benches along each side on both upper and lower decks.

The Air Force took delivery of the XC-99 on 26 May 1949 and conducted an extensive evaluation at Kelly AFB, Texas. In June the following year it made a number of 1,150ml (1,850km) flights ferrying B-36 parts to San Diego. On 14 July it lifted ten R-4360 engines and 16 propellers in a total load of 101,255lb (45,934kg) for a total weight of 303,334lb (137,592kg). But that was not the ultimate record, for it made another run lifting 104,000lb (47,174kg). In August 1953 the XC-99 made its longest flight, 12,000mls (19,308km) from the United States to the Rhein-Main Air Base, Germany, carrying 60,000lb (27,216kg) both ways.

Most of the aircraft's limited activity was with the San Antonio Air Materiel Depot at Kelly AFB but the aircraft never really did have a chance with the Air Force. The XC-99 would

BELOW In flight, as on the ground, the XC-99 carries the Convair logo as it conducts a research flight in 1948. *(Convair)*

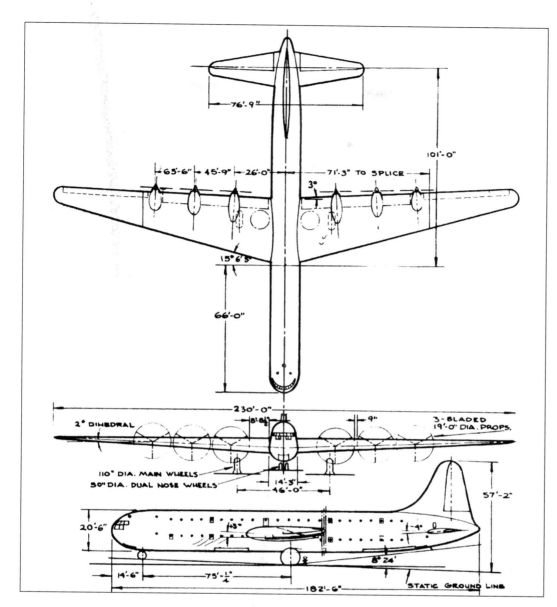

LEFT A genesis from the XB-36, initial drawings for the XC-99 shows it carrying the single wheel on each main landing leg. *(Convair)*

BELOW A side view of the XC-99 with the landing gear of the production B-36, displaying pressurised areas for personnel and a cargo area in the double-bubble fuselage arrangement. *(Convair)*

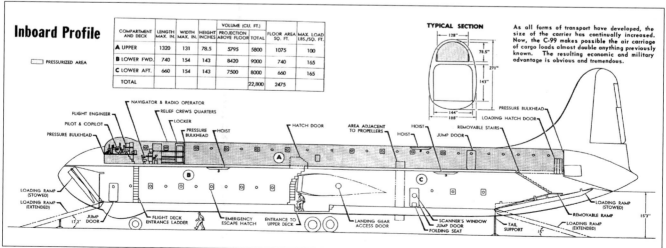

Inboard Profile

☐ PRESSURIZED AREA

COMPARTMENT AND DECK	LENGTH MAX. IN.	WIDTH MAX. IN.	HEIGHT INCHES	VOLUME (CU. FT.)		FLOOR AREA SQ. FT.	MAX. LOAD LBS./SQ. FT.
				PROJECTION ABOVE FLOOR	TOTAL		
A UPPER	1320	131	78.5	5795	5800	1075	100
B LOWER FWD.	740	154	143	8420	9000	740	165
C LOWER AFT.	660	154	143	7500	8000	660	165
TOTAL					22,800	2475	

TYPICAL SECTION

As all forms of transport have developed, the size of the carrier has continually increased. Now, the C-99 makes possible the air carriage of cargo loads almost double anything previously known. The resulting economic and military advantage is obvious and tremendous.

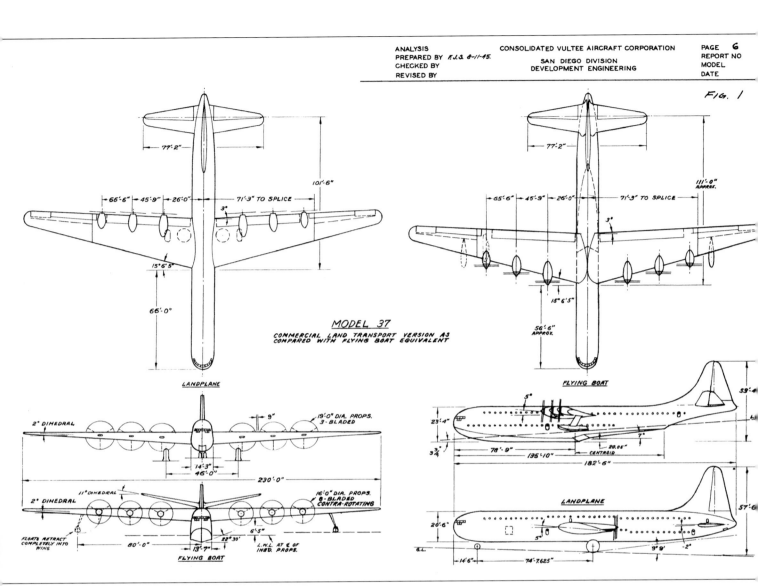

ANALYSIS
PREPARED BY *F.J.S. 8-11-45.*
CHECKED BY
REVISED BY

CONSOLIDATED VULTEE AIRCRAFT CORPORATION
SAN DIEGO DIVISION
DEVELOPMENT ENGINEERING

PAGE **6**
REPORT NO
MODEL
DATE

FIG. 1

MODEL 37
COMMERCIAL LAND TRANSPORT VERSION AS
COMPARED WITH FLYING BOAT EQUIVALENT

LANDPLANE

FLYING BOAT

FLYING BOAT

LANDPLANE

ABOVE Yet another possibility, one highly applicable to giant aircraft limited by suitable airfields, the XC-99 flying boat but with tractor engine/ propeller configuration.
(Convair)

conduct a great number of flights to Korea and impressed with its lift performance and reliability. However, most of its life up to 1957 was spent ferrying B-36 engines and supplies from Kelly to McClellan AFB, California. Interleaved with those were supply trips between intermediate bases. On sheer performance alone, the XC-99 demonstrated the tremendous potential of a heavy-lifter of this type.

But there had been plans for a production version significantly modified over the XC-99. The C-99 would have had a different nose section in common with the B-36, a different nose landing gear retracting into a bulge under the forward fuselage and a revised forward fuselage and a redefined cargo area with a pressurised upper deck capable of carrying

183 troops. The lower section remained unpressurised but with clamshell doors in the nose and tail with door sizes rearranged to accommodate the 240-mm howitzer and the Patton battle tanks. Novel about the foresight applied to the C-99 concept was its ability to fly direct to a combat area and not go through a staging area. This would not be achieved by any other aircraft prior to the introduction of the C-5A Galaxy.

In several respects the XC-99 and the proposed C-99 production design was ahead of its time and could have given the Air Force a heavy-lift cargo capability it would wait several decades to achieve. There were many reasons why this type was not adopted, subtle combinations that sent the Air Force

compartment at the aircraft centreline. Instead of having a round cross-section, the forward nose section was oval and the bubble-type canopy was replaced with a more normal, airliner-like, shape. The forward landing gear was also moved forward 6in (15.2cm) for accommodating the crew entry hatch. Sustained evaluation of the configuration went on to early 1955, with improvements to shielding, a revised instrument display panel and a new windscreen.

A very considerable reworking of the entire crew compartment produced a tightly spaced, cramped area which was completely different to the standard B-36, with connect/disconnect fittings for electrical, hydraulic and cable controls, required by the need to completely remove the forward pressurised cockpit due to the nature of the crew shielding requirement. In addition a combination of rubber and lead was bonded to the exterior of the crew compartment, designed specifically to be a plug-in/plug-out structure.

Additional shielding was required around the reactor itself with special water-jackets in the fuselage and also aft of the crew compartment for radiation absorption, in addition to a lead disc shield weighing around 8,000lb (3,629kg). The ASTR itself weighed 35,000lb (15,876kg) and produced 1,000kW of energy, installed in bomb bay No. 4 with a variety of cooling intakes and exhaust areas around the side and undersection of the aft fuselage. It was only installed for flight tests, the first of which occurred on 17 September

1955 with A. S. Witchell at the controls and accompanied in the air by a C-97 carrying US Marine parachutists ready to drop to the ground and secure the area should the NB-36H crash.

By March 1957, 47 flights had been made with the reactor on board, only 21 of which had it critical and a detailed assessment of the potential risk showed that the only real concern was if the NB-36H crashed and released fission products and that overall the risks were arguably not as high as those with other acceptable modes of transport. But the tide had turned on nuclear power for aviation and late in 1957 the aircraft was decommissioned and placed at the Nuclear Aircraft Research Facility where it remained as attempts were made to reactivate the programme. The NB-36H was scrapped in September 1958.

ABOVE Bearing the initial nose designation of XB-36H, the NB-36H nuclear-powered test airframe came as close as any other type to putting atomic energy into aircraft, here seen in formation with a B-50. *(USAF)*

BELOW NB-36H in flight from the three-quarter rear with bulges and appendages dictated by the installation of hardware supporting the nuclear propulsion system. *(USAF)*

8-G-9th AEG-25 APR 52-B-34

Chapter Five

Anatomy of the B-36

──●────────────────────────

The mighty B-36 was the largest aircraft to enter service with the US Air Force and the challenges faced at its conception and in development had no precedent. But just as the ambitious requirement placed on the design team taxed both aerodynamicists and engineers, so too would the choice of engine be equally crucial to its success.

OPPOSITE The Wasp engines were complex and not always cooperative, requiring extensive maintenance and a level of reliability which lowered the operational availability of B-36 Wings. *(Dennis Jenkins)*

The B-36 was a shoulder-wing, cantilever monoplane with a NACA laminar-flow wing section at an aspect ratio of 11:1. The wing was located slightly forward to the mid-point of the fuselage and the aircraft was of all-metal stressed skin construction. The wing had a leading edge sweepback of 15.11° and a trailing edge sweepback of 3°. The aircraft had a gross wing area of 4,772ft² (443.3m²)

supporting statically balanced ailerons with controllable trim tabs and electrically operated trailing edge flaps in three sections on each side of the fuselage. The total flap area was 519ft² (48.2m²) with heated, anti-icing surfaces.

The B-36 had a wing span of 230ft (70.14m) and a length of 162ft (49.4m) with a height of 46.75ft (14.26m). The tailplane had a span of 73.42ft (22.38m) and a total horizontal area

of 978ft² (90.85m²) and a total vertical area of 542ft² (50.34m²). Thermal anti-icing equipment was located in the leading edge of horizontal and vertical tail surfaces. With a retractable tricycle landing gear, the main gear had two four-wheel bogies on single shock-absorber struts, each unit retracting inwards into the wing. The twin nose-wheel leg retracted forward into the fuselage. The wheel track was 46ft (14m) with a wheel base of 59ft (18m).

The communication tunnel through which the crew could pass between pressurised sections had a length of 85ft (25.9m) and was 25in (0.63m) in diameter, located on the left side of the fuselage and below the wings. A four-wheel truck allowed crew access through the tunnel between forward and aft pressurised compartments. The pressurised fuselage had a total volume of 3,924ft³ (111m³). The take-off distance from first-motion to a height of 50ft (15.25m) was 5,000ft (1,524m).

Piston-power

The decision as to what type of engine to select was driven by the size of the aircraft and its specified performance requirement. It would need a lot of power for take-off and for speed over the target but it would need to be married to a clean wing for efficient airflow to ensure the greatest possible range. That pushed the design team to a tractor configuration with leading-edge air inlets and a hybrid design capturing the advantages of both radial and in-line engines. Accordingly, the Wasp Major was the only sensible choice, as it was for several very large aircraft of the period including the Hercules H-4 (better known as the *Spruce Goose*), the B-50, the Globemaster I and II and the Lockheed Constellation, to name but a few.

The origin of the company that produced the Wasp Major can be traced back to 1925 when Pratt & Whitney Aircraft was formed by Frederick B. Rentschler, formerly of Wright Aeronautical, who felt that a degree of complacency had overcome that organisation and that it was time to break out and challenge competitors with a new level of engineering performance. He wanted to develop a nine-cylinder radial engine and persuaded Wright's chief engineer George Mead and the chief designer Andy Willgoos to join him. Rentschler had resigned from Wright on 21 September 1924 and took his ideas to the Pratt & Whitney machine tools division of the Niles-Bemont-Pond company at Hartford, Connecticut, creating the Pratt & Whitney Aircraft Company on 23 July 1925.

BELOW Hand tooled, the first Pratt & Whitney Wasp R-4360 completed on 28 September 1943, selected from very few optional candidates acceptable as the powerplant for the B-36. *(Dennis Jenkins)*

ABOVE A cutaway teaching model of the Wasp R-4360 showing the spiral arrangement of seven cylinders in four rows, an arrangement optimised for efficient cooling. *(Moto1000)*

Designed to a target specification of 400hp (298kW) for a weight of only 650lb (295kg), the first Wasp radial engine was fired up for the first time on 29 December 1925. Delivering 425hp (317kW), it had a two-piece crankshaft in two roller bearings for load sharing and a specially designed rotary induction system which provided effective fuel distribution through a single carburettor. It was an immediate success and quickly found application with aircraft built by Curtiss, Boeing and Vought. With a designation R for radial engine and a number approximating the engine's capacity, the basic Wasp R-1340 displaced 1,344in³ (22 litres) and became one of the most successful radial engines of all time, almost 35,000 being produced over its life.

Several years later the 14-cylinder R-1830 Twin Wasp became available with 1,000hp (745.7kW) output and by the time America entered the war in 1941 the 18-cylinder R-2800 Double Wasp was in production producing 2,000hp (1,491kW). A year earlier, work had begun on the X-Wasp, which would quickly become the Wasp Major. Run for the first time in a ground facility on 28 April 1941, the test revealed several areas for modification which were incorporated into the test engine for its second run on 8 May. Operating for over two hours, it produced 1,325hp (988kW) and was designated R-4360 indicating its approximate displacement in cubic inches. But this was only the beginning of a major development programme which would see the X-Wasp develop into the most technically

OPPOSITE Sectional diagram of the Wasp engine with propeller drive and reduction gear assembly at top left. *(Pratt & Whitney)*

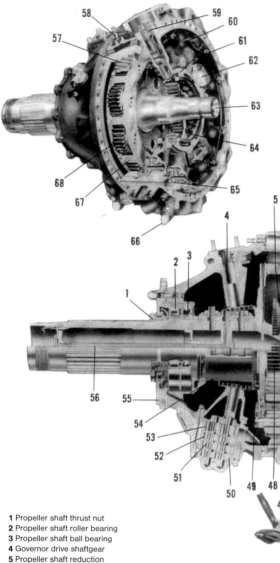

1 Propeller shaft thrust nut
2 Propeller shaft roller bearing
3 Propeller shaft ball bearing
4 Governor drive shaftgear
5 Propeller shaft reduction drive gear outer coupling
6 Spark advance control valve
7 Crankcase pressure oil line
8 Crankshaft front counterweight
9 D row masterod assembly
10 Cam small drive shaftgear
11 Cam large drive shaftgear
12 Crankshaft centre main bearing
13 Crankshaft oil slinger
14 B row linkrod
15 Inlet valve pushrod
16 Inlet valve rocker
17 Crankshaft
18 Inlet valve springs
19 Inlet valve
20 Pistonpin
21 Piston and rings
22 Pushrod cover
23 Impeller drive damper
24 Impeller intermediate drive
25 Impeller and shaft assembly

26 Accessory drive shaft
27 Impeller shaft rear rings breather
28 Fuel feed valve
29 Tachometer drive shaftgear
30 Fuel pump drive shaftgear
31 Fuel pump intermediate drive
32 Rear oil distributor ring
33 Starter drive shaftgear
34 Generator or accessory drive shaftgear
35 Rear accessory drive gear
36 Rear accessory drive oil pressure reducing valve
37 Pressure oil strainer
38 Collector case oil pump
39 Crankcase scavenge oil line
40 Crankcase scavenge oil pump
41 Exhaust valve rocker

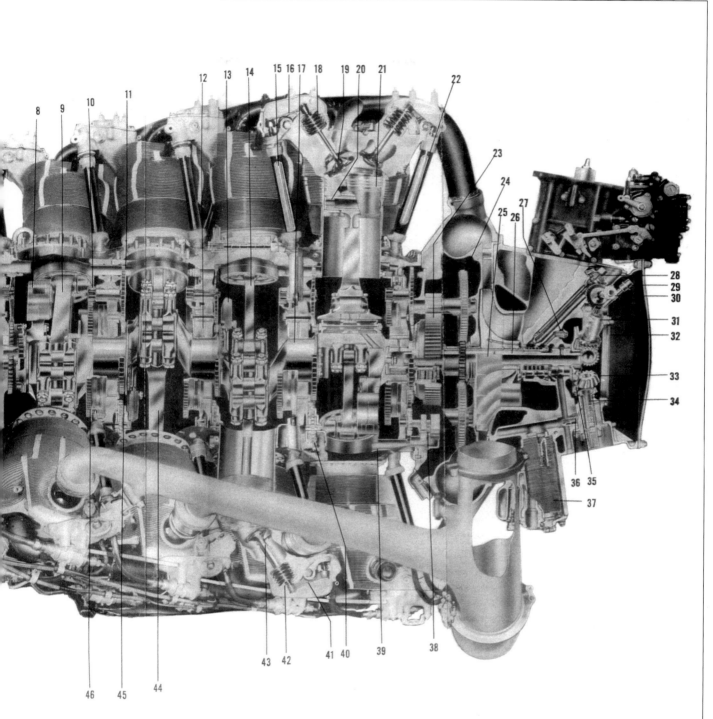

42 Exhaust valve springs
43 Exhaust valve
44 C row masterod
45 Cam drive gear
46 Cam
47 Magneto intermediate drive gear
48 Propeller shaft reduction drive gear
49 Front accessory drive gear
50 Torquemeter pump

51 Front power section scavenge pump
52 Rocker drain scavenge pump
53 Front section scavenge pump
54 Propeller shaft oil transfer bearing
55 Thrust cover
56 Propeller oil feed tube
57 Propeller shaft reduction drive fixed gear
58 Torquemeter oil pressure transmitter
59 Magneto drive shaft

60 Spark advance oil feed tube
61 Magneto drive fixed gear
62 Spark advance cylinder
63 Propeller shaft
64 Magneto drive shaftgear
65 Torquemeter master piston
66 Torquemeter oil pressure relief valve
67 Propeller shaft reduction pinion support
68 Propeller shaft reduction pinion

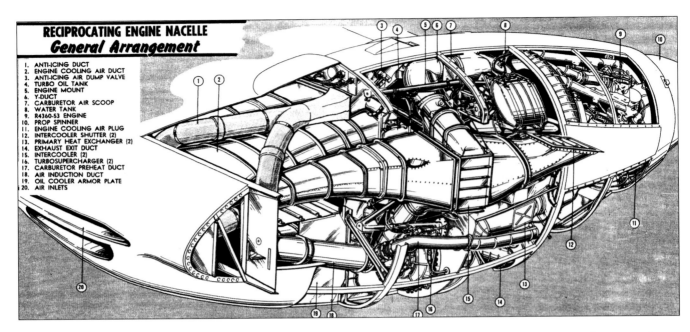

RECIPROCATING ENGINE NACELLE
General Arrangement

1. ANTI-ICING DUCT
2. ENGINE COOLING AIR DUCT
3. ANTI-ICING AIR DUMP VALVE
4. TURBO OIL TANK
5. ENGINE MOUNT
6. Y-DUCT
7. CARBURETOR AIR SCOOP
8. WATER TANK
9. R4360-53 ENGINE
10. PROP SPINNER
11. ENGINE COOLING AIR PLUG
12. INTERCOOLER SHUTTER (2)
13. PRIMARY HEAT EXCHANGER (2)
14. EXHAUST EXIT DUCT
15. INTERCOOLER (2)
16. TURBOSUPERCHARGER (2)
17. CARBURETOR PREHEAT DUCT
18. AIR INDUCTION DUCT
19. OIL COOLER ARMOR PLATE
20. AIR INLETS

ABOVE A general arrangement drawing of the R-4360 with position of the turbo-supercharger and intercooler. Note the location of the anti-icing duct. *(Convair)*

advanced engine ever put into mass production for the US Air Force.

The Wasp Major engine had 28 cylinders arranged in a spiral in four rows of seven which allowed the frontal area to be no greater than that of the Double Wasp and only 1in (2.5cm) longer than the original Wasp of 1925. It had a displacement of 4,363in³ (71.5 litres) with each cylinder presenting a bore of 5.75in (14.6cm) and a stroke of 6in (15.24cm) at a compression ratio of 6.7:1. The engine itself was 96.5in (245.1cm) long, enclosed in a maximum diameter of 55in (139.7cm) and weighed 3,670lb (1,665kg)

but these parameters do not take account of accessories such as reduction gears and turbochargers. Consumption rates varied with derivative versions of the Wasp Major but averaged 2,500lb (1,134kg) of 115/145 grade fuel with 25,000lb (11,340kg) of air per hour.

The design was a marvel of ingenuity, output and flexible development capability, the starting point in design being the front row of cylinders of the R-2800, the spiral shape of the cylinder alignment being for optimum cooling for each pot. Inherited from the R-2800 too, the pistons were reinforced and the connecting rod assembly comprised a master rod with

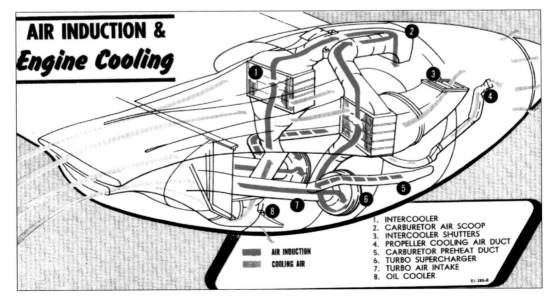

AIR INDUCTION &
Engine Cooling

AIR INDUCTION
COOLING AIR

1. INTERCOOLER
2. CARBURETOR AIR SCOOP
3. INTERCOOLER SHUTTERS
4. PROPELLER COOLING AIR DUCT
5. CARBURETOR PREHEAT DUCT
6. TURBO SUPERCHARGER
7. TURBO AIR INTAKE
8. OIL COOLER

RIGHT A sectional drawing from the familiarisation manual showing the elements of the air induction and engine cooling system. *(Convair)*

a detachable cap, a two-piece lead silver bearing and six link rods, each with a bronze bush at the piston end and riding on a silvered knuckle pin. The steel crankshaft was a one-piece forging supported by five steel-backed, lead silver main bearings with two fixed and two bifilar counterweights to balance the weight of the reciprocating parts connected to the crankpin. The power section comprised five separate elements, essentially similar except for the front and rear sections with aluminium forgings held together by bolts.

Enclosed push-rods actuated rocker arms incorporating plain bearings with double-track, self-mounted cams in the crankcase situated between the rows of cylinders which operated the exhaust valves through the forward cylinder row and the intake valves by the aft row. Reduction gears from the crankshaft drove the cams at one-sixth the speed of the crankshaft itself with single inlet and exhaust valves for each cylinder. The inlet valve was a conventional stainless steel unit and the exhaust valve was made from an exotic Inconel-M alloy. Developed by Wiggin Alloys located in Hereford, England, Inconel is a nickel-chromium-based superalloy which has applications in high temperature situations, a strength obtained through either precipitation hardening or solid solution strengthening. It would find many applications from the 1950s onwards.

Carburetion was provided by a single pressure-type Bendix-Stromberg PR-100B3 of four-barrel design with an automatic mixture control on the early engines. It had a throat diameter of 20in (50.8cm) but several versions were produced for the B-36 and it was not unusual to find several of different generations on each engine. Confusingly, each had its own specific operating conditions and the flight engineers were required to determine which was used on which engine before operation. The R-4360-53 engines used a Bendix direct-fuel injection carburettor and that had great benefits in maintenance and in reliability. In all types, however, metered fuel flowed through internal passageways and was thrown by centrifugal forces through tiny holes between the impeller blades to mix with combusted air. This fuel-air mixture was carried to the cylinders

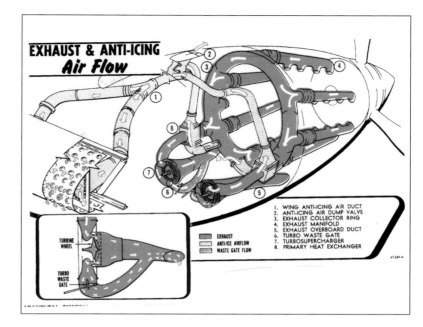

ABOVE The B-36 was not shy on altitude and the anti-icing system tapped off the airflow to deliver warm air through the wing leading edge and other surfaces. *(Convair)*

through seven intake pipes, one for each bank of four cylinders.

Each cylinder had two spark plugs with water injection on the -41 and -53 series engines, available for limited duration which was usually for take-off and for target penetration. This provided approximately 8% increase in power with each engine having a 9gal (34 litre) water supply, sufficient for five

BELOW Engine air plug positions were visually indicated by the diamond, displayed in red, between fully closed and fully open, providing verification of the selected position. *(Convair)*

CONVAIR B-36 PEACEMAKER MANUAL

minutes of operation. Although referred to as water-injection, in fact it was a solution of water and alcohol mixed in equal quantities. When selected by the flight engineer it operated automatically when the manifold pressure exceeded 53.5in (108.93mmHg).

Early engines had two magnetos per engine while the -53 series had four, controlled by a master ignition switch, separately switched for each individual engine, operated from the flight engineer's panel. There was also an emergency cut-off switch on the pilot's instrument panel, which would shut down all six engines. In addition, a setting control on the engineer's panel allowed for selecting an advance of either 20° or 35° for the ignition spark, with the normal setting at the lower value. Starting each engine could be accomplished by three switches, each controlling a pair of engines, each switch having three optional positions of OFF, L, for the left pair, and R, for the right pair.

As the engine installed in early B-36 types, the R-4360-41 would produce an output of 1,000hp (745.7kW) at 20,000ft (6,096m) but with turbocharging this would increase to 3,500hp (2,610kW) by means of two distinctly separate techniques. An internal supercharger was set in the airstream behind the carburettor and in front of the cylinders, with an impeller driven by a crankshaft and a gear train at fixed ratios. During take-off the impeller spun at 17,212rpm, with a tip speed of almost 700mph (1,126kph). This doubling of intake pressure came at a price, adding a lot of heat to the intake charge but the net benefit was to add some 1,930hp (1,439kW) after subtracting the 435hp (324.7kW) taken to drive the supercharger.

In addition each engine had two General Electric B-1 exhaust-driven, turbo-superchargers to sustain the sea-level rating to an altitude of 35,000ft (10,668m) with only a gradual fall-off in output as the aircraft climbed higher. It was not primarily designed to increase power output. But at lower altitudes in denser air the excess manifold pressure was controlled to prevent hot turbo units overcharging with an intercooler installed to remove waste heat from the air.

The necessity to increase heat rejection on the Wasp Major drove the design of the forged aluminium alloy cylinder barrel and muffs which were closely machined to provide a 30% increase in fin area over those on previous Wasp engines which were cast. The incoming cooling air taken in at the wing leading edge intakes was accelerated by a large cooling fan before being directed around a series of baffles at each engine position. A special air-plug, fixed between the trailing edge of the engine nacelle and the propeller, controlled the amount of cooling air which was allowed to enter the nacelle and these performed the same function as petals on a radial engine in tractor installations. Overheating was a persistent problem, and the cause of most failures, and the flight engineers wrestled constantly to keep a balance.

A 190gal (719 litre) oil tank was provided for each engine with shut-off valves controlled from the flight engineer's station or directly by access through the interior of the wing. Temperature was controlled automatically with air drawn through the oil cooler by fan prior to take-off and by ram air in flight with the

OPPOSITE Pratt & Whitney fitters working on the Wasp R-4360 engine, difficult to maintain and with dedicated tools for the spiral-wound configuration of the 28 cylinders. *(Dennis Jenkins)*

BELOW Fitting the propeller drive and reduction gear with the later, square-tipped propellers introduced on the B-36H. *(Dennis Jenkins)*

transition point being triggered at retraction of the undercarriage.

The number of fuel tanks increased with successive variants of B-36, increasing from six on the B-36B to eight on the B-36D to ten tanks on the B-36J, with all tanks interconnected including auxiliary tanks which could be carried in the bomb bays. Each engine had a mechanically driven fuel pump together with an engine cut-off valve to stop the flow of fuel. Normally, grade 115/145 fuel would be chosen but 100/130 grade was acceptable but with some engine operating restrictions. Fuel tanks became a serious problem on the B-36. With a propensity to leak, they would cause more than a little frustration during the operating life of the aircraft and serious problems on not a few flights.

As noted earlier in the type descriptions, the propellers were changed throughout the programme, eventually being the Curtiss Wright constant speed, fully feathering, reversible type with 19ft (5.79m) diameter blades, square-tip propellers on the B-36H replacing the rounded tip design on earlier aircraft. The variable pitch was controlled by a system tapping in to the part of the power transmitted through the rotating propeller shaft, instead of using an electric motor which was not possible due to the size of the propellers and the speed of the pitch change. Pitch change was achieved by a series of gears and four clutch mechanisms, with hydraulic pressure maintained by an oil pump and employed by either the clutch or the brake on each blade and controlled by electrical signals from the cockpit. When the engine was turning over at less than 40rpm an electric motor drove the feathering/unfeathering commands with pitch change under normal operating conditions being 2.5°/sec, increasing to 45°/sec during feathering or reversing. To prevent ice building up on the propeller blades, hot engine exhaust was channelled to the hollow blade interior.

Forward or reverse pitch could be attained both manually and automatically, synchronisation made by slaving all engines to an electric master motor, the speed of which was set by a control lever at the flight engineer's table, or a mechanically

interconnected control lever on the pilot's pedestal. An electrical indication of engine speed was provided by a propeller alternator which sent a signal to a contact assembly on the master motor. If the engine speed was out of synch with the master, electrical impulses would be sent to the pitch change mechanism until the two coincided. If the master motor failed, a relay would kick in to maintain the propeller at the same pitch as last synchronised and the flight engineer could adjust each propeller manually through switches on the control panel.

While acknowledging the frequent technical problems which arose in flight, a good Wasp could run effectively and without trouble for a long time. When this engine was applied to the XC-99 it proved reliable and could run for more than 800 hours, which represented little more than 20 flights but the standard procedure was for a major overhaul every 200–300 hours and that inability to perform longer between down-time affected operational flexibility and time on the ramp.

Jet power

The definitive B-36 arrived with the introduction of the B-36D powered by its six reciprocating engines and four reaction engines in paired pods secured to the outer wing sections. It provided the supplementary power which was to transform the aircraft into a more successful transition bomber and reconnaissance platform and as such is one of the most important stories of the aircraft and the entire development programme. As related earlier, the performance increase it provided, and the role expansion it enabled, added measurably to its value as a deterrent element with Strategic Air Command.

Selected from very few options, the General Electric J-47 was the product of desperation on the part of the designer/manufacturer, who had gained an early start in developing a jet engine made in the USA. After being picked to develop the I-A engine from the overall design of the UK's Whittle W.1X engine and the practical example of the Rover W.2B, the company was prevented from entering full scale development and production due to

those with materials playing a vital role in the engine's operation and performance; engine development in the late 1940s was as much about different metals and alloys operating at unusually high temperatures as it was about compressors and turbines.

The J-47 went into production in mid-1948 following a test flight in a B-29 on 20 April and a test run in a P-86A (later F-86A) on 18 May. On 15 September 1948 a standard F-86A with this engine established a new world speed record of 670.98mph (1,073kph). Suitably impressed, the Air Force specified the J-47 for the F-86A and for the new, all-jet Boeing B-47, the latter carrying six J-47s, four in paired pods inboard and in single pods outboard on a swept wing.

The J-47 had a 12-stage axial-flow compressor with airflow introduced at 90lb/sec (40.8kg/sec) to a single-stage axial flow turbine with eight through-flow combustion chambers. Lubrication was provided by pressure feed to primary components with a return oil system to the bearings and the accessory gears. The electrical system consisted of a GE direct-drive starter-generator, two igniter-plugs and two ignition units. Overall the J-47 had a length of 144in (365.8cm), a diameter of 36.75in (93.3cm), a frontal area of 7.4ft² (0.68m²) and a weight of approximately 2,500lb (1,135kg).

As related in a previous chapter, the trial evaluation of the B-36D configuration involved two converted B-36B aircraft. Because of the unavailability of the J-47 at that time, the converted B-36Bs had four Allison J-35-A-19 engines standing in for the J-47s. The engine assigned to production aircraft was the J-47-GE-19 turbojet with a rated thrust of 5,200lb (23,130N) but some of the early engines were of the -11 design. As a special adaptation for the B-36, the engines had collapsible aerodynamic covers over the inlets to reduce drag when they were not in use. These allowed 5% of the air to flow through and keep the compressor turning so as to prevent them freezing up through icing.

The pods were almost identical to those designed and built for the inboard pair of engines on the B-47 and initially the manufacturing continued for the B-36 with

demand for its turbo-superchargers. This, after producing the engine which powered the Bell XP-59, America's first experimental jet fighter. In further development, GE had developed the J33 for the P-80A Shooting Star, America's first operational jet fighter but the engine was licensed to Allison. With a thrust of 3,825lb (17.01kN) it formed the basis for a revival of GE design activity in jet engines.

Developed by General Electric and designated TG-180, this engine was a direct evolution of their turboprop T31 and adopted the eight-stage NACA compressor designed by GE. Designated J35, the engine had a distinguished pedigree in that it was designed alongside the centrifugal-flow J33 based on the Whittle engine from the UK and was the first production axial-flow turbojet built in the USA. With afterburner, it had a thrust of 7,400lb (32.92kN) and was placed in quantity production with Allison. But having lost both the J33 and the J35, General Electric pressed ahead with development of an axial turbojet with the exterior dimensions no greater than the J35 but with 5,000lb (22.24kN) thrust. Designated TG-190, it would become the J-47 when the Air Force supported development of this engine.

The first J-47 was test run on 21 June 1947 but problems plagued early evolution of the engine, weight being a particular challenge. Design changes solved most of

Boeing at Wichita since it was simpler to add production lots and then disperse delivery to the two programmes. From May 1951 production was switched to the Bell factory which was only 12mls (19km) from Convair's Fort Worth division. The XB-47 had made its first flight on 17 December 1947, which was the 40th anniversary of the first powered flight of a heavier-than-air machine by Orville Wright. As an interesting side note, the first flight of the XB-47 was also made with the J-35 as a stand-in for the J-47 engines with which later production aircraft were fitted. With initial deliveries to the Air Force in 1951, the B-47 accompanied the definitive B-36D into service use but as a medium bomber.

There were some differences to the jet pods used on the B-47, the single outer engines of which had outriggers attached to the underside of the casings, these not being necessary for the B-36. Modifications allowed for the use of standard aviation fuel rather than the jet fuel used on the B-47 and the B-52, which also had J-47 engines, so that feed could be configured from the existing integral tanks. This produced a slight reduction in power output but the advantage of the jet pods far outweighed the modest thrust reduction. Engine controls were situated on a panel above the pilots' heads and instruments were attached to two sub-panels below the main instrument panel but the flight engineer was only provided with fire warning lights and nothing else.

Ground technicians and personnel were made aware of the new danger from jet engine operations by intake cowlings painted bright red so as to give caution – it didn't always work and some incidents occurred when ground crew suffered burns while the jets were running on the ground together with the six reciprocating engines deadening the sound. They also provided the pilots with visible indication of the proximity of the wing tips to ground obstacles and in the air provided a visual verification of the position of the collapsible covers.

The exponential growth in engine work propelled GE into the big league, business growing from $35million at the end of the war to $350million by 1950 and after the start of the Korean War output increased at an unprecedented rate. This financed a sustained development programme with the early A-series engine producing 4,850lb (21.57kN), the C-series pushing out 5,200lb (23,13kN) and 6,000lb (26.69kN) with water injection. The J-47-GE-25 developed for the B-47E produced 6,000lb (26.69kN) dry and 6,970lb (31kN) with water injection. Production reached 950 per month shared with Studebaker and Packard, all of that a result of the big budget increases stimulated by the Korean War. In all, some 36,500 engines of

LEFT On 29 January 1949, two 43,000lb (19,500kg) T-12 bombs were loaded into the No. 2 bay on a B-36. *(Dennis Jenkins)*

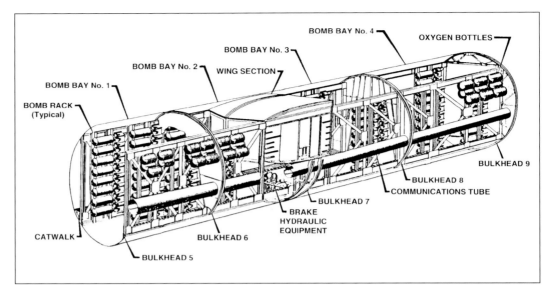

RIGHT The general configuration of the four bomb bays, divided in pairs by the substantial wing centre-section and deep root. *(Convair)*

BOMB BAY No. 4
OXYGEN BOTTLES
BOMB BAY No. 3
WING SECTION
BOMB BAY No. 2
BOMB BAY No. 1
BOMB RACK (Typical)
BULKHEAD 9
BULKHEAD 8
COMMUNICATIONS TUBE
BULKHEAD 7
BRAKE HYDRAULIC EQUIPMENT
CATWALK
BULKHEAD 6
BULKHEAD 5

BELOW The dual bomb bays 1 and 2 could accommodate two 22,000lb (9,980kg) T-14 bombs as shown here. *(USAF)*

DETAIL OF S-4 RELEASE RACK ASSEMBLY

DETAIL OF CHOCK BEAM ASSEMBLY

1. SLING RETRACTION CHUTE
2. AUXILIARY BULKHEAD
3. SLING RETRACTION CABLE HOLES
4. SLING RETRACTION MECHANISM
5. CHOCK BEAM ASSEMBLY
6. ARMING CONTROL SOLENOID
7. BOMB RACK
8. S-4 RELEASE
9. SWAY BRACE BEAM
10. FIXED SWAY BRACE
11. RETRACTABLE SWAY BRACE
12. BOMB SLING

this type were produced at a record engine production rate never surpassed to this day. However, with the Eisenhower administration (1953–61) this was to tail off but the J-47 was in big demand. Nevertheless, the definitive J-47-GE-33 produced a dry thrust of 7,650lb (34kN).

Conventional bomb loads

While it had always been understood that the B-36 programme would be capable of supporting unprecedented carrying capacity, special directives were issued to accommodate emerging bomb designs. No specified requirement existed when the B-36 was designed, only the requirement to provide as comprehensive and as diverse a range of bombs as possible. Although atomic weapons were under development during the early concept phase, they did not actually exist at that time and, in any event, were known to be under development only to a very small group outside the Manhattan Project proper, as witness the fact that until told about them after the death of President Roosevelt in April 1945, his successor Harry S. Truman knew nothing about the A-bomb.

Initially, right at the end of the war, the AAF wanted to have the B-36 carry the T-series bombs developed directly from the British Tallboy and Grand Slam bombs. In this regard, on 14 August 1945 Convair reported back to the AAF that it was making good progress with developing a capacity to carry the T-10 with a weight of 12,662lb (5,743kg), the T-14 at 25,037lb (11,357kg) and the T-12 at 44,000lb (19,958kg).

There had been some talk of a massive 75,000lb (34,020kg) bomb and Convair asked for clarification on the requirement for this in light of the use of two atom bombs on Japan, a super-

RIGHT Similarly, by removing parts of the dividing bulkhead, a single 43,000lb (19,500kg) T-12 bomb could be carried in bomb bays 3 and 4. If each of combined bays 1 and 2 and 3 and 4 carried a T-12 it was necessary to release the one carried in the forward position to prevent an aggressive pitch-up on release. (USAF)

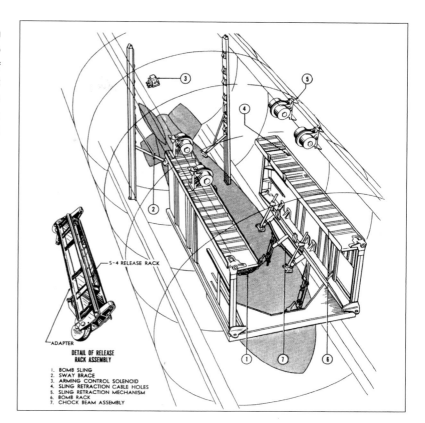

DETAIL OF RELEASE
RACK ASSEMBLY
1. BOMB SLING
2. SWAY BRACE
3. ARMING CONTROL SOLENOID
4. SLING RETRACTION CABLE HOLES
5. SLING RETRACTION MECHANISM
6. BOMB RACK
7. CHOCK BEAM ASSEMBLY

size bomb which the AAF advised was no longer needed, a requirement made redundant by the fission bombs. The bomb bays in most non-reconnaissance variants of the B-36 were fitted with 36 racks of 15 different types, maintaining the type's boast to be the most versatile bomb-carrier in the history of US air power. In fact, the B-36 could carry 67 different types of munition embracing high explosive bombs, incendiary bombs, chemical bombs and several different types of mine. Later, when configured for carrying atomic weapons, the B-36 could carry all types deployed operationally.

Adopted from a design utilised on the B-24, the doors designed for the B-36A and B series consisted of electrically controlled, cable-operated doors sliding on tracks up the side of the fuselage. The doors covering bays 1 and 4 were single-piece units sliding up the left side while the doors for bays 2 and 3 were split at the centreline and would slide up opposing sides of the fuselage because the location of the wing prevented a single-piece enclosure. Those for the B-36D and subsequent variants were modified into two opposing door pairs, each set 32.37ft (9.86m) long, hydraulically operated with a fast, double-folding action which opened and closed in two seconds. These were snap-action doors equipped with hydraulically actuated rams with each door 16.1ft (4.9m) long covering bomb bays 1 and 2 and 3 and 4, respectively. The doors had a tendency to stick, particularly in cold weather and at extreme altitude. With the early design there were severe drag problems when the doors were open, a problem solved by the new snap-action design.

RIGHT The Universal Bombing System originally facilitated in bomb bay No. 2 but later introduced in bay No. 4. (Convair)

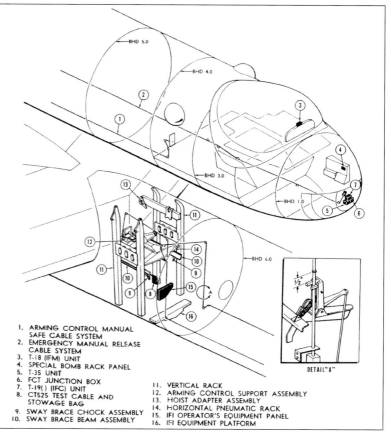

1. ARMING CONTROL MANUAL SAFE CABLE SYSTEM
2. EMERGENCY MANUAL RELEASE CABLE SYSTEM
3. T-18 (IFM) UNIT
4. SPECIAL BOMB RACK PANEL
5. T-35 UNIT
6. FCT JUNCTION BOX
7. T-19( ) (IFC) UNIT
8. CT525 TEST CABLE AND STOWAGE BAG
9. SWAY BRACE CHOCK ASSEMBLY
10. SWAY BRACE BEAM ASSEMBLY
11. VERTICAL RACK
12. ARMING CONTROL SUPPORT ASSEMBLY
13. HOIST ADAPTER ASSEMBLY
14. HORIZONTAL PNEUMATIC RACK
15. IFI OPERATOR'S EQUIPMENT PANEL
16. IFI EQUIPMENT PLATFORM

DETAIL "A"

RIGHT A B-36H (50-1086) at Eglin AFB, Florida, on a family visiting day, 12 October 1955, with two 24,000lb (10,890kg) bombs in the foreground. Note the clamshell folding bomb bay doors in the open position. *(Dennis Jenkins)*

BELOW Loading equipment for bombs up to 4,000lb (1,800kg) with relevant hoists and slings. *(Convair)*

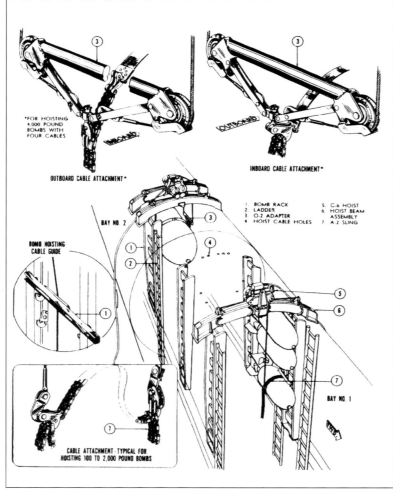

Made possible by significant structural changes, the enormous bomb-carrying capacity was set at a theoretical 86,000lb (39,001kg) in the B-36B, a 19% increase over the B-36A and the specification originally set before the US entered the war with Germany, Italy and Japan. This increase allowed the type to carry two 43,000lb (19,505kg) bombs in a system that retained the same configuration of bay doors as that on the A-series.

Eighteen B-36Bs were fitted with the required guidance equipment for two 13,000lb (5,897kg) VB-13 Tarzon guided bombs, which were controlled by a radio link to the operator viewing a TV screen showing a picture transmitted from an optical device in the nose of the weapon. Developed by Bell from the design of the British Tallboy bomb, the Tarzon was 25ft (7.62m) in length and 54in (137.2cm) in diameter. It was developed too late to see service in the war but was evaluated with the B-29 during the Korean War with 30 examples dropped between December 1950 and August 1951 displaying a success rate of around 25% against bridges and hard targets.

As said, from the outset, the B-36 was designed to carry every available bomb in the US inventory and it fulfilled that expectation, different types of munition in combinations which spanned 10,000lb (4,536kg) to

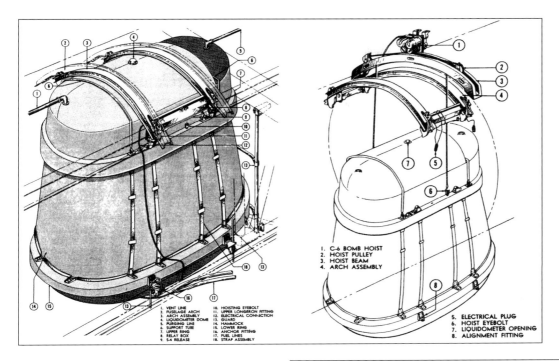

1. C-6 BOMB HOIST
2. HOIST PULLEY
3. HOIST BEAM
4. ARCH ASSEMBLY

1. VENT LINE
2. FUSELAGE ARCH
3. ARCH ASSEMBLY
4. LIQUIDOMETER DOME
5. PURGING LINE
6. SUPPORT TUBE
7. UPPER RING
8. RELAY BOX
9. S-4 RELEASE
10. HOISTING EYEBOLT
11. UPPER LONGERON FITTING
12. ELECTRICAL CONNECTION
13. GUARD
14. HAMMOCK
15. LOWER RING
16. ANCHOR FITTING
17. FUEL LINES
18. STRAP ASSEMBLY

5. ELECTRICAL PLUG
6. HOIST EYEBOLT
7. LIQUIDOMETER OPENING
8. ALIGNMENT FITTING

LEFT The bomb bay also provided stowage for the auxiliary fuel tanks, essentially a rigid shell supporting an internal rubber cell on the interior. The tank could be jettisoned after manual disconnection of lines and electrical power.
(Convair)

BELOW The navigator-bombardier station displayed from the B-36 familiarisation manual.
(USAF/Dennis Jenkins)

86,000lb (39,001kg). Bombing up required different techniques depending upon the size of the bomb, those up to 4,000lb (1,814kg) utilising standard external C6 or C10 bomb hoists attached to the upper spine of the fuselage. Holes in the upper fuselage allowed the hoists to carry through from the top of the fuselage, down to the hard stand, attach to the bombs and then be winched up to their respective positions, with all four bays being loaded simultaneously. Bigger conventional and thermonuclear bombs would be loaded by hydraulic ramps.

Although different types of bomb could be carried in individual bays, each bay was restricted to one type of bomb. At each end of the bay-spread, Nos. 1 and 4 could contain up to thirty-eight 500lb (227kg) bombs, nineteen 1,000lb (453kg), eight 2,000lb (907kg), or four 4,000lb (1,814kg) bombs. In addition, Nos. 2 and 3 bays had a different configuration because they were not as vertically spacious due to the wing carry-through structure and each could support twenty-eight 500lb (227kg), sixteen 1,000lb (453kg), six 2,000lb (907kg) or three 4,000lb (1,814kg) bombs. In a modified configuration, bay Nos. 1 and 2 or 3 and 4 could be adapted to accommodate two 12,000lb (5,443kg) bombs, one 22,000lb (9,979kg) or one 43,000lb (19,505kg) bomb.

RESTRICTED
AN 01-5EUB-1

Section IV

1. Loran Set
2. Table Lamp Rheostat
3. Circuit Breaker Panel
4. Intervolometer Control
5. Interphone Control Panel
6. Oxygen Controls
7. Radio Compass Control Panel
8. Magnetic Compass Indicator
9. Radio Compass Indicator
10. Clock
11. Altimeter
12. Airspeed Indicator
13. Check List
14. Windshield Wiper Switch
15. Servo Heaters Switch
16. Bombing Control Panel
   (See figure 4-11 for detail)
17. Interphone Control Panel
18. Oxygen Controls
19. Bomb Sight
20. Microphone Switch
21. Auxiliary Bomb Rack Control Panel

Figure 4-2. Navigator-Bombardier's Station

RESTRICTED

87

Very little work was required to open up the division between the two forward and two aft bomb bays, largely requiring the removal of dividing bulkheads. There were 15 types of bomb carriage for ordnance weighing up to 4,000lb (1,814kg), the racks being attached either side of the bay with larger bombs slung on suspension slings and shackles.

The capacity of the B-36 was considerably greater than that of the B-52, even in its 'Big Belly' modification during the Vietnam War, where a theoretical capacity of 75,000lb (34,020kg) was offered. In addition, a 3,000gal (11,355 litre) removable fuel tank could be carried in bay No. 3, although this was for special flights. Some aircraft were capable of carrying a similar tank in bay No. 2 while there has been unsubstantiated reference to bays 1 and 4 carrying tanks of similar capacity. Nothing in official documents verifies this but a considerable amount of adaptation to unit requirements was not uncommon.

ABOVE AND BELOW Two revealing shots showing the nose position with the Norden bombsight, the one above taken by Paramount Studios for their film production of *Strategic Air Command*. *(Dennis Jenkins)*

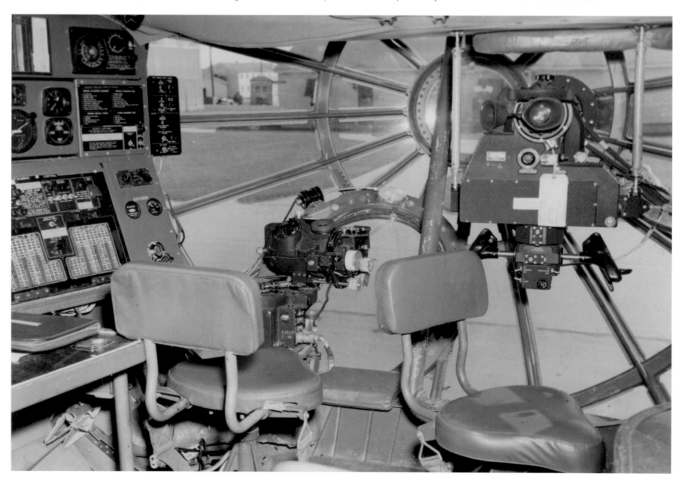

Initially, the auxiliary fuel tank consisted of a metal frame within which was suspended a fuel-proof rubberised canvas bag manufactured by Firestone Tire and Rubber Company. On later versions of the tank, produced by Goodyear at their Akron, Ohio, facility a Pliocell nylon bladder was supported by a metal encapsulating shell. Either tank design could be jettisoned during flight, after all the connections and fuel lines had been dismantled by hand. Uniquely for this aircraft, the bays could also carry support equipment including ground power start-up carts, and up to 14,000lb (6,350kg) of ancillary equipment, two carts stowed in bay Nos. 1 and 4 and a single cart in the other two.

Nuclear bomb loads

Although the B-36 was the first SAC bomber to carry the nuclear deterrent operationally, it was not designed to do so; the B-29 had been adapted to deliver fission weapons on targets in Japan in 1945 but it was not up to the job of forming a credible Cold War strike force. Designed as a conventional bomber, the B-36 was quickly assigned to the role of intercontinental air-drop nuclear delivery system and held that job throughout its operational service. When the aircraft became operational in 1948, only six B-29 crews with the 509th Bombardment Wing were proficient at dropping atomic weapons and the slow uptake of atomic weapons production and test in the Air Force allowed the B-36 time to iron out bugs and prepare the aircraft for its primary role.

Consideration of a nuclear role had argued against selection of the XB-35/YB-49 types because those aircraft did not have the size of bomb bay required for the big atomic bombs of the day. With a diameter of 5ft (1.5m) and a length of 10ft (3m), the Mk. III (Fat Man) bomb was too large for these flying wing designs. Moreover, even the B-29 and its B-50 derivative were incapable of carrying bombs with a length greater than 12ft (3.6m). One significant difficulty with the induction of nuclear weapons was the degree of secrecy that surrounded bomb development. Aircraft builders were not allowed access

ABOVE The B-36 was designed for conventional bombing and the interior of the No. 3 bomb bay illustrates the design option for carrying every weapon in the US Air Force inventory. *(Dennis Jenkins)*

BELOW When nuclear weapons came along, before the B-36 entered service, the bomb bay was adapted for a nuclear warload, as seen here on this B-36H where the suspension for a Universal Bomb System is visible. *(National Archives College Park Collection via Dennis Jenkins)*

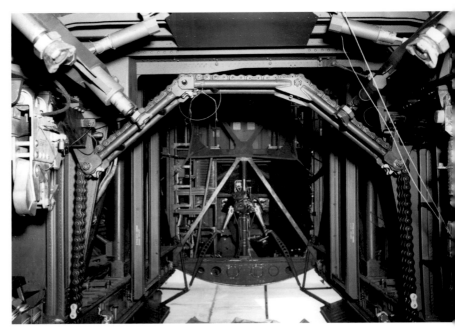

RIGHT The distribution of Electronic Control Measures (ECM) equipment varied over the life of the aircraft. Here, sets for Groups I, II and III are displayed as mounted in the forward pressurised section. *(Convair)*

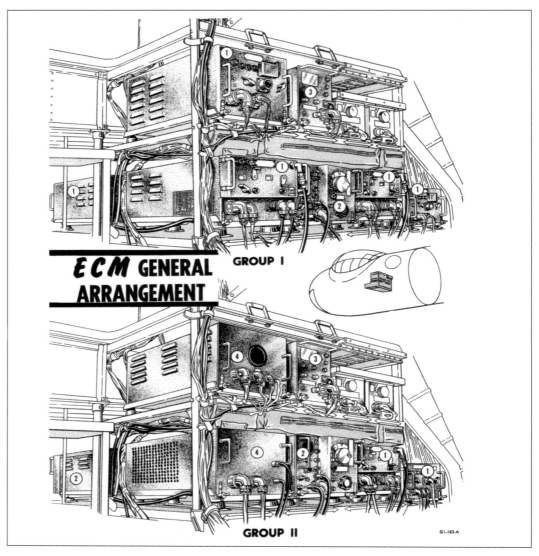

ECM GENERAL ARRANGEMENT

GROUP I

GROUP II

G1-183-A

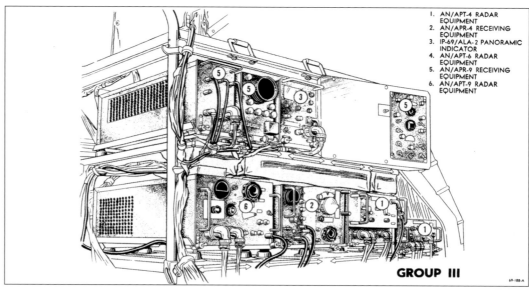

1. AN/APT-4 RADAR EQUIPMENT
2. AN/APR-4 RECEIVING EQUIPMENT
3. IP-69/ALA-2 PANORAMIC INDICATOR
4. AN/APT-6 RADAR EQUIPMENT
5. AN/APR-9 RECEIVING EQUIPMENT
6. AN/APT-9 RADAR EQUIPMENT

GROUP III

6P-188-A

to proposed bomb configurations and the definitive design frequently bore little resemblance to the original specification regarding casings and mountings.

A product of this separation of development was the uncertainty regarding what the Air Force was going to get in terms of bomb shape, centre of gravity, mounting lugs and ballistic dynamics after release – crucial in case the bomb adversely reacted to the airstream and 'floated' back up into the bomb bay – or worse! Only gradually could the Air Force convince the Atomic Energy Commission that they were working for the same country and against a common enemy, after which restrictions were lifted.

At one time it was forbidden to look up into the open bomb bay of a B-36 for fear that disclosure could lead to calculation of the size of bomb carried, thence to its destructive yield and so pose a security threat to the United States! Whether in fact true or not, the undying belief that the atom bombs dropped on Hiroshima and Nagasaki had ended a global war in which more than 50 million people perished, bestowed almost god-like powers on the capacity of nuclear weapons not only to start wars but stop them. Hence the reverence with which they were treated – at least initially.

But the problems persisted between the bomb-makers and the bomb-carrier: in 1949 the Air Force was denied access to the shape, size and weight of what would become the Mk. 6, a 'lightweight' bomb with the same size as the Mk. III but weighing 8,500lb (3,855kg), 2,400lb (1,088kg) less than the Mk. III. Introduced in 1952, it was the first production A-bomb with over 1,000 manufactured by 1955 when it was superseded. But these problems were alleviated by the time the Mk.17 was introduced, a massive thermonuclear bomb 24.6ft (7.5m) in length and 5.08ft (1.55m) in diameter weighing 42,000lb (19,051kg) and with a weaponised yield of up to 15MT. The B-36 was the only aircraft that could carry this fission weapon, together with the indistinguishably different Mk. 24 (see later).

Although the B-36 was quickly adapted to carry atomic weapons, both that work and the effort to convert B-29s to carry the developed Mk. III bomb came under the code

name 'Saddle Tree'. This required the fitting of suspension equipment and T-boxes and the first eighteen B-36Bs were thus modified by June 1948 with the last 54 B-series equipped off the production to carry the Mk. III atomic bomb in bay No. 1. Modifications to carry the Mk. 4, 5 and 6 began in December 1950 along with the Universal Bomb Suspension (UBS) system which was capable of handling any weapon up to 5ft (1.5m) in diameter and 10.7ft (3.26m) in length. These weapons had to be armed manually from the nose point on the bomb and the No. 1 bay was the optimum place for crew access.

Back in July 1950 the decision was made to equip each B-36 with more than one nuclear weapon and 30 aircraft of the D and H series were modified to carry 'units' (the reference word for nuclear bombs whether carrying a detonator or not) in all four bays by equipping each with a UBS system. The other aircraft were adapted to carry such units in bay 4 in addition to bay 1. But there is no definitive identification as to which aircraft had one, two or four bays so modified as the evolution of bomb types and SAC directives were tumbling around faster than apples and pears on a fruit machine! As designed and adopted, the UBS was installed in B-29, B-47, B-50 and B-54 types as well as the B-36.

The UBS was capable of handling the Mk. 4, Mk. 5, Mk. 6, Mk. 8 and the Mk. 18. Mk. 8 bombs

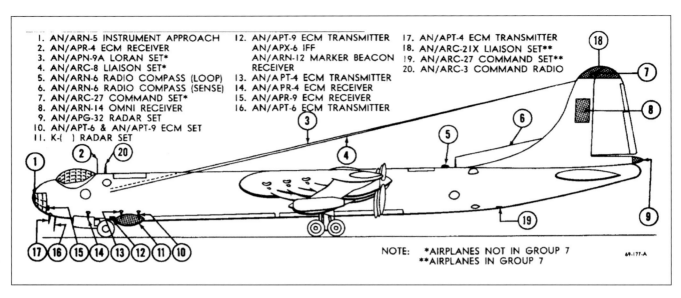

1. AN/ARN-5 INSTRUMENT APPROACH
2. AN/APR-4 ECM RECEIVER
3. AN/APN-9A LORAN SET*
4. AN/ARC-8 LIAISON SET*
5. AN/ARN-6 RADIO COMPASS (LOOP)
6. AN/ARN-6 RADIO COMPASS (SENSE)
7. AN/ARC-27 COMMAND SET*
8. AN/ARN-14 OMNI RECEIVER
9. AN/APG-32 RADAR SET
10. AN/APT-6 & AN/APT-9 ECM SET
11. K-( ) RADAR SET

12. AN/APT-9 ECM TRANSMITTER
    AN/APX-6 IFF
    AN/ARN-12 MARKER BEACON
    RECEIVER
13. AN/APT-4 ECM TRANSMITTER
14. AN/APR-4 ECM RECEIVER
15. AN/APR-9 ECM RECEIVER
16. AN/APT-6 ECM TRANSMITTER

17. AN/APT-4 ECM TRANSMITTER
18. AN/ARC-21X LIAISON SET**
19. AN/ARC-27 COMMAND SET**
20. AN/ARC-3 COMMAND RADIO

NOTE: *AIRPLANES NOT IN GROUP 7
         **AIRPLANES IN GROUP 7

69-177-A

ABOVE Antenna locations for the B-36H.
(Convair)

were of the gun-type, detonated by rapidly assembling a succession of fissile materials to create a 'bullet' which would be fired into a larger fissile core. It had a length of 116–132in (290–340cm) according to the version and a diameter of 14.5in (37cm), designed to dig deep as a bunker-buster with a yield of 25–30KT. Only 40 of the Mk. 8 were delivered, succeeded by the Mk. 11 which was in use between 1956 and 1960 as a more efficient penetrator but with the same yield. The Mk. 13 was an improved 'Little Boy' plutonium bomb, entering operational use in 1952 while the Mk. 18 was a Super Oralloy, high-yield fission device with super-enriched uranium and a yield of 500KT. Deployed from 1953, only 90 were produced exclusively for the

B-36 and B-47 before it was superseded by the thermonuclear fusion bombs. With four critical mass devices in the core it was potentially unstable and vulnerable to accidental detonation from only a minor malfunction in the triggers.

Introduced in 1954, the 39,600lb (17,962kg) Mk. 24 was a derivative of the Mk. 17 and had a yield of around 13.5MT. It was equipped with a retarding parachute which would still have left the B-36 uncomfortably close to the blast effect. The Mk. 17/24 was only capable of being lifted by the B-36, two capable of being accommodated in the paired Nos. 1/2 and 3/4 bomb bays. Development of these massive thermonuclear weapons started in 1952 at Los Alamos Scientific Laboratory.

RIGHT The general layout of the radio operator's station which also contains switching for the interphone, essential for front-end crew to communicate with those in the aft pressure compartment.

(Convair)

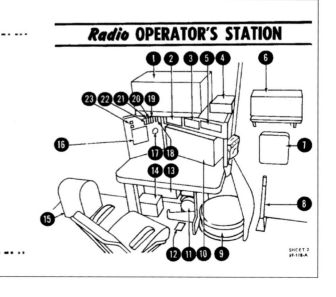

Radio **OPERATOR'S STATION**

1. LIAISON TRANSMITTER
2. INTERPHONE CONTROL PANEL
3. AN/APX-6 CONTROL PANEL
4. AN/ARC-27 RADIO CONTROL PANEL
5. CIRCUIT BREAKERS
6. AN/APT-5 RECTIFIER POWER UNIT
7. BRAKE & LANDING GEAR EMERGENCY
   HYDRAULIC RESERVOIR
8. EMERGENCY HYDRAULIC HAND PUMP
9. RT-124/APS-23 RECEIVER-TRANSMITTER
10. LIAISON RECEIVER
11. PRESSURE REGULATOR
12. MICROPHONE SWITCH
13. TRANSFORMER-RECTIFIER UNIT
14. TRANSFORMER-RECTIFIER FILTER
15. AUXILIARY HEATER
16. OXYGEN CONTROL PANEL
17. CLOCK
18. LIAISON MONITOR SWITCH
19. COMMUNICATION TUBE LIGHT SWITCH
20. DOME LIGHT SWITCH
21. SUB FLIGHT DECK LIGHT SWITCH
22. TURRET BAY & BOMB BAY LIGHTS SWITCH
23. 115 VOLT A-C RECEPTACLE

SHEET 2
69-118-A

Tested during Operation Castle at Bikini atoll in 1954, they were differentiated by the different primaries they employed, each however utilising lithium hydride rather than the rare lithium-6 deuteride.

These bombs birthed the attribution of 'city-busters' for the devastation they would cause, levelling all masonry within 10mls (16km), lethal burns within 28mls (45km), creating a firestorm 30mls (48km) across and blindness to a radius of 40mls (64km). Exceeding even this explosive yield, the B41 would be deployed as an air-drop weapon carried by the B-47 and the B-52. That had a yield of 25MT and, so far as is known, at 5.2MT/tonne carried the highest yield/weight mass ratio of any thermonuclear bomb produced to date.

For the B-36, almost all the cascading changes had been formalised by mid-1956 and each aircraft had UBS equipment in bays 1 and 4 and further changes added bays 2 and 3, usually with either Mk. 6 or Mk. 18 bombs. Within two years the B-36 would be no more, its place on the SAC roster totally replaced by the B-52, with mission capabilities expanded to embrace the B-47 medium bomber and with a nuanced mission envelope provided by the B-58A. Like the B-36, the B-58A served only a ten-year term before retirement, the supersonic strategic role gone, its potential abandoned with the cancellation of the Mach 3 XB-70 in 1961.

With the widest selection of conventional, nuclear (fission) and thermonuclear (fusion) weapons carried by any aircraft in the US inventory, the B-36 was truly the Air Force's 'Big Stick', carrying forward a role pioneered by the B-29 in the Second World War and bearing the distinction of being the world's only intercontinental bomber in history capable of delivering nuclear Armageddon to any hostile state anywhere on Earth – without aerial refuelling.

RIGHT An illustration about manual extension of the landing gear from the familiarisation handbook displays the unusually thick wing root and crawlerway (item No. 3), warning the crew not to hold on to the activation handle as it comes away with the door itself, catapulting an errant crewmember into the abyss! *(Convair)*

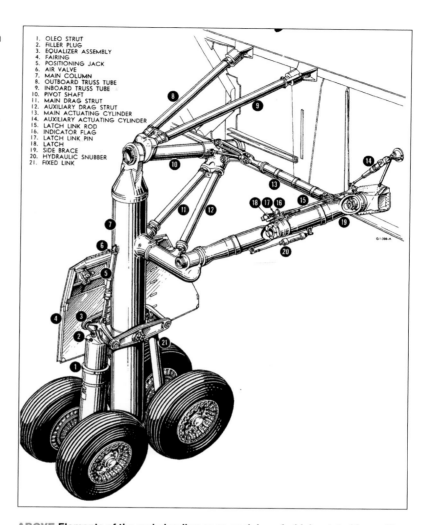

1. OLEO STRUT
2. FILLER PLUG
3. EQUALIZER ASSEMBLY
4. FAIRING
5. POSITIONING JACK
6. AIR VALVE
7. MAIN COLUMN
8. OUTBOARD TRUSS TUBE
9. INBOARD TRUSS TUBE
10. PIVOT SHAFT
11. MAIN DRAG STRUT
12. AUXILIARY DRAG STRUT
13. MAIN ACTUATING CYLINDER
14. AUXILIARY ACTUATING CYLINDER
15. LATCH LINK ROD
16. INDICATOR FLAG
17. LATCH LINK PIN
18. LATCH
19. SIDE BRACE
20. HYDRAULIC SNUBBER
21. FIXED LINK

ABOVE Elements of the main landing gear, each leg of which rotated inward to fit snugly adjacent to the fuselage where the wing root was more than 7ft (2.1m) thick. *(Convair)*

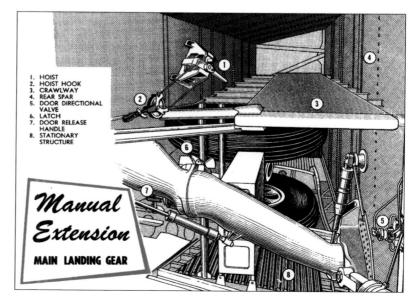

1. HOIST
2. HOIST HOOK
3. CRAWLWAY
4. REAR SPAR
5. DOOR DIRECTIONAL VALVE
6. LATCH
7. DOOR RELEASE HANDLE
8. STATIONARY STRUCTURE

Manual Extension
MAIN LANDING GEAR

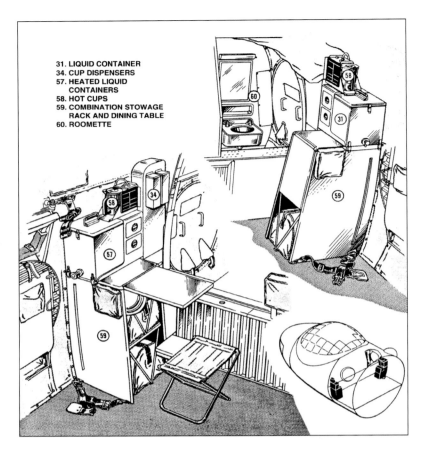

31. LIQUID CONTAINER
34. CUP DISPENSERS
57. HEATED LIQUID
    CONTAINERS
58. HOT CUPS
59. COMBINATION STOWAGE
    RACK AND DINING TABLE
60. ROOMETTE

ABOVE Extensive efforts were made for crew comfort, these provisions situated in the port and starboard sides of the forward pressure compartment in the B-36H including food table, heating containers and toilet.
(Convair)

Defensive armament

The defensive armament carried by the B-36 was the heaviest and most comprehensive suite of weapons carried by any aircraft in the history of US air power and remains so to this day. From the outset, however, the armament was troubled by design, technical, engineering and operational training flaws that made it the Achilles heel of this giant bomber.

The changing concept of defensive armament for this aircraft has been identified in the type-by-type review in Chapter 3 but the production aircraft of all variants had eight remotely controlled turrets each equipped with two 20-mm cannon. The selection of the gun was problematic and a trade-off between calibre and its effectiveness against an enemy, efficiency and weight – always a problem on the B-36. Some had suggested the use of 0.60-calibre guns which would have been a compromise between the 20-mm cannon and the 0.50-calibre gun which had been suggested, and specified, at various stages in the evolution of the aircraft. But the 20-mm gun

had better destructive capabilities albeit it was less effective in its ballistic properties.

Six of the turrets were retractable, those in the nose and tail were not. The other turrets were located in pairs on the upper forward and rear fuselage positions and on the lower aft fuselage. Readers will have noted reference to a further turret located on the lower forward fuselage position but this was not adopted for production aircraft. In fact the bomb/navigation system radome was located in that position. All retractable turrets could withdraw into the fuselage and be covered by flush-fitting doors to reduce drag and their design was cleared for use to an altitude of 50,000ft (15,240m) and to temperatures between -50°F (-45.5°C) and 122°F (50°C).

The electrically controlled turrets were operated from a sighting position located separately from the turret itself with three such positions located on each side of the fuselage, one forward and two aft. The nose section supported a sight in the glazed bombardier's position and the tail turret was controlled by a radar operator's position in the aft compartment. The sights used different methods of control. Yoke sights were set up in the four upper blisters for controlling those fore and aft turrets and they could be rotated between +90° to -45° in elevation with reference to the horizon and from 110° forward to 110° aft of the transverse axis (wing tip to wing tip). The lower turret employed pedestal sights which could cover elevation angles from -45° to +90° in elevation and rotated in azimuth from +105° forward to -105° aft. In both yoke and pedestal sights the gunners traversed the entire sight to follow a target.

Operation of the sight required some training and considerable skill to provide accurate and useable information to the computer dedicated to that sight. Each sight had a small glass plate which the gunner powered up to present a centre dot for aiming and a series of concentric dots. The gunner would set the wing span of the incoming attacker by means of a knob to align it with the dots which would set the range. By precisely tracking the motion of the attacker the computer would derive azimuth, elevation and compute the relative speed by calculating the angular velocity from the motion scan.

The nose turret was controlled from a hemispheric sight to the starboard side of the nose containing a double prism periscope for a full hemispheric view by the gunner who, from a fixed position could see 90° up, down, left or right through a fixed eyepiece. Control of the guns was afforded by handles either side of the sight. It worked much like the yoke and the pedestal sights, with the gunner using a single eyepiece for one eye but an optional left or right eye according to the visual preferences of the operator. The radar-controlled tail turret was operated by a single gunner seated in the rear compartment and facing aft but in reconnaissance variants this position was sometimes shifted to a sideways-facing orientation.

Two guns were optional for each turret, the M24A1 or the M24E2, either with a selectable rate of fire between 550 and 820 rounds per minute on the earlier production aircraft or a fixed 700 rounds per minute for later aircraft. Usually left open during taxiing, because they served as emergency ground exits, the retractable turret enclosures were unpressurised but they were accessible to the

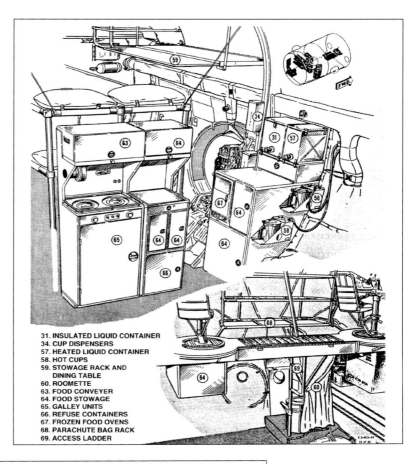

31. INSULATED LIQUID CONTAINER
34. CUP DISPENSERS
57. HEATED LIQUID CONTAINER
58. HOT CUPS
59. STOWAGE RACK AND
    DINING TABLE
60. ROOMETTE
63. FOOD CONVEYER
64. FOOD STOWAGE
65. GALLEY UNITS
66. REFUSE CONTAINERS
67. FROZEN FOOD OVENS
68. PARACHUTE BAG RACK
69. ACCESS LADDER

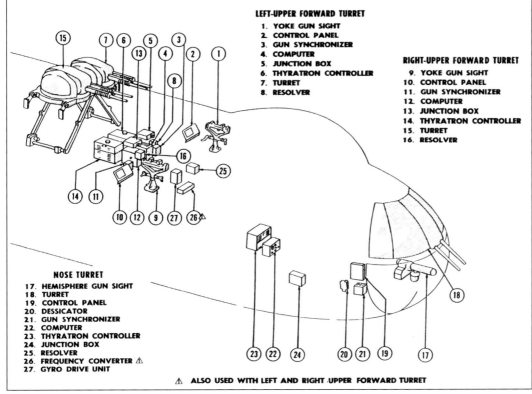

LEFT-UPPER FORWARD TURRET
1. YOKE GUN SIGHT
2. CONTROL PANEL
3. GUN SYNCHRONIZER
4. COMPUTER
5. JUNCTION BOX
6. THYRATRON CONTROLLER
7. TURRET
8. RESOLVER

RIGHT-UPPER FORWARD TURRET
9. YOKE GUN SIGHT
10. CONTROL PANEL
11. GUN SYNCHRONIZER
12. COMPUTER
13. JUNCTION BOX
14. THYRATRON CONTROLLER
15. TURRET
16. RESOLVER

NOSE TURRET
17. HEMISPHERE GUN SIGHT
18. TURRET
19. CONTROL PANEL
20. DESSICATOR
21. GUN SYNCHRONIZER
22. COMPUTER
23. THYRATRON CONTROLLER
24. JUNCTION BOX
25. RESOLVER
26. FREQUENCY CONVERTER ⚠
27. GYRO DRIVE UNIT

⚠ ALSO USED WITH LEFT AND RIGHT UPPER FORWARD TURRET

ABOVE The crew provisions in the aft pressure compartment provided full galley facilities, with frozen food, heated drinks, dispensers and refuse containers. *(Convair)*

LEFT The defensive gun positions at nose and left and right upper turret stations together with associated sights, synchronisers and control panels. *(Convair)*

crew during flight. The retractable turrets could be operated manually if required with a flush panel sliding down inside the fuselage. The gun firing system had an interrupter gear to inhibit firing during slewed angles threatening propeller tips, the vertical fin and the wings or parts of the fuselage housing crewmembers.

The weight of each gun was around 100lb (45kg) and they were 77.7in (197cm) in length of which 52.5in (133cm) was the barrel and each had a muzzle velocity of 2,730ft/sec (831km/sec). The nose turret had 800 rounds of ammunition, with 400 rounds in each of two boxes, while the other guns had 1,200 rounds, 600 in each box. There were four different types of ammunition. The M97 was a high-explosive incendiary round, the M62 was a standard incendiary, the AP-1 was an armour-piercing round and the AP-T was armour-piercing with tracer. In addition to an M95 target practice round there was also a drill-round used for practising loading and general handling of ammunition and gun in an inactive mode.

Contracted to develop and manufacture the defensive armament and the control system, General Electric had examined a wide variety of different designs for radio-controlled turrets (RCTs) and it should be noted that whereas it was common for Second World War bombers

to carry rotating turrets, the B-36 was the last USAF aircraft to have them. RCTs had seen extensive application with the B-29, the A-26 and the P-61 but the full hemispheric defence attached to the B-36 was as much a recognition of its lone role as it was a recognition that fighters would be implausible defence escorts given the range of this aircraft.

The General Electric fire control system inherited several operational schemes developed for the B-29 and its successor the B-50 but it had less authority over options. It could not pass control of turrets between gunners and the operation of the turrets was shared with the bombardier for control of the forward upper and lower turrets. The central station fire controller in the upper bubble sighting station controlled the aft upper turret and had secondary control over the upper forward turret.

Unlike the B-29 and B-50, which had a manned tail turret and had upper and lower turrets on the centreline for 360° movement in azimuth and 90° in elevation, the B-36 turrets were offset to port and starboard with only nose and tail turrets on the centreline. There was no plan for those aircraft to have manned retractable cannon turrets and weighty multi-gun unmanned central retractable turrets, the arrangement instead being simpler and with lighter 20-mm cannon, the mounts for which could be folded down inside the fuselage area for drag reduction.

There were fundamental disadvantages to this, in that each sighting station had a dedicated turret and could not be transferred should one be disabled. It also prevented a single gunner from bringing more than a pair of 20-mm cannon to bear on a single target. In theory, however, six guns operated by three gunners could bring fire to bear on a single target approaching from either flank side. Moreover, because there were parallel intercommunication connections, the gunners could throw targets verbally to each other without interference between the communication sets connecting the rest of the crew.

Other advantages included the relatively close proximity of gunners to their turrets, a maximum distance of 11ft (3.35m), eliminating the parallax problems. And because each sighting station had its dedicated control computer, avoiding the need to link them together, wiring was reduced and the electronics of the fire control system were made simpler. Considerable debate surrounded the selection of the guns employed, 20-mm cannon being felt sufficient to bring down an attacking fighter. Had the stations been interconnected, the great distance between the fore and aft compartments with their dedicated sighting stations would have made the parallax problem almost insurmountable.

Nevertheless, with the B-36's eight sighting stations, seven visual and one radar, there were three more than on the B-29. Had all the stations been interlinked, the sheer weight of the cabling and the conduits alone would have been prohibitive. But the B-29 and the B-50 did have such an integrated fire control system and this was considered by GE early on the design of the XB-36. The alternative options considered were to integrate fire control operations for the two upper turrets and their eight guns but had that been implemented there would have been a requirement for fire-interrupters to switch one pair of guns from one side of the fuselage to the other pair

LEFT The location and interior equipment for the nose sight.
(Dennis Jenkins)

1. Gunner's Control Panel
2. Interphone Control
3. Oxygen Controls

on the other side as the attacking aircraft traversed across the top of the aircraft. There were aircraft that had such an arrangement but it added complexity when a simpler solution was available with less weight. One peculiarity, however, prevented all four upper turrets from

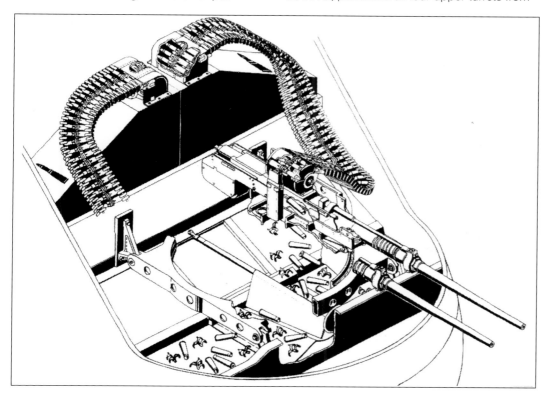

LEFT Ammunition feed trays for the nose gun and storage boxes.
(Convair)

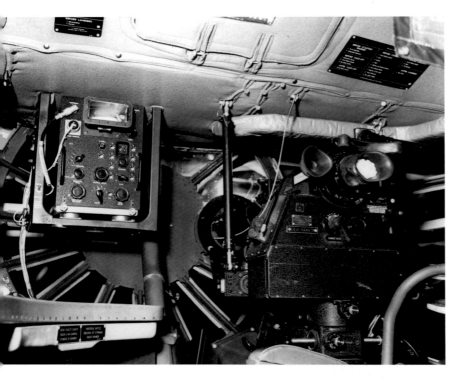

ABOVE An interior view
of the offset nose gun
sight. *(Dennis Jenkins)*

conference at Headquarters on 21 July 1949 to evaluate tests which had been conducted at SAC and at the Air Force Air Proving Ground Command. It was agreed that the configuration of the fire control system for the defensive armament was not fit for operational purpose and that the highest priority had to be attached to elimination of deficiencies.

The following month reports came in which appeared to show an even worse situation than had been stated at the conference and that a deadline of January 1950 for finding a solution would be missed. Three aircraft were assigned to evaluate 'fixes'; one for Air Materiel Command, one at SAC and one at the Air Force Proving Ground at Eglin AFB, Florida. In September 1949 an RB-36D (44-92058) was turned over for continuous evaluation and test and by May 1950 this activity had catalogued six major and 74 minor changes which would be required for the GE fire control system but all this did was solve the dispersion problem. Gunnery problems were pursued through increased air firing trials but they were brought to a halt in September when the deficiencies were judged to be a danger to 'life and property'.

Following some caustic and acerbic remarks from the senior command at SAC to news that 91 gunnery deficiencies had been identified, fresh trials on 25 October 1949 employed a B-36B (44-92042) from the 11th BG/7th BW/26th BS, modified to carry a Vitarama movie camera system in place of the

linking with all four sighting stations; the long fuselage tended to flex in turbulent air and that would have prevented proper alignment of the fore and aft upper turrets, had a single interlink been in place. This factor alone also influenced the bomb-aiming equipment.

From the outset, it was recognised that defensive armament on such an aircraft would prove problematical and the first steps to provide incremental improvement to the system really began when the Air Force convened a

RIGHT With turret
doors lowered and
a panel on the side
of the gun housing
removed showing
the ammunition feed,
this view shows the
top forward position.
(Dennis Jenkins)

1. Ammunition Box
2. Ammunition Booster
3. Ammunition Chute
4. Turret Enclosure
5. Feed Mechanism
6. Link Ejection Chute
7. Gun
8. Lower Shell Chute
9. Ejected Links and Cases
10. Elevation Drive Motor
11. Gun Charger
12. Ammunition Booster

LEFT The twin tail guns with associated equipment. *(Convair)*

faced by SAC was due to this alone, many crewmembers openly confessing to being perplexed over the sophistication of the new electronic operating systems and the computers that controlled them. Training was good and effective but not adapted to the unusual position in which these men found themselves but once harnessed, corrective procedures paid dividends.

So effective was the 'Hit More' series of tests that one B-36 (44-92054) was retained as a test aircraft for its service life, finally being retired in September 1957 after it had made 244 flights totalling 1,600 flying hours. This aircraft fired a quarter of a million rounds of 20-mm ammunition and was subject to several major modifications including the addition of a radome installed in its nose to evaluate a range of air-defence radar systems and also several antennas and other structures for electronic counter-measures. So successful were these tests that it was loaned out for evaluation of other aircraft systems, including a suite of systems for the Convair B-58 and this became the prototype for the R-4360-53 engine.

As a signal to unfriendly states in South East Asia and elsewhere in that hemisphere, in August 1953 B-36s from the 92nd BW completed a flight to bases in Japan, Okinawa and Guam. This was just after the armistice

had been signed dividing Korea into North and South and served notice that America retained a strategic and overall defence interest in the region. It was the first time an entire B-36 wing had deployed overseas and it signalled the coming of age of an aircraft which had taken a very long time to reach maturity.

BELOW The tail gunner's ECM equipment in the aft pressurised section. *(Dennis Jenkins)*

Chapter Six

Service life

The B-36 served with the US Air Force for ten years, forming the strategic deterrent wielded by Strategic Air Command. In that time it participated in the greatest transformation of air power in the history of military aviation, moving from a national deterrent force to an instrument for strategic strike, carrying the most powerful weapons ever devised.

OPPOSITE The game changer for the B-36 was the successful test of the first atomic device at Alamogordo, New Mexico, on 16 July 1945, ushering in the age of atomic weapons and a new role for the B-36 as the strategic air-launched deterrent of the United States. *(LANL)*

By the end of the Second World War it was obvious that long-range bombardment of the enemy homeland would play a significant, if not deciding factor in the outcome of any future war. Toward that end, and at a time of seriously diminishing defence budgets together with finalisation of the emergence of an independent US Air Force, Gen 'Hap' Arnold and Gen Carl Spaatz, architects of the mighty bomber forces that had played a major role with the RAF in flattening Germany and exclusively in raiding Japan, defined a unique force for a new age of atomic warfare.

On 21 March 1946 Strategic Air Command (SAC) was formed with Gen George C. Kenney, second only to Spaatz, as its first commander, that in itself signifying its top priority. In several respects, SAC mirrored RAF Bomber Command, which had itself been formed out of the 'Command' restructuring in 1936. Diminished from their mighty formations in the Second World War, the 15th and 8th Air Forces were assigned to SAC, which would only grow in size and capability over the next decade.

Initially equipped with obsolescent B-17s, B-29s and some ageing B-26s, as well as three P-80 jet fighters, SAC's mission was to conduct long range operations, anywhere in the world at any time. By the end of its first year, SAC had 148 B-29s, 85 P-51s, 31 F-2s and 15 C-54 transport aircraft but the nucleus of its offensive operation was the 509th Composite Group which had been set up to handle operations with the atomic bomb. Its first operation came on 30 June 1946 when a B-29 dropped a Nagasaki-type plutonium bomb on 73 ships at Bikini Atoll, sinking five and damaging nine.

From meagre beginnings, SAC grew into a potent force capable of delivering a devastating nuclear strike, its resources ultimately including manned penetrating bombers, air-dropped thermonuclear gravity bombs, stand-off weapons and Intercontinental Ballistic Missiles (ICBMs). The B-36 saw service in SAC between 1948 and 1958, the last of the prop-driven strategic bombers to serve in the US Air Force, concurrently with the first US all-jet bomber, the B-45 (1949–52), the B-47 (1951–66) and the B-52 (from 1955), the latter outliving SAC itself!

In 1946 SAC boasted 37,093 personnel. When the B-36 departed from SAC in 1958 the organisation had 258,703 people on its books and 3,031 aircraft in the inventory, of which 1,769 were bombers and close to the highest number it would ever have. SAC ended its days on 31 May 1992 when it was largely superseded by Air Combat Command. The Cold War had been effectively over for two years, since when, the collapse of the Soviet state and the unification of Germany determined that the US Air Force was operating to a new world order.

LEFT **Strategic Air Command was established on 21 March 1946 as one of three major combat commands of the US Army Air Forces and, under the authority of an independent US Air Force from 18 September 1947, became the strategic bomber command covering both conventional and nuclear weapons until dis-establishment began on 31 May 1992.** *(USAF)*

The B-36 came to Strategic Air Command in the year SAC moved its headquarters from Andrews AFB, Maryland, to Offutt AFB, Nebraska, officially moving across from 9 November. In this year there were officially 35 B-36 aircraft on line but that means very little. Definition of 'strength' usually indicates a date in which aircraft were accredited to a unit or air force and in the case of these B-36s, that was no clear indication of an operational capability. In all cases subsequent, readers should treat annual on-strength numbers as indicative of a relevant strength only.

The first B-36A delivered (44-92004) arrived on 26 June and went on strength with the 7th BG at Carswell AFB. From this date the categorisation of other SAC bombers was adjusted: going defunct as a category, 'very heavy' B-29 and B-50 types became medium bombers and the B-36 became a heavy bomber. In this vein the B-47 replaced the B-29/B-50 as a medium bomber and the B-52 replaced the B-36 as a heavy bomber. With integration and shakedown evaluation completed, this year the B-36s were

bedding in and SAC was solving manpower, management and expansion problems, with difficulties in getting a credible and accurate bombing capability.

In 1949 SAC had 36 B-36s on strength, a year in which the Air Force placed top priority on equipping SAC and standing it up as the strategic deterrent stick of the United States. Training reached high levels of commitment and intensity and recruitment was a major driving force in building up personnel from 51,965 the previous year to 71,490 by the end of 1949. Emphasis was still on the B-29/B-50 types and personnel were on a war footing, with high stress levels and a driving imperative to strengthen the deterrent arm, reacting to a worsening global crisis, epitomised by the Berlin blockade, which began on 24 June 1948 and ended on 12 May 1949.

On 12 March the B-36 began to flex its muscle, with a record flight of 9,600mls (15,446km) by an aircraft of the 7th BG, completed in 49hr 37min, starting and finishing at Fort Worth using a crew of 12 piloted by Capt Roy Showalter. The first

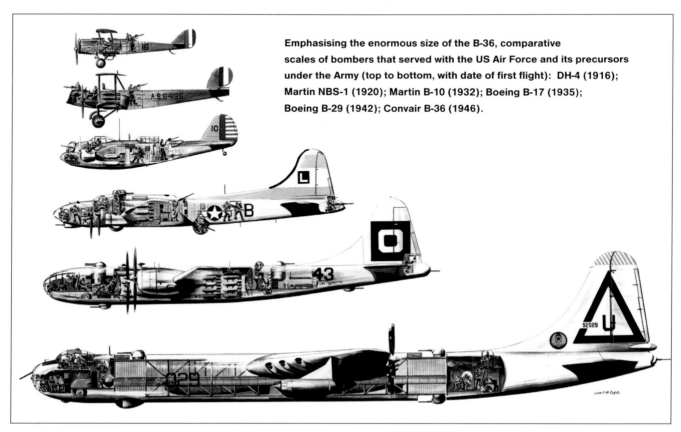

Emphasising the enormous size of the B-36, comparative scales of bombers that served with the US Air Force and its precursors under the Army (top to bottom, with date of first flight): DH-4 (1916); Martin NBS-1 (1920); Martin B-10 (1932); Boeing B-17 (1935); Boeing B-29 (1942); Convair B-36 (1946).

bombing competition involving the B-36 took place 3–7 October with a 28th BG crew winning the individual crew trophy. Nevertheless, the build-up of aircraft on strength was slow, for reasons that will be obvious to the reader having understood by now the ponderous and simultaneous preparation of the aircraft, incorporating both design and development with production in the flawed concept of 'concurrency' explored in the early chapters.

In 1950, SAC boasted 38 B-36 bombers and 20 RB-36 types on strength with personnel now 85,473 and a total of 962 aircraft, up from 837 in 1948 and 868 in 1949. This was the first year of the Korean War but the B-36 was in no fit state to commit and bombing operations in theatre were handled by B-29/B-50 units. But it was the first time that the B-36 began to bed in and serve as a seminal and polarising factor for SAC in the more balanced organisation it was becoming. Of only incidental relevance, this was also the year the RB-45 entered service with the 91st SRS at Barksdale AFB, Louisiana, with reconnaissance becoming an accelerating priority for the Air Force and for SAC in particular.

The big jump in the B-36 inventory came in 1951 when SAC had 163 on strength, of

which 65 were reconnaissance variants, the personnel level had jumped to 144,525 and a total force of 1,186 aircraft were listed for the Command. During the year, two wings operated the B-36 with a third transitioning from the B-29s. On 16 January six aircraft of the 7th BW, Carswell AFB, flew to Lakenheath, England, giving British citizens their first look at the B-36, returning four days later. On 3 December six B-36s of the 11th BW arrived at Sidi Slimane after a non-stop flight during the first visit by these aircraft to French Morocco. They returned five days later.

The sustained expansion of SAC saw 268 B-36s on strength in 1952 in a total inventory of 1,830 aircraft, the Command growing a fourth wing of Convair bombers and a third and fourth wing of reconnaissance variants. Held 13–18 October, four B-36 wings joined ten B-29 and five B-50 wings in the fourth annual bombing competition out of Davis-Monthan AFB, Arizona, with the B-36s operating out of Walker AFB, New Mexico. Following this, the SAC reconnaissance and navigation competition was held from 23 October to 1 November, involving B-36 aircraft out of Rapid City AFB, South Dakota, forming two of the four wings competing. The highest score was achieved by the 28th SRS/8th AF, recipient of the P. T. Cullen Award named after Brig Gen Paul T. Cullen, who was killed in a C-124 crash on 23 March 1951.

The following year SAC stood up 322 B-36s of which 137 were reconnaissance variants with four wings and 185 were bombers in six wings. Action in the Korean War ceased on 27 July 1953 when the ceasefire was signed by both sides in a conflict that had permanently divided the country, an armistice that remains to this day. During August and September the 92nd BW conducted the first mass B-36 flight to the Far East with visits to Japan, Okinawa and Guam, appropriately named 'Big Stick' in a demonstration of the US commitment to maintaining peace in the region. This was the first appearance of the B-36 in that area and underscored the intention to use whatever force was necessary to shut down a resurgence of violence.

The fifth annual bombing competition held from 25–31 October was joined by four B-36 wings alongside four B-29 and two B-29 wings out of Walker AFB. But the writing was on the wall: seven B-47 wings out of David-Monthan AFB joined the competition. Nevertheless, four B-36 wings joined one RB-50 wing, an RB-29 wing and one YRB-47 wing in the annual reconnaissance competition out of Ellsworth AFB, South Dakota, held 18–27 October in which an RB-36 from the 15th AF won the P. T. Cullen Award.

B-36 strength reached its peak in 1954 with 209 bombers and 133 reconnaissance variants, 342 aircraft in a total SAC inventory of 2,640 aircraft of which 795 were medium B-47 bombers. This was a time of tremendous growth and overall expansion in SAC, with 142,000 air refuelling hook-ups in the year and over 3,400 transatlantic and transpacific crossings.

The great advance in air-to-air refuelling erased the distinct advantage with the B-36 and in that emergence of extended capability was demonstrated a non-stop flight from March AFB, California, to Yokota Air Base, Japan, on 21 June. The 6,700ml (10,780km) flight took under 15 hours and involved two in-flight refuelling hook-ups from KC-97s. Another advantage with the B-36 was self-defensive armament, all but eliminated on the fast B-47s and the B-52s, the latter of which would appear

in service during the following year, as fighter escorts were more readily available by the same process of in-flight refuelling.

The first B-36 rotation to Guam occurred on 15–16 October when the 92nd BW stationed at Fairchild AFB, Washington, deployed to Andersen AFB on a 90-day training visit. This marked the first time a complete B-36 wing

ABOVE The design of the B-36 shared several similarities with the B-29, the latter having a glazed nose section and forward bombardier position. *(USAF)*

RIGHT Development of the Pratt & Whitney R-4360 was pioneered on the XB-44, a B-29A-1 (42-93845) fitted with redesigned nacelles for what would have been the B-29D but was designated B-50. *(USAF)*

deployed to an overseas base. From 16 June the four B-36 reconnaissance wings were shifted to a bombing role as their primary mission, albeit reserving reconnaissance as a secondary capability. The B-36s dominated the six events in the reconnaissance and navigation competition held 9–14 August and six B-36 wings from Walker AFB joined the annual bombing competition 23–29 August, two crews permitted from each wing, joining the 15 B-47 wings and two B-50 wings. Testament to the refinement of their capabilities, the B-36s took the top three placings in both the bombing and the reconnaissance stakes, significantly outclassing the B-47s which had yet to demonstrate an equivalent bombing capability.

In 1955 as the SAC inventory soared to 3,068 aircraft, of which 338 were B-36s (205 bombers and 133 reconnaissance types), the B-47 continued to dominate with 1,086 listed together with the first 18 B-52s on strength. The re-designation of RB-36 reconnaissance wings continued with a further four allocated as bomber wings on 1 October, retaining some reconnaissance capability now as a secondary role. While much of the heavy-lift to overseas bases was being taken up by B-47 wings, rotating to Lakenheath, Upper Heyford, Fairford, Mildenhall and Brize Norton

in England, B-36 wings were deployed to Nouasseur Air Base, French Morocco, to Burtonwood and Upper Heyford in England and Andersen AFB, Guam.

As the B-50 was at the terminal end of its phase-out plan, only B-47s and B-36s were available for the seventh bombing competition held 24–30 August with ten B-36 wings each putting up two crews from Fairchild AFB, Washington. The B-47s showed tremendous improvement in both bombing and navigation and the 15th AF's 320th BW won the Fairchild Trophy. As all the RB-36s had been formally re-designated as bomber wings only the RB-47s could compete in the reconnaissance and navigation competition, held 24–30 September.

Significant waves of change were transforming the tactical equipment in SAC from a prop-force to an all-jet Command and by the end of the decade Intercontinental Ballistic Missiles (ICBMs) would begin to deploy, shifting SAC to a multi-mode Command divided between aircraft and missiles. Formally organised in 1954, the decision to develop the Atlas, and then the Titan ICBMs had been contested, fiercely at times by Curtis LeMay, while the missiles would be muscled into force by Gen Bernard Schriever, as noted earlier.

In 1956, while the number of SAC

BELOW **Operating largely in parallel with the B-36, SAC utilised the effective performance increase of the B-50 to produce variants such as this KB-50J cargo-tanker as a support ship for internal and overseas deployments.** *(USAF)*

personnel reached 217,279 officers, airmen and civilians and the total tactical inventory reached 3,218 aircraft of all types, the B-36 force retracted to 247 as combined bomber and reconnaissance aircraft, in that order of priority. But this was also the year the last B-47 was delivered, the inventory reaching 1,560. Of the 42 wings competing the bombing, navigation and reconnaissance competition

held 24–30 August, only eight B-36 wings participated. This year the B-36s got their own back on the B-47s, beating the latter to the Fairchild Trophy, won by an aircraft from the 2nd AF, 11th BW.

Responding to an increasing concern that Soviet ICBM deployment was imminent, SAC began to transition toward a one-third ground alert operation so that a significant fraction

of the retaliatory force would be away from airfields that could be hit in a pre-emptive first strike by the time warheads reached their targets. Crews and aircraft would be prepared for immediate take-off so as to get airborne on alert of an attack. But SAC was not equipped for this and a structural reorganisation was essential to implementing the new strategy.

It was in synergy with preparations for one-third ground alert that in 1957 SAC began the phase-out of the KB-29 as well as the B-47, at a time when the B-36 force was in decline, with 127 remaining in a force that had a total complement of 2,711 aircraft and the personnel level had reached 224,014. The annual bombing and reconnaissance competitions were held 30 October to 6 November and 43 bomber wings put up from Pinecastle AFB, Florida, and Carswell AFB, Texas. Of those, five were B-36 wings which won the crew and wing navigation awards with the B-47 wings winning out over the B-36 each time they competed in the bombing competition.

In 1958 the transition to one-third ground alert accelerated which brought about considerable change to the organisational infrastructure of SAC, which now had a personnel strength of 258,703 and 3,031 aircraft including the last 22 B-36 bombers to serve on official strength with the US Air Force. In this year, the last two B-36 crews to participate in a bombing competition, held

13–18 October, participated out of Carswell AFB but the B-47 crews dominated the event and the operational life of the B-36 was over.

This was the year in which SAC received the 1st Missile Division from the Air Research and Development Command (ARDC) at Cooke AFB, California, soon to be renamed Vandenberg AFB, beginning the transition to operational ICBMs through a crew training programme. It was a time of great change; the Space Age had been born, satellites were being routinely launched by Russia and America and the age of the piston-engine bomber had passed into history. The number of jet bombers with SAC would peak at 3,207 in 1959 and then start a decline as the Command divided resources between aircraft and missiles. Within ten years, there would be fewer than 1,200 aircraft in SAC, personnel would be down by 94,000 and there would be 1,065 ICBMs in underground silos capable of launch at short notice.

Nuclear tests

Throughout its service life the B-36 participated in many trials and tests of equipment, processes and procedures which related to the overall mission of Strategic Air Command and to the nuclear weapons programme in certain select areas. The development of the atomic (fission) bomb

LEFT The B-36 played a major role in influencing the design of the B-52, the latter seen here with the ADM-20 Quail, jet-powered decoy. (USAF)

ABOVE The primary role of the B-36 was as a strategic deterrent. The 25MT, Mk. 17 thermonuclear bomb on display at the Castle Air Museum, Atwater, California, alongside a B-36H. *(Nehrams2020)*

OPPOSITE Engines stacked awaiting use, their size belied by the lack of perspective scale. *(Dennis Jenkins)*

BELOW Another role, one for which the B-36 was uniquely capable, was photographic reconnaissance and saw the use of the powerful Boston camera taken aloft, designed by Dr James Baker. Built by Boston University in 1951, it was capable of showing a golf ball from 45,000ft (13,700m). *(McChizzle)*

and then thermonuclear (fusion) weapons required involvement of the aircraft that would carry these ultimate weapons of retribution and destruction. Five B-36s were applied for extended duration to supporting this research and development programme. In several respects it can be thought of as another arm of the concurrency programme under which the aircraft itself evolved, since both the aircraft and the war load it would ultimately carry were developed at the same time.

A B-36D-5-CF (49-2653) was employed for extended periods on effects testing for most of the detonations in the early phase of evaluation. Four other aircraft, all B-36H models (50-1083, 50-1086, 51-5726 and 52-1386) were assigned to the 4925th Test Group (Atomic) at Kirtland AFB, New Mexico, to provide support for nuclear tests. For photographic support to obtain images of the mushroom clouds two RB-36H-15-CF aircraft (51-5748 and 51-5750) were assigned equipped with upward looking cameras.

Concern over the effect a nuclear detonation within relative close proximity might have on various materials, including the fabric still used on the B-29 and B-50, pushed the effects research programme toward the B-36 as an ideal platform, an aircraft big enough to carry a meaningful weight of measuring equipment and science instruments to obtain this information. In the bigger effects programme concerns were raised about the overall effect that nuclear explosions may have on the operability of electrical, mechanical and structural elements of the carrier aircraft that had dropped the device. Only the B-36 and later the B-47 were capable of carrying out these measurements.

Modification to the effects aircraft (49-2653) were carried out between 9 May and 15 June 1952 which included fitting a metal rudder, already in the mix for retrofit to all B-36 aircraft. It carried thermocouples for measuring the intensity of the heat, several accelerometers to measure, and record, motion in the three axes caused by the blast, strain gauges and recording meters and oscilloscopes. Wire recorders and cameras could record the test on board. Had telemetry been available at the time it would likely have been rendered

inoperable by the electromagnetic pulse (EMP) of the blast. The calibration of sensors was completed on 15 August 1952 and the aircraft was flown to Carswell AFB for maintenance and from there on to Kwajalein Island in the Pacific where it arrived, along with a B-47B, on 2 October.

A full-scale rehearsal of the Operation IVY test had been conducted on 13 August in the Gulf of Mexico under Operation TEXAN, during which 39 aircraft took part in simulated drops, sampling exercises and cloud-tracking tasks. Three of the aircraft involved were B-36Hs, including 49-2653, which dropped a Mk. 4 bomb shape standing in for the Mk. 18 which would be dropped at Eniwetok. As part of the preparation, the Wright Air Development Center issued guidelines regarding the altitudes at which a B-36 could operate at a safe distance from the detonation point. For a 100KT device a ground burst required an altitude of 19,100ft (5,822m) or 21,800ft (6,645m) for a 3,000ft (914m) air burst.

Operation IVY would involve thermonuclear fusion bombs in the megaton range. Being too heavy to drop from an aircraft, a liquid-fuelled thermonuclear device would be detonated on the ground in a test known as Shot Mike. When the device was detonated, the B-36D from Kwajalein was at an altitude of 40,000ft (12,192m) and a distance of 15mls (24km)

from the point of detonation, which had a yield of 10.4MT creating a crater 164ft (50m) deep and 6,240ft (1,902m) in diameter. When the blast wave reached the effects aircraft it was at a height of 38,500ft (11,582m) and a range of 25mls (40km). The overpressure on the aircraft was only 0.33lb/in² (2.275kPa), about two-thirds the design limit of the aircraft's structure.

The results, while more benign at this range than expected, indicated that the B-36 could not drop a thermonuclear bomb and survive the blast effect, driving pressure for SAC to apply retarding parachutes to bombs of this yield. Resistance to this prevented early adoption of that technology but eventually all nuclear bombs were fitted with them.

Next up was the Shot King test in Operation IVY on 16 November 1952, a device of much less yield (500KT) which was released from the B-36H at an altitude of 40,000ft (12,192m) for an air burst at 1,480ft (451m). The bomb detonated only 215ft (65.5m) off target but the drop aircraft was out of position when the blast hit, incurring some damage as the effect imposed forces equivalent to 80% of the aircraft's structural design limit. Some changes were made to thermal protection devices, including a change of material from which the blast curtains were fabricated and it was from this test that the decision was made to paint under-surfaces of the B-36 a reflective white.

OPPOSITE The nose turret of a B-36 with offset gun sight and a good view of the glazed area. *(Dennis Jenkins)*

LEFT Production of the B-36 provided Strategic Air Command with a credible deterrent force, the message of which was not lost on Soviet observers noting the build-up in capability throughout the 1950s. *(Convair)*

Further tests involving the B-36 took place in 1953 with Operation UPSHOT-KNOTHOLE, a widely variable series of 11 tests over the Nevada Test Site beginning in March and ending on 4 June with Shot Climax, when a B-36H dropped a tactical Mk. 7 bomb. With a 61KT yield, the highest of any test conducted on US soil to that date, it demonstrated the core which would be used on the Mk. 14, 17 and 21 devices which would be tested in Operation CASTLE. But components of a B-36 fabricated for test were used in ground measurements as to exactly how nuclear effects from UPSHOT-KNOTHOLE detonations

LEFT Between 1946 and 1958 Bikini Atoll in the Pacific Ocean played host to 23 nuclear tests, such as Operation Crossroads, involving participation by the B-36. *(LANL)*

BELOW Nuclear tests were supported by B-36 participation alongside the B-47 and the B-52, as with this detonation under Operation Crossroads-Baker. *(LANL)*

would stress or affect elements of a B-36 both structurally and thermally.

The effects aircraft (49-2653) participated in all six shots in Operation CASTLE which ran from 1 March to 14 May 1954, conducted at Eniwetok in the Marshall Islands. Supporting this aircraft were three other B-36s for sampling the air, one aircraft of which was a control aircraft for the other two. These detonations were high yield, all but one between 6.9MT and 15MT. Considerable damage was reported and unprotected areas were adversely affected by the heat, burning panels, charring paint, blasting away landing gear bay doors with light even penetrating the curtains specially designed to block out the flash, reported by the crew as a double pulse of light.

In the final report on the effects of CASTLE, a delivery profile was designed in which the aircraft would drop the device(s) at 40,000ft (12,192m) and a speed of 397mph (639kph) before immediately executing an aggressive turn away from the target. In this way it was believed that a B-36 could survive a surface

ABOVE In a continuing search for more diversified operations, a B-36F was recruited to a programme supporting the 1950 GEBO (Generalised Bomber) study which envisaged a parasitic, delta-wing aircraft incorporating a weapons pod similar to that eventually proposed for the XB-58. *(USAF)*

BELOW A wide range of proposed developments included the possible adoption of four Curtiss-Wright XT35-W-1 turboprop tractor engines for the basic B-36 airframe, instigated to deflect criticism of the aircraft's slow speed, an idea which was superseded by the advent of the all-jet bomber fleet. *(Convair)*

burst of a 10.8MT bomb or a 100MT bomb on a parachute retarded drop; no operational nuclear device with a yield greater than 25MT was ever deployed by the United States, either on an aircraft or a missile. But if set for an air burst, the survivable yield of the detonated device was reduced considerably, 1.5MT for a gravity fall or 35MT for a retarded drop.

Ironically, one of the objects of the tests was to give a crew experience of what it was like to be in the proximity of a nuclear detonation. This had a noted effect on the mental attitude of crews who experienced this and similar experiences have been noted for other military personnel on the ground and at sea when observing such events. The mental attitude of those who participated was measurably affected and it was believed at very senior level that this had a negative effect on the operational smoothness of a crew sent in a real war to carry out these duties. So much so that the practice of placing operational personnel in close proximity for no other purpose than to impose a sense of familiarity, an acceptance of the event as 'normality' should cease as it might interfere with the prosecution of duty. In other words, some crews began to question the magnitude of the expectations placed upon them. In this way, the B-36 and its involvement in nuclear tests opened a new chapter in the way military personnel were selected, and from that point monitored, in preparing for war and the implication that several million lives could depend upon their individual actions.

Other support operations followed, in Operation TEAPOT during March and April 1954 where personnel and aircraft were involved in measuring effects, testing procedures and defining the optimum way to fly an aircraft on a live drop mission. Radiation exposure was becoming an important aspect; already after the UPSHOT-KNOTHOLE test series there had been concerns regarding the radiation levels in neighbouring areas where small towns were in the path of clouds of contaminated particles. The liberal use of film badges registering radiation levels was already becoming an important aspect in determining the collateral damage, not least to 'friendly' forces moving in to areas where nuclear detonations had taken place.

The first air drop of a thermonuclear weapon was scheduled for Operation REDWING, conducted between April and July 1956, and was to have employed a B-36 to drop the device but it was determined that the aircraft could not escape fast enough to survive. A B-52B (52-013) was employed for that instead and a B-36 did drop a low-yield TX-28 on Shot OSAGE on 17 June. It was the last nuclear test in which the B-36 took part and ended a corner of that type's history, picked up and amplified during live tests involving the B-52. But this was not the end of the B-36 and its association with the development of nuclear weapons.

Under Operation MIAMI MOON in May and June 1957, four B-36s were employed on sampling flights. With two external pods on each side of the fuselage, the filters they contained would trap radioactive particles for post-flight analysis. The pods were entirely separate from the interior of the aircraft itself and only accessed by scientists after the aircraft landed. The operation supported British tests with each sampling flight lasting 19hr of which 2.5hr was spent inside the mushroom cloud at 40,000ft (12,192m).

Sampling was not only directed at US tests, with a need to measure the precise level of contamination both within the mushroom cloud and outside it at various distances, but also at Soviet tests where the constituent atomic particles could disclose the specific type of bomb and hence gather data on the level of

direction, and the state of development, with Russia's nuclear weapons programme.

After supporting both direct nuclear and thermonuclear tests, and conducting intensive sampling operations, four B-36 aircraft (49-2653, 50-1083, 50-1086 and 52-1386) were significantly contaminated. Unaware of the very nature of radioactive contamination that would be uncovered during the 1960s, efforts to 'clean' the aircraft involved standard maintenance procedures conducted, at length, by ground personnel who became directly exposed to dangerous levels of radiation, a fact testified to in the official report in assessing the manpower intensive activity. Revised procedures had each aircraft cool for 44 hours before personnel protected by gloves and special clothing washed down the aircraft with a formulated mixture of gunk and kerosene, a process which took 17 men four or five days to complete.

As the seriousness of the situation became self-evident, after Operation TEAPOT an intensive programme of decontamination was carried out and certain badly affected parts of the aircraft were replaced, especially external skin panels, but the aircraft, once cleaned, were returned to the Air Force between April and August 1955 and then utilised for the sampling tests in Operation MIAMI MOON. Those four aircraft were cleaned at Hickham Field, Hawaii in a process similar to that applied after Operation CASTLE.

ABOVE The last Peacemaker, as B-36J 52-2827 is about to leave the Fort Worth facility. *(Convair)*

Chapter Seven

Flying the B-36

Flying the Peacemaker was not for the faint hearted, for this most unconventional of aircraft had its idiosyncrasies and 'bad boy' behaviour in abundance. Nevertheless, it was a product of its day, unique and with a flying experience, as one pilot put it: "rather like sitting on your front porch and flying the house around!"

OPPOSITE From Lot 4, the much photographed B-36A 44-92021 presents a pleasing profile showing the difference between the dull magnesium and effective aluminium skins along the fuselage of the bomber variant. *(Dennis Jenkins)*

Francis H. Potter, Colonel USAF Retired

I was a 1st Lt, with about 1,500 flying hours, recently returned from a tour flying cargo aircraft on the Berlin Airlift. I was assigned to the 9th BWH, flying primarily B-29s. We were to transition to the B-36s as they became available from the factory at Fort Worth, Texas. We soon had three or four of these wonderful, modern, new aircraft, with crews formed to man them. Since we had pilots with more experience than I, my assignment was as a crew co-pilot. My crew was somewhat down the line on the check-out list, so we spent our free time ogling this beauty, and talking about it with those already in the programme.

During this time the Air Force set up a ground school for prospective aircrews at Rapid City AFB, South Dakota, which I attended in the fall of 1949. I believe it was the first training school where crew members came from other bases to a central location to receive training. This proved an effective operation and was used from then on. The B-47 had such a school in Florida, the B-52 in California, etc. It proved a most efficient way of training.

My first flight, a round robin which kept us airborne for 30 hours, came on 18 January 1950. There were several pilots on board, all scheduled to receive training. My instrument check was due which gave me priority to be aboard. Can you imagine, taking an instrument check on your first flight in a new aircraft, one of this enormity and complexity? The newest and most sophisticated bomber in the world at the time! I don't remember much about it, except the check pilot was satisfied. My white instrument card was renewed.

Although the new bomber was interesting and fun to fly, it had one rather naughty problem that gave the maintenance men a real fit. It wouldn't hold its gas. That's right. We were plagued with gas leaks. I recall seeing several leaks seeping from the wing sections and at the same time, drips in the bomb bay. Burning high-octane aviation gasoline, this was not a problem to ignore. It didn't take too long to become evident that this was a problem that could not be fixed by on-base band-aids, it would require something more drastic. So, after having them for less than a year our B-36s were returned to the company to fix their leak problems.

Here is other trivia data that really impressed all who qualified to fly this bird. The wing was more than seven feet (2.1m) thick at the root. A person could climb into the wing and work his way outboard of the centre engine. The 19ft (5.79m),

BELOW Another view of 44-92023 with red tail and outboard wing sections.
(Dennis Jenkins)

square tipped props were geared to turn approximately one half engine speed to keep them sub-sonic, which gave that unforgettable throbbing. Each aircraft used 336 spark plugs, a big portion of which required replacing after each mission.

My next association with the B-36 came in late summer 1954. I was assigned to the 92nd BWH at Fairchild AFB, Washington. The 92nd had three squadrons, flying the D and J models. Shortly after I checked in, the wing departed for a 90-day deployment to the island of Guam. By now I had 3,200 hours of four-engine flying time. I had been checked out as an aircraft commander, bomb commander and instructor pilot on the B-29. So I was put into the programme to be an aircraft commander. The wing had left a couple of aircraft along with three or four instructor pilots at the home station. After seven instructional flights and two ferry flights, I was a checked-out aircraft commander, and soon after upgraded to instructor status.

I still remember the first time my crew and I took off with me at the controls, and no instructor personnel on board. Although I felt entirely comfortable with my check out and the many simulator hours had taught me emergency procedures, there is still something special about that first mission in the left seat. Without an instructor you feel all alone and have that somewhat 'now or never' attitude. As we lifted off and climbed into the clouds (there were always clouds at Fairchild) I recall

thinking, 'I hope I can get this big mamma back on the ground all in one piece.'

Many interesting occurrences happened during the nearly 1,200 hours I was to spend in this aircraft. One, that earned my crew the coveted 'SAC Crew of the Month' award for January 1956, occurred in late 1955. We were flying a routine bombing navigational

training mission. We had been out quite a few hours and, due to a turbo compressor problem, were operating with less than full power on two engines. We were on a night navigation training leg when the gunners reported the exhaust shroud around one of the engines had failed. This let the very hot exhaust gas shoot back through the engine nacelle and was considered very much a fire hazard. We shut the engine down which solved that problem. In less than 10 minutes the gunner reported the same problem on another engine. We shut it down. So, with two of six shut down and two with partial power, we headed home. We started the jets, which were normally shut down during cruise, and used them to help hold altitude sufficient to get over the mountains. Arriving at Fairchild AFB, we had low visibility and a ceiling of 500–600ft (152–183m). But, true to their advertising, the GCA unit brought us in through the clouds and mist perfectly lined up with the runway. After landing, a servo did not close, so the nose wheel steering would not work. Just another mission, but one we didn't need to repeat.

Many other [memories] come to mind. The first time I landed on packed snow was

interesting. It was on a deployment to Eielson AFB, at Fairbanks, Alaska. We were briefed we'd be landing on an inch or more of 'packed snow'. We were also advised that if we were aligned properly at touchdown, it would make the landing much more pleasant. Our landing, as well as the others, all went well. For this deployment, we had 'snow' tyres installed. These were tyres with what appeared to be steel wool moulded into the tyre. If you ran your hand along the tread, you'd get a hundred scratches. They seemed to do a lot of good. In the other temperature extreme, I remember the 'greenhouse' effect you got in that big glass cockpit, when on the ground in the hot sun. There was no air-conditioning, just a small fan which just moved the hot air. The sun would beat in through the glass and the temperature would soar. Many times I would be completely soaked with sweat before take-off.

We were required to fire our guns each training quarter. To do this we usually went several hundred miles over the ocean. When we were in position and had no ships visible on radar, we'd give the command to fire! What a racket they made. It seemed that if several turrets fired in the same direction, you could feel the recoil through the aircraft controls. To keep from over-heating the gun barrels, the gunners were to practice shooting in short bursts, then take so much cooling time before continuing to fire. The extended turrets were into the slipstream which caused added drag, requiring more power to hold air speed.

And then there were the super-secret 'sniffer missions'. This was during the Cold War and Russia as well as we were doing tests using atomic explosives. When our intelligence got wind of a proposed Russian test, we would fly out near Attu, on the Alaskan chain and hold for hours. All such missions would run 20 hours plus, so we could stay at our assigned location for many hours. Our aircraft were equipped with air pumps and a filter system which would extract particles from the air. Upon return these special filters would be analysed and the 'smart' people could tell the approximate yield of the detonation. While in the air we had no way of knowing if we were getting a 'hot' filter or not. If the detonation was delayed, we'd go out the next night. One time, I believe we went out three times before the Ruskies actually let it go.

We also ran missions giving the Tactical Air Command a chance to show their expertise in defence of the ADIZ (Air Defense Identification Zone). An exercise would be

LEFT Convair photographer Frank Kleinwechter braving the weather at Goose Bay, Labrador, with B-36F 49-2680 in the background on 23 January 1952. *(Dennis Jenkins)*

scheduled. The defenders would know it was scheduled sometime during a period of several days. Sometimes we would go single ship, sometimes several aircraft together. I recall going north, to near Alaska, then heading toward Hawaii, then turning east

LEFT Eielsen AFB, Alaska, in February 1959, displaying its usual winter covering presenting harsh and difficult working conditions. *(Dennis Jenkins)*

ABOVE De-icing has a different meaning for ground crew using wood spade brooms to remove snow and ice – note the total absence of any safety gear as personnel work on the top of the fuselage and the inboard wing section. *(Don Pyeatt via Dennis Jenkins)*

to enter the ADIZ around mid-to-northern California. If there were ten bombers in the exercise, there could be ten different flight paths. Or you could have one bomber follow another, 10–15 minutes later.

We bombers would be at our optimum altitude and airspeed watching for the fighters. I recall seeing the fighters, probably F-89s, come in for a head-on attack. They'd pass us by with a closure speed of around 850mph (1,367kph). That was usually the only pass they could make. By the time they turned around, we were fairly hard to catch. After the fighters with afterburners came into use, that would change. We were also permitted to intercept their radio frequencies, except for emergency channels and give false instructions. We often disrupted their games using this medium, anything to confuse them!

I had one especially exciting take-off from Eielson AFB at Fairbanks, Alaska. At that time their runway ran through some fairly dense woods. The trees had been cleared perhaps 200–300 yards (183–274m) on each side. I had a young third-pilot on board and was letting him make the take-off. He was a husky individual, just like a football player. As we started our acceleration down the runway and the nose started to lighten for lift-off, the aircraft wanted to go to the right. I told the young pilot to 'give it some left rudder'. I could see no change, the nose still wanted to go right. I repeated my instructions and looked at his legs at the same time. I could see him

straining so hard on the left rudder, his leg was actually quivering. I tried applying left rudder too, but it would not budge. By this time we were a good distance down the runway with the nose getting lighter all the time. So I called to abort the take-off.

I pushed the nose firmly onto the runway, and reversed all six recips while still at take-off power. I didn't think I had time to bring them to idle, reverse, then increase power. My first co-pilot was watching the take-off from between the pilots' seats. He beat me to retarding the throttles on the overhead panel that controlled the four jets. We were able to stop, stay on the runway and not blow any tyres, but talk about the noise! By reversing all six engines at take-off power, that baby really screamed, bounced and bucked! The noise and vibrations in that cold air were horrendous. As we taxied back to the parking area, all the workers in the nearby buildings were out watching to see what made all that noise. The maintenance people found that the electrically controlled hydraulic servo that locked the huge rudder while on the ground had failed to release, preventing the rudder from moving. There was no way the aircrew could check this on the ground, since the rudder pedal moved only the servo trim tab, which along with the slip-stream caused the rudder to move. I felt I never needed to repeat that exercise.

In August 1956, my crew was picked to give a short, four-hour orientation flight to 18 AF ROTC cadets. We took off, climbed to a medium altitude and showed them the sights of the area. Grand Coulee Dam, the Columbia River and the large lake behind the dam, Mt Rainier, etc. They all seemed to enjoy the flight; none got airsick. Years later, I was approached at different times by two individuals who told me they were one of the cadets who participated and remembered that flight! Just shows what a small world it really is.

In April 1956 our wing again deployed to Guam for our 90-day rotation. We had my crew of 15 aboard, along with some 20–25 ground crew members. In those days we did not have the support of cargo aircraft, so carried most of our freight and support personnel with us. We departed Fairchild at full gross weight, flew west to the coast and set up our flight

at 5,000ft (1,524m). We held that altitude for perhaps eight to ten hours, then being lighter, we climbed to perhaps 12,000ft (3,657m). After some time, we'd increase altitude again. We stair-stepped all the way to Guam.

After 30 flying hours we arrived at Guam. When we extended the landing gear lever for landing, the left main gear would not unlock. This required one of the flight engineers to go into the wing, go to the wheel well and pull the manual 'unlock' handle. After doing this the gear came down and locked. We landed without further incident. Ninety-some days later, we returned to Fairchild. The Wing Commander, Col. Roland Campbell decided he would return

aboard my aircraft. This was somewhat an honour and let us be the first aircraft to depart Guam and the first to arrive back home. This time, they led us to the base operations area, usually reserved for transient and special aircraft. After we parked, a red carpet was rolled out along the Commander's exit path. Course, we crew members told our wives it was rolled out for us!

My crew and I were picked to 'get rid' of one of the (Mk. 17) practice bombs we had on base. It was the same dimensions as the real thing, but instead of having explosives, was filled with concrete to give the same weight. Its purpose was to give loading crews

ABOVE B-36B 44-92028 shows off the clean wing of the early A- and B-series as another Red Tail takes to the air. *(Dennis Jenkins)*

BELOW B-36B 44-92037, converted to D-series configuration, on display with the four podded jet engines. *(Dennis Jenkins)*

experience in handling and loading that large a weapon. So one of them was loaded onto our aircraft. To 'get rid' of it, our flight path took us 400mls (644km) out over the Pacific Ocean. It was well after sundown when we got to the designated spot. We cleared the area with radar, and seeing nothing on the water, dropped that 41,400lb (18,598kg) hunk of steel and concrete. We had talked about the possible reaction the aircraft would display, losing that much weight so quickly. I remember we retarded the throttles slightly, but felt no great bounce. I often wondered how deep into the floor of the ocean that 'bomb' went.

Other memories are also vivid. We had a lot of instrument flying here at Fairchild, so we were on a first name acquaintance (almost) with the GCA (ground control approach) operators. During the winter months nearly all landings were actual GCAs and during the good weather we practiced the procedure. It was hard to get the B-36 to settle down on a specific heading and hold it without wavering a degree or two

to each side. It seemed like you just orbited around the heading you desired, sloshing back and forth, until you were on the ground.

The nose of this aircraft was a series of windows, each held in its place in a metal framework. When in moist, warm air, we could get some terrific St Elmo's fire. It would snap and jump across the windows and run up and down the wings. Just a bluish ribbon of light 'dancing' all over, back across the top of the wing, etc. It was fascinating to watch. It was so bright at times you could read by it. I am not aware of it ever doing any damage and when you were used to it, it was fun. Newer crew members sometimes didn't agree. Some were quite apprehensive.

The only time I ever got even slightly airsick was in July 1955. The AF Academy at Colorado Springs, Colorado, was to be opened and dedicated soon. There was to be a three-ship B-36 flyover. My crew and another were picked to fly down and make some practice 'runs' to get a feel for the area.

ABOVE Showing its characteristic slight nose-down attitude at rest on the ground, a B-36F (49-2652) of the 7th BG at Carswell AFB. (USAF)

ABOVE, RIGHT AND OPPOSITE Under Operation Big Stick, the 92nd BW conducted the type's first mass flight to the Far East, here seen at Okinawa during August 1953.
(Dennis Jenkins)

One aircraft was provided by each of three different wings. We met the other two aircraft in the Academy area, joined into a three-ship formation and made quite a number of low altitude passes over the grounds. Seems I flew for an hour or so, then the other crew took over. I went downstairs to sit out the remaining time. The air was extremely turbulent, and being at low altitude for such a long time, the air inside the aircraft was quite warm. This warm, somewhat foul air, along with the constant bouncing, gave me a minor case of airsickness. When the time came a few days later for the actual dedication and flyover, my crew was not chosen. I did not have to make the trip a second time and didn't mind a bit.

In 1956, like all things, the era of this magnificent monster was to end for us. My wing was scheduled to transfer into the newer eight-engine all-jet B-52s. What a change that was going to be. Instead of lumbering along at 200mph (322kph), we'd do our cruise at .77 Mach, about three quarters the speed of sound. Instead of returning to our home station

and taking nearly an hour to get on the ground, we could accomplish the same thing in about 10 minutes. So, no one felt we'd rather hang onto the 'old' 36s. As 1956 progressed, we started flying the big old birds to re-assignment bases. On 25 March 1956, my crew was assigned to fly the last B-36 aircraft (a J model) away from Fairchild. We delivered it to the bomb wing at Biggs AFB, El Paso, Texas. Fittingly it was another cloudy, rainy day. After take-off, about mid-morning and while still below the clouds we made a circular trip around the base. What a change! Instead of seeing some 35–40 big birds roosting on the ground, all we could see was wet concrete. Sad!

Since retiring I have heard a time or two of an operational B-36 being flown at altitudes I find difficult to believe. Certainly I'm not the last nor best expert, but when I see figures of 50,000ft (15,240m) plus and at one time better than 55,000ft (16,764m) I'm curious. I don't know what they were fuelling their birds with, but ours, using high-octane av/gas

gasped and struggled to get to and maintain 45,000ft (13,860m). All ten throttles were at or near the firewall to maintain that altitude. In rechecking the Dash 1, both the D1 and the D2 oxygen pressure demand regulators were rated as adequate for altitudes only to 43,000ft (13,106m). From 43,000–45,000ft (13,106–13,716m) they were rated as 'marginal'.

A caution states that at 50,000ft (15,240m), (when unpressurised) no more than two to three minutes of consciousness can be anticipated using either regulator. Hopefully this would give enough time to initiate a descent. And wasn't the figure of 55,000ft (16,764m) what the altitude chamber people used to give as the atmospheric pressure point where a person's blood will boil when unpressurised? I never heard of any crew in our outfit being so daring or foolhardy.

So, the big bird really earned its nickname, 'The Peacekeeper'. It never dropped a bomb nor fired its guns in anger. It was truly the most

effective deterrent during the long Cold War with the communist countries. Its retirement truly signalled the end of a great era. I would never wish to punch the delete or diminish button on any of the great, fond and vivid memories I have. It was really the era of the 'BIG BOMBERS'!

Bob Miller

I was in the USAF 1952–56 thru Lowry B-29 gunnery thence to Carswell AFB tng. for B-36 as tail gunner. Eventually formed with other transfers as a member of a combat-ready crew and shipped to Limestone (Loring AFB, Maine).

After the final phase-out of B-29s out of Korea and everywhere else (no match for MIG-15s) a further diminished number of us found ourselves at Carswell AFB, Fort Worth, Texas the home of the famed B-36. Essentially we were then processed into a cram-course on 20mm cannon, remote-controlled turret mechanics, 'newer' pedestal and yoke-sights, AN- APG 32 gun-laying radar and a dry school on 'enemy' target recognition. Some of us, myself included, also took a hands-on black-box orientation to radar fundamentals, waveguides, magnetrons, dish di-poles, and CRT image recognition of range, azimuth and elevation. The training seemed rushed and left me and my pals with huge ring-binders

of scanner's and gunner's S.O.P. and a later tome of 'Emergency Procedures' for the B-36 Heavy Bomber.

In about five Texas months, where my most vivid recollections are the very hot summer, car trips to the flesh-pots of Dallas for a weekend, ice-frozen beers on the road between Fort Worth and Dallas (although I was still, legally, under age) – and a vain attempt to join a sorority dance and other disappointments! Nevertheless, by mid-August 1953 we had completed the B-36 gunnery school orientation flights on that huge aircraft and after just eight hours' total 'inflight instruction' we were introduced to the 12 members of our student crew which to me was fairly frightening.

My AC (Aircraft Commander) looked to be at least 50 years old (actually in his early 40s). Captain Mailander, who was a veteran pilot who 'Flew the Hump' in WWII, who smiled at me and then asked 'how many days ago was it that you left your momma?' I think I just grimaced for about 30 seconds, and then said slowly 'My momma's been dead for quite a few years Sir'. After that introduction Captain, (later Major) Mailander and I never exchanged a word beyond required intercom talk for as long as he was my AC.

Other members of my crew were more congenial, but there was a natural rift or distance from the officers up front who were all career Air Force and the aft compartment

BELOW A B-36D (44-92033) gets an escort in the form of a Lockheed F-94B (51-5450) of the Oregon Air National Guard. *(Dennis Jenkins)*

ABOVE Only the sound is lacking in this aesthetic shot of a B-36 running up its engines. *(Dennis Jenkins)*

BELOW AND BOTTOM B-36H 50-1086 *Miss Featherweight* during bombing up activities which show the bomb hoist attached to the top of the fuselage. *(Dennis Jenkins)*

who were, essentially, raw, young recruits. Our Pilot was Captain Roy Kirkland, a veteran of WWII and Korea. He was a quiet man very professional and (I learned later) looking to a day when he could retire back to his farm in Louisiana. Other officers were1st Lt Ford, Bombardier, Captain Martin, Navigator, (a graduate of Annapolis – I never found out how he made it to SAC) and also a Second Lt West Pointer, as 'Third Pilot' whose name I can't recall. Later, Maj Mailander was 'kicked upstairs' to Omaha, I think, replaced by Captain (later) Major Black Barney, a much more outgoing, cheery, happy leader, whom we all (I think) got to respect and love.

Among the enlisted crew we had a Staff Sergeant Radio Operator and a WWII B-17 Master Sergeant First Radio Operator and another Master Sergeant as second Flight Engineer. After that our 'Senior Gunner' (Tony Giamanco) was just recently made a 'Buck Sergeant' and the rest of us 'aft people' were all corporals: John Pfor from Nebraska, Rich Kunzman from Iowa and K.Y. Landsdale from Kentucky plus me from Oregon. I wondered how these old veterans like Mailander trusted any of us!

There were six bunks in the aft compartment of all the models I rode also an electric stove with four burners where we presumably could cook ham and eggs but we seldom, if ever did that, even on long missions of more than 30 hours. Inflight 'box lunches' were not all bad, except for the ubiquitous 'Purple Plums in Syrup', and the vitamin fortified chocolate bar. Advancement for combat-ready crews was more rapid than in the rest of the Air Force, (we were told) our AC, Pilots, and Radar/Nav/Bombardiers all gained heavier metal within the first 18 months after passable flight safety records and good bombing scores.

In early August 1953 we had some small wings awarded to us which looked like miniature Bombardier wings, and were given a three week furlough home along with new orders to go to 'Limestone Maine'. My trip home was aided by a C-47 hop to San Francisco, from where I took a Greyhound Bus to Portland, Oregon. My reporting date to Limestone ME was 5 September and accomplished by a long train ticket with transfers in Chicago, New York and Hartford, and, finally Presque Isle Maine where I was met by a blue bus and a sergeant who knew my name.

Four days without a bunk or a change of underwear, and it was already cold and wet when I processed into a long line of new people at Limestone Maine. My attitude changed when I finally was driven to my assigned quarters, a brand new barracks but it was brick, with large windows, hardwood floors, rooms with bunks much wider and deeper than anything I had seen before, beautiful sanitary latrines (comparatively speaking) a day room with a television, a gymnasium, and even special mess halls and open hours for flight crews. Maybe this wasn't going to be so bad.

First hand events that I experienced, between September 1953 and 17 January 1956 when I left the service, included almost regular in-flight malfunctions of our reciprocating (R-4360) engines. After the first couple of feathering events preceded by 'smoke and flame' or just a decision to shut down a misbehaving engine 'running too rich' – we all just took such events in our stride most of the time. One day en route to England in 1954 we feathered the No. 3 (inboard starboard engine) just as we left the east coast of Greenland. We were probably cruising at about 25,000ft (7,620m) or 28,000ft (8,534m) flying into night with daylight behind us.

Before long, after a nap, I replaced Johnny Pfor as left scanner. He told me something strange about losing altitude and to be sure to wake him if necessary. I wasn't sure what he was talking about, but I learned more after listening to intercom chatter for a few minutes. Our flight engineer(s) and the pilots were apparently discussing options about carburettor icing, or wing icing and losing power across the board. Within about ten minutes after taking over for Johnny Pfor we were instructed to locate our 'water survival suits' and be ready to review ditching procedures. I don't recall any exact sequence of events after that message but I do know that we all got very alert in the aft compartment. We all were doing exactly what was asked, without a curse or complaint but I felt horrible because I knew that we (after many missions) had still never reviewed or practiced deployment of our 20-man life raft and we all knew that our 'Water Survival Suits' were absolute bullshit, prone to be less than water tight, to tearing and hard to

get into in the cramped aft compartment.

The end of this episode was after about four hours of fighting with the engines and losing then gaining then losing altitude, we got to within radio distance of Keflavik, Iceland and then at no higher than 1,800ft (549m) we were able to start the jets, notice a change in outside temperature and decide to neither ditch nor attempt an emergency landing in Iceland but to climb to a reasonable altitude and, after taking inventory of our remaining fuel, proceed to Upper Heyford, UK.

I don't have a clue about the particulars of how our aircraft 'healed itself' but our flight engineers and pilots wrote it up as a victory of 'out thinking the malfunctions'. I don't know if this episode was ever reported or recorded in

Flight Safety Reports but I do know that it was, by far, NOT the most serious event concerned with malfunctioning engines or icing that other crews from Loring AFB had experienced. One of my roommates, John Yost, of Lawrence, Kansas, gave us a vivid account of a No. 6 engine literally burning the nacelle off its engine mounts and the whole unit, (prop blades, engine and all) falling off into the ocean.

I think I became disillusioned with the whole notion of the B-36 during my last months of service. I had learned to put up with the rather frequent gun jamming incidents where we almost never were able to expend our 20mm ammunition beyond a few bursts. No matter how many times we critiqued our ammo belts, or torqued our electric breech loaders, some of our guns jammed or just quit, again and again. This was not only my crew, it was an epidemic in the 69th, 70th and 75th. Such malfunctioning lost emphasis, or actually went unreported, simply because after about May of 1955 we were flying H and J models, with either no guns, or just tail guns, and we almost never carried ammo or engaged in shooting rounds into the ocean.

Even after becoming an 'elite' crew, or elevated to the exalted role as an 'instructor' I began to sense that the mighty B-36 was probably no more than a political victory of the Air Force that got way out of hand. That our vaunted capabilities were never fully revealed, for good reasons: we were a long

range bomber when our major load was gas and thus loaded we could and did fly for 40hr and nearly 10,000mls (16,090km). But with a bomb load or the featured nuke of that day our radius was much, much shorter.

In the Loring enlisted barracks, it dawned on several of us that we might just be part of a yet undisclosed scam that had fooled enough people (including enemies) for just long enough to build a new generation of effective and new (jet) aircraft, that were actually lethal, that is, actually capable. I guess I began to think that this deception was my reason for being rather than the notion that the B-36 was anything like a survivable war machine. Logically our aircraft was just a 'Peacemaker-threat' that I had to stand behind regardless of the facts that I became aware of. I never expressed this feeling to anyone outside my own circle of friends. We were all far too obedient, too willing to execute our duties as well as possible. Quite frankly, I think we also were afraid to voice our reservations. We were also reasonably certain that those 'profile' missions we had been flying would more than likely never happen.

But what I did know was that we seldom even reached a true airspeed above 287mph (462kph), that headwinds like the jet stream from West to East made a simple flight from Loring to Fairchild ten hours or more going direct. So we made it look good by going out of our way and 'bombing' Boulder Dam and attacking Mt. Hood en route.

We aft cabin people learned that even the jets could get us into a sprint of no more than 402mph (647kph) or a bit faster with J series or 'featherweights'. Then, on one mission in late summer 1955, we simulated a broad 'attack' on the Northeast coast of the USA. I think all our squadrons were involved, perhaps 30 aircraft. Somewhere in the West Atlantic maybe 300mls (483km) from Boston we hit a headwind of (probably) 138mph (222kph). Our ground speed was reported by the navigator to be 'less than 86mph (138kph)'. We were swarmed by East Coast Air Defense Command (ADC), noticeably by F-89 Scorpions from Otis AFB and a number of swept-wing types. To get to my point, we began to know just how obsolete we were when, at the debriefing of this exercise,

ABOVE The flight crew of the last of 383 Peacemakers, B-36J 52-2827 (*City of Ft. Worth* – and not *City of Fort Worth*, which was the first aircraft 44-93015, delivered to SAC) pose for a publicity shot. *(USAF)*

BELOW The last B-36J now resting at Pima Air & Space Museum, Arizona. *(David Baker)*

by the prototype B-52, still with the tandem cockpit. Looking at that thing convinced me that 'they' (SAC, Curtis LeMay et al) were probably done with us and with a huge sigh of relief that we had kept the myth of the B-36 alive...just barely long enough to be useful. I also began to realise at age 22, just how ignorant I was and I was determined to leave the service and go to college.

Ken Wallis, Wing Commander RAF

I was a Senior Specialist Armament Officer in the RAF on exchange posting to Strategic Air Command, Offutt AFB between 1956 and 1958. As one of the four pilots on board it was of the giant RB-36H of which I have the strongest memories. I would go down to Carswell AFB, Fort Worth, Texas, and be kitted out with clothing intended to ensure survival at the North Pole if necessary. An early morning start would be made on the pre-flight inspection of the huge aircraft involving some climbing in the wings, etc. By the time the inspection was finished it was as though one had done a day's work but it was time to climb aboard and start the very long flight.

ABOVE Born in 1916 at Ely, England, Wing Commander Ken Wallis famously became a leading exponent of the autogyro, with 34 world records to his credit as well as being credited with the 'hot seat' in a B-36. *(Via David Baker)*

it was noted that ALL, as in EVERY 45th bomb Wing B-36, was 'shot down' multiple times, some as many as 20 times according to gun-camera results.

I kept noticing that SAC was now far more interested in B-47 capabilities and deployments, that air-to-air refuelling and speed were factors. Several 47s began remaining parked on our tarmac for extended days. In late 1955, we were greeted with a visit

When taxying, the aircraft was steered by a large hand-wheel on the port side of the cockpit. Take-off would be at a very heavy weight with the six piston and four jet engines at full power. The take-off run would go on and on until a very gentle detachment from the ground and a very slow climb. At an altitude of 10,000–15,000ft the engines would be shut down and the umbrella-like seals in the jet air intakes would be adjusted to allow just enough air in to keep the engines wind-milling to prevent icing up. The long cruise to the simulated target would then start, passing north over the USA and Canada and heading for the region of the North Pole.

During the flight two pilots would take four-hour shifts at the controls before handing over to the other two pilots. Most of the time we would be on autopilot but at intervals we would revert to manual to re-trim the aircraft as the immense fuel load was consumed. In fact, for about the first 10 hours the attitude would be distinctly nose-up to maintain height at such a weight. The cockpit area and forward part of the aircraft was pressurised as was an area aft accessed via a small pressurised tunnel 84ft long. A small trolley allowed a crewmember to lie flat on his back

but such was the aircraft's pitch angle for the first 10 hours of the 33 hour flight that a small handbrake down the right side of the trolley was needed to prevent an overshoot at the other end! Small windows in the tunnel allowed us to see the atomic bomb we always had on board – just in case war broke out during the flight and orders came to divert to a real target. There was always an A-bomb on board.

After the four-hour stint of flying, much of it in darkness, we would look forward to a little sleep in a hammock but the sounds of cabin pressure changes, the note of the piston engines and general noise prevented anything other than fitful rest. We could, however, heat up ready prepared meals. Trouble with one or two of the piston engines was not uncommon but we always seemed to have enough power. As we approached the target the jet engines would be started and we would climb to 45,000ft for a simulated bombing run followed by a turn to starboard from where we would head north of Sweden and turn for England and a landing at Burtonwood. While ground crew performed the odd engine change and other work I sometimes had the opportunity to nip home for a day or two!

BELOW B-36J 52-2220 displayed in the Cold War Gallery at the National Museum of the United States Air Force, Wright-Patterson AFB, Ohio. *(NMUSAF)*

Specifications and data

The B-36 remained essentially the same in all its exterior dimensions throughout the range of variants in its operational life. However, the data presented on these pages reflects the subtle changes in capability and performance and in the development which resulted from the addition of supplementary jet engines which increased overall performance to a level where the H and J series variants were able to take on ever more ambitious roles.

No single table could contain all the various performance advantages which accrued from these evolutions and the tables and charts shown here allow the reader to define the nature of these changes between the early A and B series aircraft and the later bomber and reconnaissance types.

Development of the B-36 into the world's first intercontinental nuclear deterrent and its variation into a reconnaissance type allowed successors to pick up the mantle and build on the pioneering role of the Peacemaker.

RIGHT A B-36J (55-2217) located at the Strategic Air and Space Museum in Ashland, New England. *(Peoparmr)*

RIGHT Prior to its present location at the National Museum of the US Air Force (NMUSAF), Wright-Patterson AFB, B-36J 52-2220 was moved from building 1 to building 3 in 2002. *(NMUSAF)*

TOP Installed in its proud position of honour at the NMUSAF, the interior of 52-2220 has been extensively imaged for a 'virtual' tour of the crew areas available to view on the museum's website. *(NMUSAF)*

ABOVE An RB-36H (51-13730) at Castle Air Museum, the site celebrating the contribution of Castle AFB to the story of the Peacemaker. *(Perry Clarke)*

LEFT The technical complexity of the B-36 was driven as much by the emerging technology of the day as by its sheer size. Located near the engineer's station, some of the 27mls (43km) of electrical wires that made up a Peacemaker. *(David Baker)*

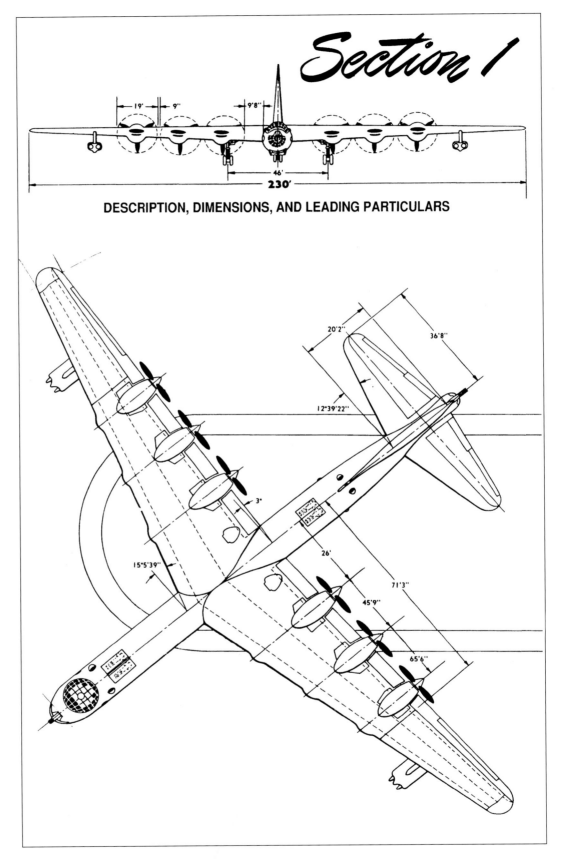

Section 1

DESCRIPTION, DIMENSIONS, AND LEADING PARTICULARS

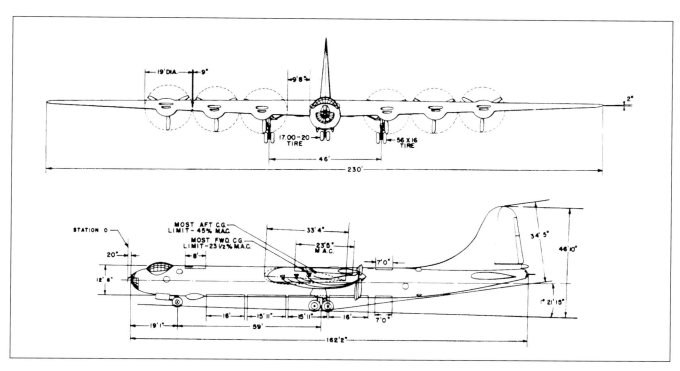

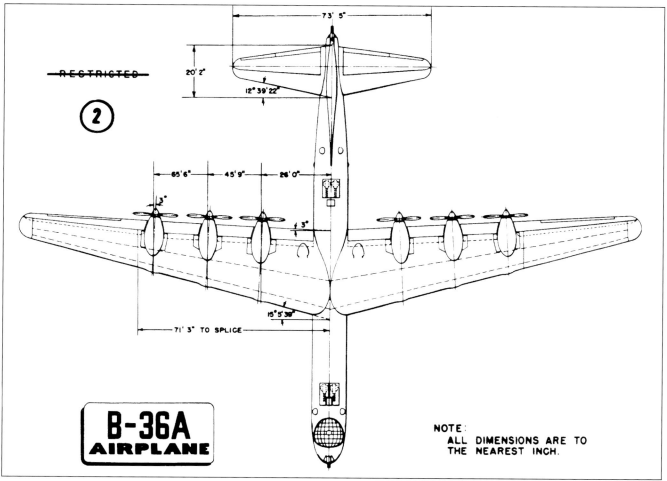

②

B-36A AIRPLANE

NOTE:
ALL DIMENSIONS ARE TO
THE NEAREST INCH.

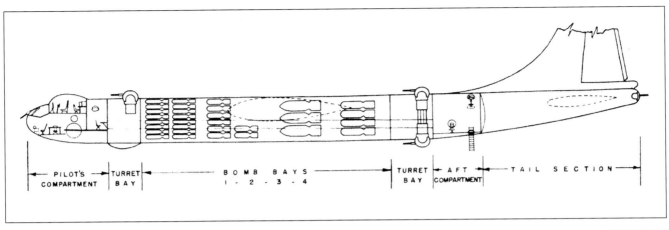

PILOT'S COMPARTMENT | TURRET BAY | B O M B   B A Y S 1 - 2 - 3 - 4 | TURRET BAY | AFT COMPARTMENT | T A I L   S E C T I O N

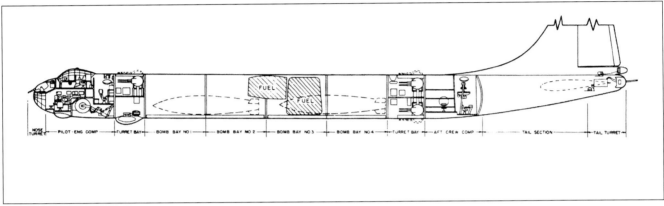

NOSE TURRET | PILOT-ENG COMP | TURRET BAY | BOMB BAY NO 1 | BOMB BAY NO 2 | BOMB BAY NO 3 | BOMB BAY NO 4 | TURRET BAY | AFT CREW COMP | TAIL SECTION | TAIL TURRET

TOP A typical conventional general-purpose bomb load configuration for a B-36A. *(Convair)*

ABOVE A B-36B displaying the orientation in coupled bomb bays for two 43,000lb (19,500kg) bombs. *(Convair)*

RIGHT The application of magnesium skin and structure applied on external surfaces of the B-36. *(Convair)*

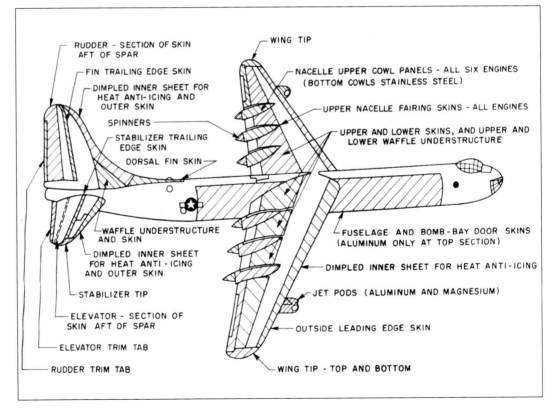

RUDDER - SECTION OF SKIN AFT OF SPAR

FIN TRAILING EDGE SKIN

DIMPLED INNER SHEET FOR HEAT ANTI-ICING AND OUTER SKIN

SPINNERS

STABILIZER TRAILING EDGE SKIN

DORSAL FIN SKIN

WAFFLE UNDERSTRUCTURE AND SKIN

DIMPLED INNER SHEET FOR HEAT ANTI-ICING AND OUTER SKIN

STABILIZER TIP

ELEVATOR - SECTION OF SKIN AFT OF SPAR

ELEVATOR TRIM TAB

RUDDER TRIM TAB

WING TIP

NACELLE UPPER COWL PANELS - ALL SIX ENGINES (BOTTOM COWLS STAINLESS STEEL)

UPPER NACELLE FAIRING SKINS - ALL ENGINES

UPPER AND LOWER SKINS, AND UPPER AND LOWER WAFFLE UNDERSTRUCTURE

FUSELAGE AND BOMB-BAY DOOR SKINS (ALUMINUM ONLY AT TOP SECTION)

DIMPLED INNER SHEET FOR HEAT ANTI-ICING

JET PODS (ALUMINUM AND MAGNESIUM)

OUTSIDE LEADING EDGE SKIN

WING TIP - TOP AND BOTTOM

Loading and Performance - Typical Mission

CONDITIONS		BASIC RADIUS I	BASIC RANGE II	MAXBOMBS RADIUS III	HIGH ALT. RADIUS IV	MAX.SPEED RADIUS V	FERRY RANGE VI
TAKE-OFF WEIGHT	(lb)	310,380	310,380	311,000	310,380	310,380	311,000
Fuel/Oil	(gal)	24,121/965	24,121/965	14,434/577	24,121/965	24,121/965	26,745/1070
Military Load	(lb)	10,000	10,000	72,000	10,000	10,000	None
Total Ammunition	(rds/cal)	9200/20mm	9200/20mm	9200/20mm	9200/20mm	9200/20mm	None
Wing Loading	(lb/sq ft)	65.04	65.04	65.17	65.04	65.04	65.17
Stall Speed-(power off)	(kn)	98	98	98	98	98	98
TAKE-OFF DISTANCE SL ④							
Ground Run (no wind)	(ft)	6000	6000	6000	6000	6000	6000
To Clear 50 ft Obst	(ft)	8000	8000	8000	8000	8000	8000
CLIMB FROM SL							
Rate of Climb at SL ③	(fpm)	502	502	500	502	502	500
Time To 10,000 Feet ③	(min)	22.3	22.3	22.5	22.3	22.3	22.5
Time To 20,000 Feet ③	(min)	53.0	53.0	53.5	53.0	53.0	53.5
COMBAT RANGE or RADIUS	(n.mi)	3370	6320	1830	2485	1860	7934
Avg. Cruising Speed	(kn)	189	181	187	231	269	189
Total Mission Time	(hr)	35.6	35.08	19.57	21.52	13.83	42.17
Cruising Altitude	(ft)	⑤	⑤	⑤	⑤	⑤	⑤
COMBAT WEIGHT	(lb)	212,800	165,570	182,100	207,800	220,800	—
Combat Altitude	(ft)	25,000	25,000	25,000	35,000	34,400	—
SPEED							
Max Speed (combat alt) ②	(kn)	290	295	294	292	288	—
Max Speed ②	(kn/alt)	300/31,600	310/33,000	307/32,400	302/31,800	293/31,400	—
CLIMB							
Rate of Climb (combat alt) ②	(fpm)	1023	1617	1380	620	545	—
Rate of Climb at SL ②	(fpm)	1447	2045	1810	1500	1367	—
CEILING							
Combat Ceiling ②	(ft)	35,800	39,400	38,400	36,300	34,900	—
Service Ceiling ③	(ft)	39,100	41,300	40,700	39,500	38,600	—
LANDING WEIGHT SL	(lb)	158,080	—	153,850	158,080	158,080	153,200
Ground Roll ⑥	(ft)	1490	—	1450	1490	1490	1440
From 50'Obst ⑥	(ft)	2650	—	2600	2650	2650	2590

NOTES
① Take-off power
② Max power
③ Normal power
④ Take-off and landing distances are obtainable at sea level using normal technique. For airport planning add 25% to distances shown.
⑤ Detailed descriptions of the RADIUS & RANGE missions are given on page 6.

CONDITIONS:
(a) Performance Basis: NACA standard conditions, no wind, single airplane.
(b) Fuel consumption used in computing RADIUS & RANGE is based on manufacturer's estimates and flight tests increased 5%.
(c) Performance based on powers listed on page 6.
(d) RADIUS & RANGE are based on operation where maximum continuous BMEP (178 psi) is maintained in all auto-rich power settings except as modified by propeller restrictions.

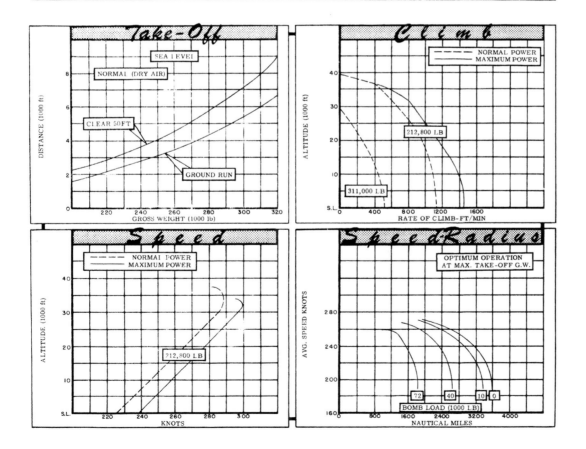

LEFT The performance and operating capabilities of the B-36A, the first model to enter production.
(Convair)

Loading and Performance - Typical Mission

CONDITIONS		BASIC RADIUS I	BASIC RANGE II	MAX. BOMBS RADIUS III	HIGH ALT. RADIUS IV	MAX. SPEED RADIUS V	FERRY RANGE VI
TAKE-OFF WEIGHT	(lb)	326,000	326,000	317,500	294,000	326,000	326,000
Fuel & Oil	(gal)	25,880/1025	25,880/1025	12,646/506	21,067/844	25,880/1025	28,070/1123
Military Load	(lb)	10,000	10,000	86,000	10,000	10,000	None
Total Ammunition	(rds/cal)	9200/20mm	9200/20mm	9200/20mm	9200/20mm	9200/20mm	None
Wing Loading	(lb/sq ft)	68.32	68.32	66.53	61.60	68.32	68.32
Stall Speed -(power off)	(kn)	100	100	99	95	100	100
TAKE-OFF DISTANCE SL ④							
Ground Run (no wind)	(ft)	5900	5900	5350	4170	5900	5900
To Clear 50 ft Obst	(ft)	8030	8000	7250	5610	8000	8000
CLIMB FROM SL							
Rate of Climb at SL ③	(fpm)	500	500	540	670	500	500
Time To 10,000 Feet ③	(min)	23.2	23.2	19.8	16.7	23.2	23.2
Time To 20,000 Feet ③	(min)	59.5	59.5	46.5	36.7	59.5	59.5
Service Ceiling (100 f.p.m.) ③	(ft)	24,100	24,100	25,200	30,000	24,100	24,100
COMBAT RANGE	(n.mi)	——	6946				8478
COMBAT RADIUS	(n.mi)	3710		1610	2850	2462	
Avg. Cruising Speed	(kn)	193	185	195	260	286	192
Total Mission Time	(hr)	38.45	37.55	16.5	21.92	17.1	44.35
Cruising Altitude	(ft)	⑤	⑤	⑤	⑤	⑤	⑤
COMBAT WEIGHT	(lb)	221,400	171,360	181,420	205,000	216,600	——
Combat Altitude	(ft)	25,000	25,500	25,000	40,000	35,000	——
SPEED							
Max Speed (combat alt) ②	(kn)	314	322	319	309	330	
Max Speed ②	(kn/ft)	327/35,000	338/35,500	336/35,000	331/34,000	329/35,000	
CLIMB							
Rate of Climb (combat alt) ②	(fpm)	1130	1720	1600	290	870	——
Rate of Climb At SL ②	(fpm)	1530	2160	2008	1710	1578	——
CEILING							
Combat Ceiling ②	(ft)	37,500	40,800	40,150	38,600	37,800	——
Service Ceiling ③	(ft)	40,500	43,700	43,100	41,600	40,800	——
LANDING WEIGHT SL	(lb)	163,321	——	156,918	159,530	163,321	160,401
Ground Roll ④	(ft)	1530	——	1470	1500	1530	1510
From 50' Obst ④	(ft)	2720	——	2680	2710	2720	2680

NOTES
① Take-off power
② Max power
③ Normal power
④ Take-off and landing distances are obtainable at sea level using normal technique. For airport planning add 25% to distances shown
⑤ Detailed descriptions of the RADIUS & RANGE missions are given on page 6
⑥ Radius mission if radius is shown

CONDITIONS:
(a) Performance Basis: NACA standard day, no wind, single airplane
(b) Fuel consumption used in computing RADIUS & RANGE is increased 5% based on manufacturer's estimates
(c) Performance is based on powers shown on page 6.
(d) RADIUS & RANGE are based on operation where maximum continuous BMEP (188.6 psi) is maintained in all normal power settings.

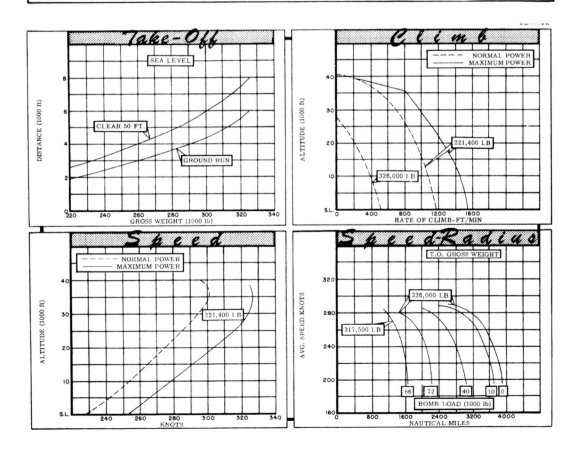

LEFT A significant
improvement
in performance
and capability
demonstrated by the
RB-36D and E series
aircraft incorporating
the podded jet engines.

(Convair)

Loading and Performance — Typical Mission

CONDITIONS		BASIC MISSION I	MAX BOMBS II	MAX ATTAIN.ALT. III	HIGH SPEED IV	FERRY RANGE V		
TAKE-OFF WEIGHT	(lb)	370,000	370,000	370,000	370,000	370,000		
Fuel at 6 lb/gal (Grade 115/145)	(lb)	188,431	175,520	188,431	188,431	192,249		
Payload (Flash bombs)	(lb)	2256	15,040	2256	2256	None		
Payload (Chaff)	(lb)	1408	1408	1408	1408	None		
Wing Loading	(lb/sq ft)	77.5	77.5	77.5	77.5	77.5		
Stall speed (power off)	(kn)	107	107	107	107	107		
Take-off ground run at SL ①	(ft)	4400	4400	4400	4400	4400		
Take-off to clear 50 ft ①	(ft)	5685	5685	5685	5685	5685		
Rate of climb at SL ③	(fpm)	950	950	950	950	950		
Rate of climb at SL (one eng. out) ②	(fpm)	1005	1005	1005	1005	1005		
Time: SL to 10,000 ft ③	(min)	12	12	12	12	12		
Time: SL to 20,000 ft ③	(min)	26	26	26	26	26		
Service ceiling (100 fpm) ③	(ft)	33,000	33,000	33,000	33,000	33,000		
Service ceiling (one eng. out) ②	(ft)	31,100	31,100	31,100	31,100	31,100		
COMBAT RANGE ④	(n.mi)	—	—	—	—	7765		
COMBAT RADIUS ④	(n.mi)	3225	2910	2955	1425	—		
Average cruise speed	(kn)	188	191	192	338	176		
Initial cruising altitude	(ft)	5000	5000	5000	31,200	5000		
Target speed ③	(kn)	344	343	304	342	336		
Target altitude	(ft)	39,900	39,200	44,800	27,100	27,100		
Final cruising altitude	(ft)	27,100	27,700	27,100	39,300	27,100		
Total mission time	(hr)	33.9	30.2	29.5	8.9	44.2		
COMBAT WEIGHT	(lb)	251,900	245,000	248,700	265,700	188,320		
Combat altitude	(ft)	39,900	39,200	44,800	37,500	27,100		
Combat speed ②	(kn)	355	359	321	355	336		
Combat climb ②	(fpm)	575	700	90	645	2085		
Combat ceiling (500 fpm) ②	(ft)	40,700	41,200	40,800	39,400	46,300		
Service ceiling (100 fpm) ③	(ft)	44,200	45,000	44,400	43,100	48,900		
Service ceiling (one eng. out) ③	(ft)	42,000	42,600	42,300	41,000	47,400		
Max rate of climb at SL ②	(fpm)	2220	2315	2270	2080	3150		
Max speed at optimum altitude ②	(kn/ft)	360/37,200	361/38,000	360/37,500	355/37,000	373/39,500		
Basic speed at 25,000/35,000 ft ②	(kn)	339/358	340/360	339/359	337/354	345/367		
LANDING WEIGHT	(lb)	188,280	187,760	188,280	188,280	188,320		
Ground roll at SL	(ft)	1840	1835	1840	1840	1840		
Ground roll (auxiliary brake) ⑤	(ft)	1610	1605	1610	1610	1610		
Total from 50 ft	(ft)	3280	3275	3280	3280	3280		
Total from 50 ft (auxiliary brake) ⑤	(ft)	3050	3045	3050	3050	3050		

NOTES
① T.O. power
② Max available power
③ Normal power
④ Detailed descriptions of Range and Radius missions given on page 6
⑤ Props reversed

PERFORMANCE BASIS:
(a) Data source: Calculated data based on flight test of B-36D Aircraft with configuration adjustments
(b) Performance is based on powers shown on page 6

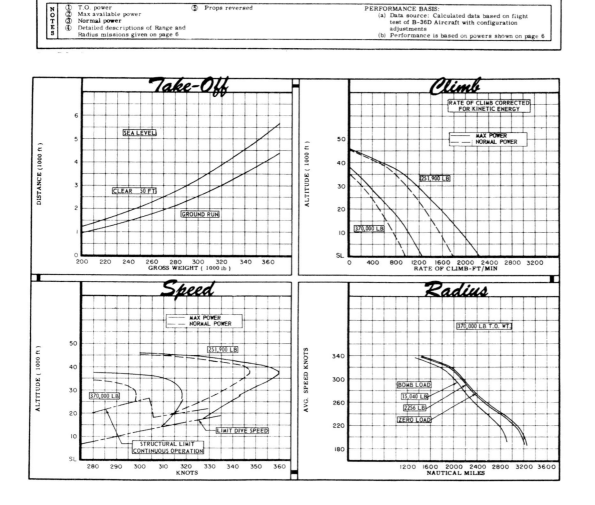

Loading and Performance—Typical Mission

CONDITIONS		BASIC MISSION I	MAX BOMBS II	MAX ATTAIN. ALT. III	HIGH ZONE ALT. IV	HIGH SPEED V	FERRY RANGE VI
TAKE-OFF WEIGHT	(lb)	370,000	370,000	370,000	370,000	370,000	370,000
Fuel at 6 lb/gal (Grade 115/145)	(lb)	188,640	175,030	188,640	188,640	188,640	192,160
Payload (Flash bombs)	(lb)	2256	15,040	2256	2256	2256	None
Payload (Chaff)	(lb)	1408	1408	1408	1408	1408	None
Wing Loading	(lb/sq ft)	77.5	77.5	77.5	77.5	77.5	77.5
Stall speed (power off)	(kn)	107	107	107	107	107	107
Take-off ground run at SL [1]	(ft)	3990	3990	3990	3990	3990	3990
Take-off to clear 50 ft [1]	(ft)	5110	5110	5110	5110	5110	5110
Rate of climb at SL [3]	(fpm)	940	940	940	940	940	940
Rate of climb at SL (one eng. out) [2]	(fpm)	955	955	955	955	955	955
Time: SL to 10,000 ft [3]	(min)	11	11	11	11	11	11
Time: SL to 20,000 ft [3]	(min)	26	26	26	26	26	26
Service ceiling (100 fpm) [3]	(ft)	33,300	33,300	33,300	33,300	33,300	33,300
Service ceiling (one eng. out) [2]	(ft)	30,200	30,200	30,200	30,200	30,200	
COMBAT RANGE [4]	(n.mi)					—	7210
COMBAT RADIUS [4]	(n.mi)	3145	2875	2910	2965	1420	
Average cruise speed	(kn)	208	209	211	209	346	197
Initial cruising altitude	(ft)	5000	5000	5000	5000	32,000	5000
Target speed [3]	(kn)	351	349	322	339	348	370
Target altitude	(ft)	40,000	39,500	44,500	43,000	37,800	34,100
Final cruising altitude	(ft)	34,100	34,200	34,100	34,100	38,600	34,100
Total mission time	(hr)	29.9	27.2	27.1	27.8	8.6	36.6
COMBAT WEIGHT	(lb)	254,600	247,500	252,700	251,600	263,300	188,450
Combat altitude	(ft)	40,000	39,500	44,500	43,000	37,800	34,100
Combat speed [2]	(kn)	360	362	332	344	359	370
Combat climb [2]	(fpm)	530	625	125	250	565	1545
Combat ceiling (500 fpm) [2]	(ft)	40,300	40,900	40,500	40,600	39,400	47,200
Service ceiling (100 fpm) [3]	(ft)	43,900	44,300	44,000	44,100	43,300	50,200
Service ceiling (one eng. out) [2]	(ft)	41,400	41,800	41,500	41,600	41,000	48,000
Max rate of climb at SL [2]	(fpm)	2050	2130	2070	2080	1960	2950
Max speed at optimum altitude [2]	(kn/ft)	362/38,000	364/38,100	364/38,100	364/38,100	359/37,600	375/39,000
Basic speed at 25,000/35,000 ft [2]	(kn/kn)	341/360	342/362	342/361	342/361	340/358	349/371
LANDING WEIGHT	(lb)	188,410	188,260	188,410	188,410	188,410	188,450
Ground roll at SL	(ft)	1840	1840	1840	1840	1840	1840
Ground roll (auxiliary brake) [5]	(ft)	1620	1620	1620	1620	1620	1620
Total from 50 ft	(ft)	3290	3290	3290	3290	3290	3290
Total from 50 ft (auxiliary brake) [5]	(ft)	3040	3040	3040	3040	3040	3040

NOTES:
[1] T.O. power
[2] Max power
[3] Normal power
[4] Detailed descriptions of Range and Radius missions given on page 6
[5] Props reversed

PERFORMANCE BASIS:
(a) Data source: Calculated data based on flight test of B-36F and H Aircraft with configuration adjustments
(b) Performance is based on powers shown on page 6

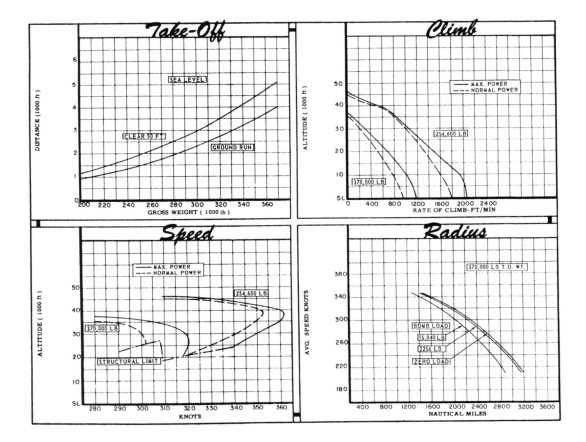

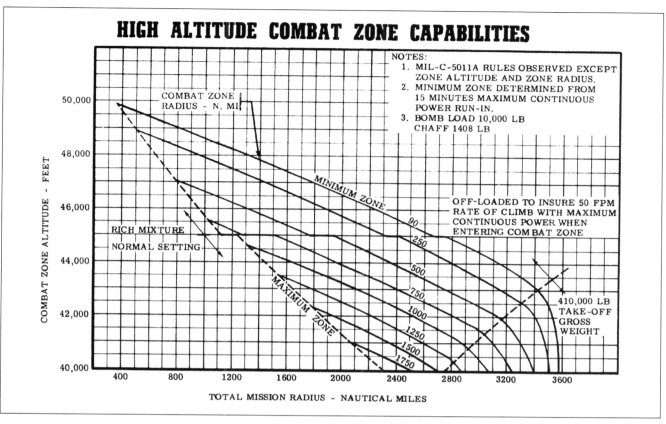

HIGH ALTITUDE COMBAT ZONE CAPABILITIES

NOTES:
1. MIL-C-5011A RULES OBSERVED EXCEPT ZONE ALTITUDE AND ZONE RADIUS.
2. MINIMUM ZONE DETERMINED FROM 15 MINUTES MAXIMUM CONTINUOUS POWER RUN-IN.
3. BOMB LOAD 10,000 LB CHAFF 1408 LB

COMBAT ZONE RADIUS - N. MI.

MINIMUM ZONE

OFF-LOADED TO INSURE 50 FPM RATE OF CLIMB WITH MAXIMUM CONTINUOUS POWER WHEN ENTERING COMBAT ZONE

RICH MIXTURE NORMAL SETTING

MAXIMUM ZONE

410,000 LB TAKE-OFF GROSS WEIGHT

COMBAT ZONE ALTITUDE - FEET

TOTAL MISSION RADIUS - NAUTICAL MILES

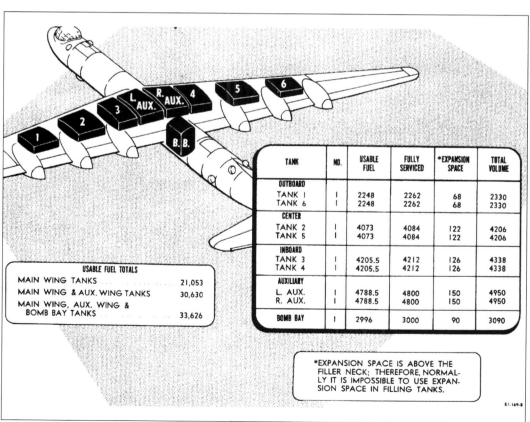

USABLE FUEL TOTALS

MAIN WING TANKS	21,053
MAIN WING & AUX. WING TANKS	30,630
MAIN WING, AUX. WING & BOMB BAY TANKS	33,626

TANK	NO.	USABLE FUEL	FULLY SERVICED	*EXPANSION SPACE	TOTAL VOLUME
OUTBOARD					
TANK 1	1	2248	2262	68	2330
TANK 6	1	2248	2262	68	2330
CENTER					
TANK 2	1	4073	4084	122	4206
TANK 5	1	4073	4084	122	4206
INBOARD					
TANK 3	1	4205.5	4212	126	4338
TANK 4	1	4205.5	4212	126	4338
AUXILIARY					
L. AUX.	1	4788.5	4800	150	4950
R. AUX.	1	4788.5	4800	150	4950
BOMB BAY	1	2996	3000	90	3090

*EXPANSION SPACE IS ABOVE THE FILLER NECK; THEREFORE, NORMALLY IT IS IMPOSSIBLE TO USE EXPANSION SPACE IN FILLING TANKS.

EI-169-B

ABOVE There have been many tales of the B-36 achieving great altitude, far higher than officially noted in the performance charts. However, this high-altitude capabilities chart testifies to that possibility. *(USAF)*

LEFT Fuel tank capacities for the B-36H. *(Convair)*